Education in the Age of the Screen

This edited volume brings together experts from across the field of education to explore how traditional pedagogic and didactic forms and processes are changing, or even disappearing, as a result of new technologies being used for education and learning.

Considering the use, opportunities and limitations of technologies including interactive whiteboards, tablets, smart phones, search engines and social media platforms, chapters draw on primary and secondary research to illustrate the wide-reaching and often salient changes that new digital technologies are introducing into educational environments and learning practices around the world. Neither claiming that traditional forms of learning must be replaced, nor calling for a restoration of the school, *Education in the Age of the Screen* offers a nuanced exploration of the implications of digitization for education. Taking a broad view on education as a social and cultural phenomenon, the volume focuses on three major dimensions: the wider conditions against the background of which we educate and are educated today, detailed examples of aesthetic practices and educational initiatives in the current media culture, and concrete answers to the challenges that come our way.

A comprehensive and timely consideration of the state of education in the digital age, this will be of interest to researchers, academics and post-graduate students in the fields of education and pedagogy, media and cultural studies, as well as teacher educators and trainee teachers.

Nancy Vansieleghem is coordinator of the educational master in fine arts at LUCA School of Arts, Belgium, and of the research group Art, Practices and Education.

Joris Vlieghe is Assistant Professor in Philosophy and Theory of Education at the University of Leuven, Belgium.

Manuel Zahn is Professor for Aesthetic Education with a focus on contemporary media culture at the University of Cologne, Germany.

Theorizing Education

Theorizing Education brings together innovative work from a wide range of contexts and traditions which explicitly focuses on the roles of theory in educational research and educational practice. The series includes contextual and socio-historical analyses of existing traditions of theory and theorizing, exemplary use of theory, and empirical work where theory has been used in innovative ways. The distinctive focus for the series is the engagement with educational questions, articulating what explicitly educational function the work of particular forms of theorizing supports.

Series Editors

Gert Biesta, Brunel University, UK
Stefano Oliverio, University of Naples "Federico II", Italy

Inoperative Learning
A Radical Rewriting of Educational Potentialities
Tyson E. Lewis

Religious Education and the Public Sphere
Patricia Hannam

Art as Unlearning
Towards a Mannerist Pedagogy
John Baldacchino

Education in the Age of the Screen
Possibilities and Transformations in Technology
Edited by Nancy Vansieleghem, Joris Vlieghe and Manuel Zahn

For more information about this series, please visit: www.routledge.com/Theorizing-Education/book-series/THEOED

Education in the Age of the Screen

Possibilities and Transformations in Technology

Edited by
Nancy Vansieleghem, Joris Vlieghe and Manuel Zahn

LONDON AND NEW YORK

First published 2019
by Routledge
2 Park Square, Milton Park, Abingdon, Oxon OX14 4RN

and by Routledge
52 Vanderbilt Avenue, New York, NY 10017

Routledge is an imprint of the Taylor & Francis Group, an informa business

© 2019 selection and editorial matter, Nancy Vansieleghem, Joris Vlieghe and Manuel Zahn; individual chapters, the contributors

The right of Nancy Vansieleghem, Joris Vlieghe and Manuel Zahn to be identified as the authors of the editorial material, and of the authors for their individual chapters, has been asserted in accordance with sections 77 and 78 of the Copyright, Designs and Patents Act 1988.

All rights reserved. No part of this book may be reprinted or reproduced or utilised in any form or by any electronic, mechanical, or other means, now known or hereafter invented, including photocopying and recording, or in any information storage or retrieval system, without permission in writing from the publishers.

Trademark notice: Product or corporate names may be trademarks or registered trademarks, and are used only for identification and explanation without intent to infringe.

British Library Cataloguing in Publication Data
A catalogue record for this book is available from the British Library

Library of Congress Cataloging-in-Publication Data
Names: Vansieleghem, Nancy, editor. | Vlieghe, Joris, editor. | Zahn, Manuel, editor.
Title: Education in the age of the screen : possibilities and transformations in technology / edited by Nancy Vansieleghem, Joris Vlieghe, and Manuel Zahn.
Description: Abingdon, Oxon ; New York, NY : Routledge, 2019.
Identifiers: LCCN 2019009965| ISBN 9781138323339 (hb : alk. paper) | ISBN 9780429451478 (eb)
Subjects: LCSH: Educational technology. | Education--Effect of technological innovations on.
Classification: LCC LB1028.3+ | DDC 371.33--dc23
LC record available at https://lccn.loc.gov/2019009965

ISBN: 9781138323339 (hbk)
ISBN: 9780429451478 (ebk)

Typeset in Bembo
by Taylor & Francis Books

Contents

List of illustrations vii
List of contributors viii

Introduction 1
JORIS VLIEGHE, NANCY VANSIELEGHEM AND MANUEL ZAHN

SECTION 1: CONDITIONS 7

1 The academic lecture (1800–present): subject, medium and performance 9
  NORM FRIESEN

2 Education and world disclosure in the age of the screen: On screens, hands and owning the now 23
  JORIS VLIEGHE

3 Screening the classic: A case of re-mediation?: The new chronotope and some possible educational consequences 36
  STEFANO OLIVERIO

SECTION 2: MAPPINGS 49

4 Classroom spaces in the making: a sociomaterial account of digital screens in BYOD schools 51
  SAMIRA ALI REZA BEIGI AND MATHIAS DECUYPERE

5 Beyond the Screen: Hatsune Miku in the Context of Post-Digital Culture 68
  ANNEMARIE HAHN AND KRISTIN KLEIN

6 Beyond digital screens – media ecological perspectives on artistic practices in the digital media culture 80
MANUEL ZAHN

7 Next school's art education 92
TORSTEN MEYER

SECTION 3: INTERVENTIONS 105

8 Looking at ourselves looking through a screen. A case study of media education 107
ANNA CATERINA DALMASSO

9 Digital literacy in the age of the screen? Re-imagining the social pedagogy of the archive 127
D.-M. WITHERS AND MARIA FANNIN

10 Scholastic practices in digital education: on grammatization and poetization in bMOOC 140
NANCY VANSIELEGHEM

11 Reframing the making of school in digital times: How art can(not) change digitization 158
FRANK MAET

12 Epilogue 171
NANCY VANSIELEGHEM, JORIS VLIEGHE AND MANUEL ZAHN

Index 179

Illustrations

Figures

1.1	Philosopher Bertrand Russell eyes the microphone at one of his many BBC lectures. Source: BBC, used with permission	14
7.1	The scope of teaching teachers [see text for details]	94
8.1	Teenagers taking selfies in front of Vincenzo Amendola's grave, Naples, February 2016 (c) La Repubblica: https://napoli.rep ubblica.it/cronaca/2016/02/20/news napoli_gara_di_selfie_ all_ uscita_da_scuola_ucciso_un_ragazzo_mando_la_foto_a_casa_ -133829397/	109
8.2	Still from *Vedozero²* (2016)	115
8.3	Still from *Vedozero²* (2016)	117
8.4	Still from *Vedozero²* (2016)	120
8.5	and 8.6 Premiere of *Vedozero²* (2016) at the Filmmaker Festival in Milan (c) Massimo Schiavon [same caption for 8.5 and 8.5]	122
9.1	Images of handwritten description using Dublin Core	135
9.2	Images of handwritten description using Dublin Core	136
10.1	Screenshot of the opening page of bMOOC	148
10.2	Screenshot of contributions within one particular topic on bMOOC	149
10.3	Screenshot of two images alongside each other on bMOOC	149
10.4	Screenshot of the instruction page that pops up when the user wants to add a new contribution to bMOOC	150
10.5	Screenshot of the topic of the ignorant schoolmaster – an example of educational commonality	151
10.6	Screenshot of the topic of the ignorant schoolmaster – an example of educational commonality	151
10.7a,	10.7b and 10.7c. Different forms of media visualizations: a network, a tree, and a grid	154

Contributors

Samira Ali Reza Beigi is a doctoral student at the research groups of Methodology of Educational Sciences, and the laboratory of Education, Culture and Society, University of Leuven, Belgium. She has also collaborated with the department of Art Education at the University of North Texas as a visiting scholar. Her research interests include digitization and new media, qualitative research methodologies, sociomaterial approaches, and philosophy of education.

Anna Caterina Dalmasso is postdoctoral fellow at the *Centre Prospéro* of Saint-Louis University – Brussels. She is the author of a thesis on Merleau-Ponty's philosophy of the visual and its implications for our contemporary scopic regime, recently published in a book (*Le corps, c'est l'écran*, Mimesis, 2018), and the editor, with Mauro Carbone and Jacopo Bodini, of two interdisciplinary volumes addressing the screens as dispositives of reference of our time: *Vivre par(mi) les écrans* (Presses du réel, 2016) and *Des pouvoirs des écrans* (Mimesis, 2018). She is also filmmaker and she has worked in cinema and audiovisual literacy workshops.

Mathias Decuypere is an assistant professor at KU Leuven (Belgium). Primary research interests are directed at developing and using qualitative methodologies for researching the (role of the) digital in higher and regular education (policy), open education and education for sustainable development. Furthermore, the role and position of (sociomaterial and sociotopological) theories in qualitative research methods, and their embeddedness within contemporary sociologies of education, are a central focus.

Maria Fannin is Reader in Human Geography at the University of Bristol. Her research interests include cultural and ethical aspects of human tissue technologies and the histories and legacies of feminist social movements for health.

Norm Friesen is Professor in the College of Education, Boise State University. Dr. Friesen has written over 100 articles in journals ranging from *C-Theory* to AERA's *Educational Researcher*, and has published 10 books. He recently completed *The Textbook and the Lecture: Education in the Age of new Media*, a monograph from Johns Hopkins University Press exploring how textbook and lecture remain preeminent in educational practice to this day. Professor Friesen is active in the areas of educational technology, philosophy of education and qualitative research. He studied German philosophy and critical theory at the Johns Hopkins University, and has worked as a visiting researcher at the Humboldt University (Berlin), the Leopold-Franzens-University (Innsbruck) and the University of British Columbia (Vancouver).

Annemarie Hahn is a research associate at the department for Art and Art Theory of the University of Cologne, Germany. She studied art education, German language studies and educational sciences in Cologne and also has a professional background in graphics and design. In her PhD thesis, she addresses issues of artificial creativity in the context of inclusive learning.

Kristin Klein is a research associate at the department for art and art theory at the University of Cologne, Germany. She studied cultural and educational sciences, German and art education at the Humboldt University of Berlin, the TU Dresden und Boston University. She recently published the Workbook Arts Education (myow.org) with Gila Kolb, Torsten Meyer, and Konstanze Schütze. In her PhD thesis, she addresses aspects of art after the internet and art education in the context of post-digital societies.

Frank Maet is a lecturer in philosophy of art and philosophy of technology at LUCA, School of Arts and special guest lecturer in the arts at KU Leuven (Belgium). Previously he held a position as lecturer at Rietveld Academy Amsterdam (the Netherlands). He published on contemporary art theory (Danto, de Duve, Fried), contemporary artists (Sikander, Murakami, Snibbe), and philosophy of technology (McLuhan, Latour, Stiegler, Nancy). Currently his research focuses on the question how art and aesthetics can contribute to the understanding as well as the development of the digitization.

Torsten Meyer is Professor of Art Education with a focus on contemporary media ulture at the University of Cologne (Germany). His academic work focuses on next art education, post-internet arts education and the reform of schools and development of higher education in the 21st century. His publications include: *What's Next? Vol. 1: Kunst nach der Krise* (2013), *Next Art Education* (2013), *Subjekt Medium Bildung* (2014), *What's Next? Vol. 2: Art Education* (2015), *Where the Magic Happens – Bildung nach der Entgrenzung der Künste* (2016), *Arts Education in Transition* (2018). http://medialogy.de

Stefano Oliverio is senior lecturer of Education at the Department of Political Sciences of the University of Naples Federico II. He publishes and teaches in the areas of philosophy of education, philosophy for children, intercultural education, and educational theory. Over the last few years he has been exploring, from a philosophical viewpoint, how new technologies appeal to a revision of our ways of thinking of and practicing education.

Nancy Vansieleghem is coordinator of the educational master in fine arts at LUCA School of Arts (Belgium). She is also special guest lecturer in the arts at KU Leuven. She publishes and teaches in the areas of educational theory, philosophy of childhood/children, art education, radical pedagogies, and the educational turn in the arts. She is mainly interested in issues such as thinking, seeing, speaking, teaching and learning in post-critical times with special focus on the impact of digital technologies. Over the last few years she has also co-edited two documentaries on inclusive education: DIS_ORDER (2011) and BREEDHOEK (2016).

Joris Vlieghe is an assistant professor of philosophy and theory of education at KU Leuven (Belgium). With Naomi Hodgson and Piotr Zamojski he recently published a *Manifesto for a Post-critical Pedagogy* (Punctum Books, 2018). He is also interested in the impact of digital technologies on education, and more specifically in how fundamental notions such as schooling, attention, community, transformation, literacy and creativity change when a culture of the screen is (rapidly) substituted for a culture of the book.

D.-M. Withers is currently a Research Fellow at the University of Sussex, working on the Leverhulme-funded project *The Business of Women's Words*. The research engages with the cultural heritage of feminist social movements and the politics and pedagogy of the archive. D.-M.'s 2015 book *Feminism, Digital Culture and the Politics of Transmission: Theory, Practice and Cultural Heritage* won the 2015 Feminist and Women's Studies Association book prize. D.-M.'s most recent book is *The Feminist Revolution: the Struggle for Women's Liberation*, published in 2018.

Manuel Zahn studied educational science, philosophy and psychology at the University of Hamburg and received his doctorate with a book on aesthetic film education. He is Professor of Aesthetic Education at the Institute for Art and Art Theory at the University of Cologne. He previously worked as Professor of Art Education at the Academy of Fine Arts Brunswick, and as a research assistant at the universities of Oldenburg and Hamburg. His fields of work are: philosophy of education; media pedagogy, especially film education; and arts education in digital media culture.

Introduction

Joris Vlieghe, Nancy Vansieleghem and Manuel Zahn

One of the most salient changes in the contemporary world is the increasing digitization of our lives. Digital media, and screen technologies more generally, are ubiquitous and seem to have become indispensable (cf. Introna, Ilharco 2006; Vlieghe 2015). This evolution has major consequences for the issue that is central to this book: how to conceive of and to give shape to the education of the young – and future – generation. Indeed, digital devices and techniques (e.g., interactive whiteboards, tablets, smart phones, social media platforms, search engines, translation software, automatic text completion, collaborative online learning tools) are rapidly, if not in a rampant manner, and on an ever larger scale, also introduced and deployed in the contemporary classroom. In the case of open education initiatives, such as MOOCs, it could even be argued that classrooms, or more generally schools and universities, might disappear one day: if, in the (near) future, learning (and teaching) becomes an entirely onscreen enterprise, there is no longer the need for leaving our homes behind and moving ourselves into specific architectural settings, such as school buildings or university campuses. Also, this allows pupils and students to study alone, driven by their own interests and according to their own life rhythm, and to actually study whatever they prefer – anywhere and at any time.

Therefore, the main idea behind this book is that the rise in digital technologies challenges *in a fundamental way* what it means to educate and to be educated, as well as the concrete ways in which education takes shape. This is, digitization might impact ways of thinking about education (and how it is organized) that have existed for a long period of time, such as the often taken for granted assumption that education is by definition *school* education. Or, that it is only possible to gain an academic understanding of the world thanks to an introduction into a tradition and a canonic (fixed and limited) set of knowledge, or as the result of studying (text)books (and learning by heart the facts, insights, and formulae contained in them). In view of recent developments, however, these are no longer self-evident claims. Hence, the future of education becomes a pressing question for which we first need to develop an adequate theoretical language and approach to be able to respond accurately. And responding here may first of all mean to observe closely or to pose the 'right' questions about current media culture and their effects on us. This is the focus of this edited volume.

Of course, there is no shortage as far as educational literature on this shift towards the digital is concerned. This book, however, is different from these accounts, which often take a purely instrumental and didactical stance. By this we mean that these studies are predominantly interested in applying new technologies to the field of education, as well as in optimizing learning outcomes. This testifies to a 'what works' approach that compares the efficacy and efficiency of old and new ways of doing education. Questions that arise are for instance: have we really become less literate and have our attention levels dropped now that we no longer read 'real' books? Is it true that e-learning platforms are engaging youngsters and stimulating their intrinsic motivation much more than traditional school settings ever can? Although these questions, and many others, are valuable ones, they presume that essentially nothing has changed except for the technologies we use. And this entails that the relevant question for educationalists is finding out what technology works best.

In this book, we want to take a step further and explore the idea that, maybe, the very meaning of education *itself* is transformed when we enter the era of screen-based digital media. As such, we set about a broader view of education, viz., education as a cultural and societal phenomenon (rather than merely individual processes of learning). This means that education is to be understood against the background of wider conditions that define a particular culture and society. For instance, learning and teaching in Ancient Greece and in the Late Modern European world are, most likely, *not* the same phenomenon. Hence, education is subject to broader (technological, social, and cultural) evolutions, and today digitization comes in the picture as setting new social conditions (cf. Stiegler 2010; Hörl 2011, 2015).

By social conditions, we mean historically situated parameters within which we commonly think, experience, speak, and act and which determine (to a large extent) what we can think, feel, say, and do. A condition is, more specifically, a background to which one must relate and in view of which our subjectivities get defined. A good example of a change in conditions is the invention of the printing press. Due to the dissemination and ubiquity of printed books, life changed drastically: being illiterate became as enormous a disadvantage, or even impairment, as lacking hearing or vision was before (Eisenstein 1979). Therefore, being able to read and write defines who we are. Obviously, one is not forced to become literate, but even if one might prefer not to learn how to read and write, one can only make this choice negatively: as a response to the fact that one lives in an era of the book. Analogously, one can refuse today to use digital means, but only as a choice against an inescapable condition (cf. Fogel, Patino 2013).

In much contemporary media theory, it is also a commonplace that technological and media-cultural transformations change the ways in which people experience and understand the world and communicate with one another. This assumption is all the more true from an educational perspective, from which it makes sense to defend the following thesis: changes in mediality come with changes in subjectivity (cf. Jörissen, Meyer 2015). Hence, nothing is as important for the self-understanding of a society and its subjects as the leading media technologies. From this perspective, digitization is a process that deeply intervenes in social conditions and thus in the ways people relate to the world, to others, and to themselves. This is the result of modifications in subject configurations, identity building, memory practices, ways and means of communication, and critical references to culture, to name just a few examples.

Therefore, the first series of contributions to this book (Norm Friesen, Joris Vlieghe, Stefano Oliverio) attempt to analyze these *conditions*, and focus – more specifically – on shifts in culturally and societally dominant technologies, which bring about new and unforeseen ways of understanding ourselves and the world (and hence of how education gives the new generation access to this world). Actually, the impact of the (old and new) technologies we use on how we understand and give shape to education constitutes a thread running through the whole of this book.

It is our claim that the conditions we face today are so novel and so complex that we currently don't possess an adequate understanding of what is happening in front of our eyes, let alone that we would have a vocabulary at our disposal to come to terms with the consequences of digitization for the domain of education. This book wants to take a first step in the direction of a theorization of education in the age of the screen. In order to achieve this, we must also take stock of the concrete situation we are in and therefore, in the second part of this volume (Samira Ali Reza Beigi and Mathias Decuypere, Annemarie Hahn and Kristin Klein, Manuel Zahn and Torsten Meyer), we have gathered contributions that aim at *mapping* our digital educational present. These chapters articulate what is new about digital screen media and media education today, by zooming in on detailed examples of aesthetic practices in the current media culture, and on concrete digital learning and teaching initiatives.

But, taking an educationalists' perspective, it is also important to give answers to the challenges that are coming our way. This is, we are called on to relate to the changes that present themselves as in need of an educational answer. Hence, in the third part, we have brought together contributions (Anna Caterina Dalmasso, D.-M. Withers and Maria Fannin, Nancy Vansieleghem and Frank Maet) that discuss concrete responses to the new societal, cultural, and technological conditions of our time. These could be called educational *interventions* in that they present, analyze, and discuss in a detailed manner ideas of how educators can deal with particular issues that arise today.

These analyses of conditions, mapping exercises, and presentations of interventions are closely connected as they all aim at coming to terms with education in the age of the screen. And yet this book covers a large variety of chapters that draw from many different (theoretical) resources, that apply a variety of methods, and that are diverse in style. Rather than trying to reach one overarching perspective, these chapters are themselves illustrations of certain unresolved tensions that come with theorizing education in digital times.

First, some contributions to this book aim at developing general theorizations, which entail claims about digital technology *as such* or *the* screen as a universal category. Other contributors, in turn, emphasize the importance of distinguishing between various digital *technologies* and between different forms of *screens* – always in plural. Furthermore, in some chapters, it is argued that we need to disclose the meaning of the digital by remaining at the surface of the screen (and what appears on it), whereas other authors in this book hold that we need to come and see what is happening 'behind' or 'beyond' the screen (and which often goes unnoticed), i.e., data (digital objects), software (digital code), and the whole digital network (of networks) in which the screen devices are embedded.

A further point of discussion that arises is that it is not decided whether we can and should start from established concepts and ways of thinking, or whether we have to forge completely new ways of thought and develop an original idiom. This is particularly the case when the issue of the school is concerned. On the one hand, one can just start from the idea that the school is a particular pedagogical form with well-defined and unique features, and that it forms the heart of what education is all about: the question is then whether or not it is still meaningful to have schools in the age of the screen (Masschelein, Simons 2013). On the other hand, one can also begin with an altogether different assumption and try to understand the educational without being concerned about the question of the school, and just look – and analyze – contemporary phenomena that are, at face value, connected with education. All this is related to a fourth opposition, viz., between merely descriptive and normative approaches, the last of which almost necessarily emerges when discussing the impact of the digital. It is easy to hold strong opinions about whether digitization will facilitate a bright future or lead us straight to a cultural abyss, and, hence, whether digitization is to the benefit or the detriment of (school) education. However, it is also possible to start from a more neutral and non-judgmental position, and hence to try and stay away from making normative claims. In sum, the chapters collected in this volume are not an attempt to bring a coherent analysis or theory. Rather, each tries to investigate and do justice to what is at stake today in education.

This book is the result of a three-part series of International Research Seminars 'Making School in the Age of the Screen.' This event was held in the academic year 2016–2017 at Liverpool Hope University (UK) and LUCA School of Arts Ghent (Belgium), and it was sponsored by the Philosophy of Education Society of Great Britain (PESGB) Large Grant Scheme. We are grateful for the institutional and financial support we received from these organizations, and we would likewise like to thank the many colleagues and students who participated to the seminar series, as well as the editorial team of Routledge we worked with.

The book consists of a selection of reworked keynotes and papers delivered during the seminars. However, during the research seminars we also read and discussed texts that gave an input to our further discussions and, eventually, to this book. Among others, we explored texts by Giorgio Agamben (2017), Erving Goffman (1981), Lucas Introna and Fernando

Ilharco (2006) and Lev Manovich (2001). Alongside this, we have watched and discussed films together, in particular *Father and Sons* (2014) by Wang Bing, *Lo and Behold* (2016) by Werner Herzog, *The Human Surge* (2016) by Eduardo Williams, *For Now* (2017) by Herman Asselberghs, and *Hyper-Reality* (2016) by Keiichi Matsuda. These collective exercises account for the consistency over the different chapters in terms of problems and issues that are discussed, and of authors/schools of thought that are referred to. One of the central issues taken up in these (film) seminars was the question of what it means to be involved with a subject matter when it appears on a screen: how can things be pointed at, how can attention be drown, and how can something interesting be touched on under digital conditions? And, how can we as spectators be together with others and things when we look at a screen? The main aim of these exercises was to experience and to discuss 'screen learning' as an educational practice, and to focus on the forms of gathering and attention formation that (can) take shape. In other words, this exercise was an attempt to turn the screen into an issue: to make it visible and to experience the screen *as screen*. The selection of the films and the idea of watching these together was an attempt to provoke thinking: to draw the participants into the present, and to articulate our current digital condition. At the same time, it was an attempt to think about ways of how to make experience possible today. This is also what this book aims to be. An attempt to face the present and to call for attention. Provoking thinking, but also speaking about education in the age of the screen.

References

Agamben, G. (2017). *From the Book to the Screen. The Before and the After of the Book*, translated by Lorenzo Chiesa, in *The Fire and the Tale*. Stanford, CA: Stanford University Press, pp. 83–108.

Eisenstein, E. (1979). *The Printing Press as an Agent of Change: Communications and Cultural Transformations in Early Modern Europe* (2 vols.). Cambridge: Cambridge University Press.

Fogel, J.F. and Patino, B. (2013). La condition numérique. Comment internet bouleverse nos vies. Paris: Grasset et Fasquelle.

Goffman, E. (1981). The Lecture, in *Forms of Talk*. Philadelphia, PA: University of Pennsylvania Press, pp. 160–195.

Hörl, E. (2011) (Ed.). *Die technologische Bedingung. Beiträge zur Beschreibung der technischen Welt*. Berlin: Suhrkamp.

Hörl, E. (2015). The Technological Condition, translated by Anthony Enns. *Parrhesia: A Journal of Critical Philosophy*, 22/2015, 1–15.

Introna, L.D. and Ilharco, F.M. (2006). The Meaning of Screens: Towards a phenomenological account of screenness. *Human Studies*, 29(1), 57–76.

Jörissen, B. and Meyer, T. (2015) (Eds.). *Subjekt Medium Bildung*. Wiesbaden: VS Verlag.

Manovich, L. (2001). The Screen and the User, in *The Language of New Media*. Cambridge, MA: MIT Press, pp. 94–115.

Masschelein, J. and Simons, M. (2013). *In Defence of the School. A public issue*. Leuven: E-ducation, Culture & Society Publishers.
Stiegler, B. (2010). *Taking Care of Youth and the Generations*. Stanford, CA: Stanford University Press.
Vlieghe, J. (2015). A Technosomatic Account of Education in Digital Times. Neil Postman's views on literacy and the screen revisited. *Studies in Philosophy and Education,* 35(2), 163–179.

Section 1

Conditions

Chapter 1

The academic lecture (1800–present): subject, medium and performance[1]

Norm Friesen

> … *unconstrained oral communication to an audience… includes a significant number of intelligences thinking in unison with the lecturer.*
> —Wilhelm von Humboldt, ca. 1810

> *One speaking mouth, with many ears, and half as many writing hands—there you have the external academic apparatus.*
> —Friedrich Nietzsche, 1872

Introduction

Friedrich Kittler asserts that communicative processes in and around 1800 are *unified* through *spirit*. If this is true, then the time since has been marked by their increasing disaggregation and disenchantment. This applies also to the lecture. Around 1800 in Jena and Berlin, Fichte and others came to understand the reflective self—whether in the audience or at the lectern—as manifest through spirit rather than in the dead letter of the text. Instead of being 'a static thing with fixed properties,' the lecturing (and listening) self was seen as 'a self-producing process' (Bowman 2017, n.p.) with the possibility of such production even happening together in unison, as von Humboldt says. Later, in the wake of Nietzsche's famous dissection of the lecture into 'one speaking mouth … many ears, and half as many writing hands,' new media—including that of the screen—have ushered in a new era of mechanics, electronics and what Kittler calls "psychophysics." It is one that Kittler associates above all with the year 1900, and in which the physics of communication—whether occurring via radio, gramophone, film or typewriter—supersede 'the meaning and thoughts of text' (1990 p. 92). For the lecture, this marks the triumph of style and performance over intention and substance. As Rudolf Arnheim noted of the radio lecture in the 1930s, it becomes 'less a question of … what is said than of *how* it is spoken*'* (1936, p. 36). Form and diction replace content, at times even the identity of the speaker him or herself, as the principal concern. Despite being ignored by all but a few observers in the decades since, the reconfiguration of media, performance and the subject in the lecture is again of explicit interest.

This paper briefly traces both this renewal of practical interest and intervening theoretical neglect. It concludes by considering how, in the age of YouTube, podcast and TED Talks – as well as of contingent academic labor – the ongoing importance of the lecture and the lecturer appears as contested as it is irrefutable. The first section begins by exploring the lecture as a manifestation of spirit in the 19th century.

1800: Intelligences thinking in unison

Johann Gottlieb Fichte was a Romantic philosopher, a landmark university administrator, and author of the *Wissenschaftslehre*, the 'system of philosophy' or of 'knowledge' or 'science.' Fichte was an outstanding lecturer and public speaker. He was described by his fellow romantics Goethe and Hegel as 'extraordinary,' even 'rapturous' (Ehrlich 1977, p. 38). Fichte was also outspoken. He criticized the university and its lecturers as being utterly redundant at a time when books were both plentiful and accessible:

> books have become extremely common … making it easier to disseminate one's [ideas] in writing than through the spoken lectures. Even though there is no branch of study for which there is not an overabundance of books, people still feel that the university needs to recapitulate the entire world of books once again—to *recite* what lies printed on the page for all to see. (as quoted in Kittler 2013, p. 146)

In an age when book printing was becoming industrialized and books ever more plentiful, Fichte is saying that lecturing from a prepared text is hopelessly redundant and outmoded. But Fichte did not just talk about this. Indeed, in

> the 1790s in the University of Jena Fichte became one of the first German professors who began officially lecturing without a set text … Fichte and other Romantics began lecturing on their own work without any pretense that they were glossing a text or recapitulating a tradition. (Clark 2006, p. 410)

Fichte produced, articulated and extemporized his theory, his science of knowledge, directly at the lectern; and, in so doing, he can be said to have literally brought its fundamental principles to life. Fichte's theory begins with the self, the 'I,' representing or positing itself through its own thought and action, through its own existence, freedom, self-reflection or self-awareness (all of these things were fundamentally united for Fichte). Fichte called this reflective awareness of oneself, one's thought and action, and of the world around one *Geist*, meaning spirit, thought, or intellect. Lecturing on *the Difference between the Spirit and the Letter within Philosophy*, Fichte explained that spirit and its reflection could become transcendental and absolute through successive steps of self-reflection, or through various *levels* of reflection: I can reflect upon my own act of representing, I can reflect in turn upon my act of representing this act of representing, and I can continue to reflect in this manner indefinitely ... until one has generated a pure, general logic. [...] Through the least self-reflection one can once more lift oneself into the realm of pure reason and pure truth, and one can dwell and wander in this higher world—at least spiritually. (1993, p. 201)

Fichte envisions this compounded self-reflection as a kind of hall of mirrors of the spirit. Caught between multiple specular images, the self can study successive reflections of itself. The most reflected images or representations are not the most obscure ones, however; they are rather the ones most infused with spirit and light. In this way, the individual can enter a realm of ever more rarefied reflection, of ever greater reason and truth.

As suggested above, this observing and reflecting self or 'I' for Fichte was not 'a static thing with fixed properties, but rather a self-producing process' (Bowman 2017, n.p.). Using the terms of his own philosophy, one can venture the following: In speaking at the lectern, Fichte not only brought into existence his theory of the production of both self and knowledge; he can also be said to have 'produced' himself through this act of body and spirit. Fichte as a lecturing self emerges as a kind of self-producing process.

Of course, this self-production must happen, as Fichte himself says, as a 'spontaneous' expression of spirit, rather than through the 'unhelpful' 'empty, dead letters' of the text. He explains:

I set before you a product, into which I believe I have breathed a few ideas. But I do not give you the ideas themselves, nor can I do so. I give you the mere body. The words which you hear constitute this body. Taken in themselves, my words are no more than an empty noise, a movement in the air which surrounds us. You place a meaning in these words *for yourself*, just as I place a meaning in them *for myself*. (Fichte 1993, p. 196)

Each student must, in other words, develop his own *Wissenschaftslehre*, using his self or 'I' as his own self-positing starting point. But this activity cannot be entirely personalized in nature:

No teacher can make his teaching completely individualized, and no teacher should do this. Everyone must discover for himself *how* something is construed in accordance with his own manner of thinking and how this is to be squared with what he previously considered to be true and settled. (1993, p. 212)

Like many others in the Romantic tradition – and in education more broadly (Friesen 2015) – Fichte privileged the spoken word over writing. But he did not see it merely as a more authentic and natural form of expression, but rather, as the direct expression of thought, intellect, spirit, or *Geist* itself. Fichte describes this 'spirit' in terms of a kind of emotional flicker and ignition, a *spark* that 'comes from somewhere invisible to you and to all mortal eyes.' Still writing, or rather, speaking, in his *Spirit and Letter*, Fichte brings his oration to an end as follows:

> I conclude today's lecture [with] the wish that, unnoticed by me, a great deal of spirit may be found among you, and that from time to time I can succeed in scattering in your souls fiery sparks which will arouse and stir them. (Fichte 1993, pp. 198–199)

Fichte, in short, was an exemplary media theorist *avant la lettre*. He articulated a consistent theory of communication in relation to the media of text and speech before 'media' as such were explicitly 'theorized.' What's more, Fichte brought this into clear and theoretically consistent connection with a fully articulated theory of the *self*.

Fichte's ideas are reflected in what has come to be known as the 'Humboldtian' research university. Together with other Romantic academics, Wilhelm von Humboldt designed and founded what is known today as the Humboldt University of Berlin, an institution that has been called 'the mother of all modern universities' (Humboldt-Universität zu Berlin 2016, n.p.). It was founded on principles of freedom of faculty research (also known as 'academic freedom'), the freedom of students to choose their areas of study, the relative autonomy of the university from the state, and the founding unity of teaching and research. It was consciously used as a model in setting up the University of Chicago, the University of Toronto, Johns Hopkins University, and many others. In this institutional setting, the lecture and the lecturer played a central role, which Humboldt understood as a kind of generation or production of communal knowledge:

> For unconstrained oral communication to an audience, which includes a significant number of intelligences thinking in unison with the lecturer, inspires those who have become used to this mode of study just as surely as does the peaceful solitude of a writer or the less institutionalised activities of the members of an academy. (Humboldt 1970, p. 247)

The academic lecture for Humboldt, in other words, represented a kind of communal, 'scaled' or 'massified' version of the writing and research that a professor generally undertakes outside of the classroom. In a chapter on 'Humboldtian and Contemporary Notions of the Academic Lecture,' Thomas Karlsohn explains:

> The task for the lecturer in this new age was thus not to pass on what had been handed down, but to embody the creation of new knowledge. In addition to his teaching duties, he had also to act as a researcher. Those

who were to be capable of guiding others had themselves to produce new knowledge. It was here that the axiom was postulated as to the irrefutable connection between teaching and research that is nowadays associated with Humboldt's name. (Karlsohn 2014, p. 49)

Not only are research and teaching unified in this model, so too are the intelligences in the lecture hall that Humboldt characterized as 'thinking in unison.' This phrase might have a familiar ring to it. It is echoed by Nietzsche's reference to one speaking mouth and many listening ears and writing hands that was juxtaposed with Humboldt's at the outset of this chapter. It is difficult to imagine that Nietzsche could not have had Humboldt in mind in writing this. However, instead of focusing on intelligences thinking in unison, or of Fichte's sparks and flammable spirits, Nietzsche characterizes his vision of a 'University culture machine,' saying:

> There you have, to all appearances, the external academic apparatus: there you have the University culture machine (*Bildungsmaschine*) in action. The proprietor of the one mouth is severed from and independent of the owners of the many ears; and this double autonomy is enthusiastically called academic freedom. What is more, by increasing this freedom a little, the one can speak more or less what he likes and the other may hear more or less what he wants to—except that, behind both of them, at a carefully calculated distance, stands the State, wearing the intent expression of an overseer, to remind the professors and students from time to time that *it* is the aim, the goal, the be-all and end-all of this curious speaking and hearing procedure. (Nietzsche 2016, pp. 36–37)

The university is an apparatus or machine, a 'curious speaking and hearing procedure,' consisting of a mouth, and many ears and hands – rather than spirits being aroused or intelligences thinking in unison. It is the state, rather than the lecturer and his audience, that then 'places meaning' in the words of the lecture, that determines their final value and significance. Nietzsche effectively declares the self-producing, self-transcending Romantic self or 'I' dead on arrival. He anticipates the formation of a rather different self, one that becomes more clear, and also more explicitly machinic or technological in the century after his death.

1900–present: one speaking mouth, with many ears

The second half of the 20th century produced many important examples of lecturers and lectures, such as the inaugural 'Reith Lectures' given by Bertrand Russell (Figure 1.1), and lectures held by Michel Foucault over 14 years at the *Collège de France*. There is an important difference, however, between these last two examples and all other lectures or lecturers mentioned so far. These lectures of Russell and Foucault are *not* known today primarily because of students' faithful note taking,

Figure 1.1 Philosopher Bertrand Russell eyes the microphone at one of his many BBC lectures. Source: BBC, used with permission

or even thanks to the lecturer's own typescript. Instead, they came into being because of electromechanical audio and video media. Russell, who has recently been described as 'the first intellectual star of the modern media age' (Reisz 2012, n.p.) made many appearances on the British Broadcasting Corporation (BBC), and was keen to broadcast his ideas to a wider audience. And Foucault's lectures at the *Collège de France* were tape recorded by an audience of eager students.[2]

Russell's lectures had notable political impact, despite complaints that he '"had a bad voice,"' and that he "read us a lecture" rather than giving a more informal "talk"' (Ince 2012).

However, Foucault viewed his audience's efforts to electronically record his words slightly differently. He responded with equal measures of irritation and indifference. One witness to his famous talks at the *Collège* recalls:

> When Foucault enters the amphitheater, brisk and dynamic like someone who plunges into the water, he steps over bodies to reach his chair, pushes away the cassette recorders so he can put down his papers, removes his jacket … and sets off at full speed. (Gérard Petitjean, as quoted in Foucault 2008, p. xiii)

Foucault, like Fichte, was an electrifying speaker. But unlike with Fichte, you can judge this for yourself. You can search for online archived clips taken from cassette recordings and other media, some of these in English. Of course, it is easy to see the availability of such recordings – their virtual 'broadcasting' on the web – as offering an enormous advantage for students and researchers alike. We all get a chance, in a sense, to relive the experience of Foucault operating 'at full speed.'

But, at the same time, these recording devices meant that Foucault had to contend with something that Fichte – or for that matter Nietzsche, or even Socrates – *never* had to face. What awaits Foucault at his podium is not a faithful student-stenographer like Plato, or even the many listening ears and writing hands described by Nietzsche. Instead, Foucault is confronted, much more immediately and obtrusively, by an array of cassette recorders that he needs to 'push away.' How do the slowly turning wheels, the blind and indifferent operations of these silent machines affect the lecture? What does it mean that their recording is not of Foucault's words or thoughts, but rather electromechanical registration of the 'movement in the air which surrounds us,' which Fichte viewed so dismissively? And what does it mean, furthermore, that this record is considered as superior to even the most faithful efforts of his students?

Let's return to the account:

> At 19.15 [after exactly two hours] Foucault stops. The students rush toward his desk, not to speak to him but to stop their cassette recorders. There are no questions. In the pushing and shoving, Foucault is alone. Foucault remarks: 'It should be possible to discuss what I have put forward … However, [a] … question never comes. The group effect in France makes any genuine discussion impossible. And as there is no feedback, the course is theatricalized. My relationship with the people there is like that of an actor or an acrobat. And when I have finished speaking, a sensation of total solitude.' (Ibid., pp. xiii–xiv)

Foucault attributes his sensation of solitude, and his role as a theatrical performer to the 'group effect in France' – to his status as a French intellectual celebrity.

Foucault, however, could have thought of this in a different way. In focusing on discourse as his principle unit of analysis, Foucault steered clear of discussions of media in his work, even saying at one point that 'this is not about McLuhan' (Foucault 1970, n.p.). But he might have begun by considering the significance of the recording media so obtrusively arrayed around him. Foucault, in other words, could have looked to the new medium of the recorder, and *its* message. This message, of course, is only indicated tacitly or indirectly in many ways in the passage above: It is suggested in the students' rush 'toward his desk' at the end of his lecture, and in the 'pushing and shoving' that ensued. These attendees apparently have no questions in mind for Foucault, no expectation of dialogue with him. The fiery sparks, the thinking in unison, the 'discovery' of meaning of words for oneself, for one's own manner of thinking, are not at all in evidence here. The single point of urgency is instead to stop and retrieve one's recording. As happens so often today, the experience of a singular event seems to be the experience of capturing it on some sort of device. And one could also say that Foucault, whose observation of the self in society was always acute, is indeed an actor: Without his lines or his 'act' to fall back on, the presumption seems to be that he has nothing to say; in a space filled by an eager audience, pushing and shoving, he is left only with 'a sensation of total solitude.'

The transformation of the lecturer into a kind of actor or performer can be readily illustrated in conjunction with an event that is of special importance to the topic of the screen – namely the emergence of broadcast television in the 1950s and 60s. The introduction of this technology into domestic life brought with it a veritable tsunami of excitement and funding. The Ford Foundation spent over $100 million on both fostering and studying the educational use of this new medium. New academic journals were founded on the subject, studios were built on university campuses, and further waves of televisual change were eagerly awaited. However, in all of this excitement, few seemed to notice that television resulted in a rather different, more 'intimate and personal' experience than the lecture hall. It placed very different demands on the lecturer that were difficult for many to accommodate. For example, the *New Scientist* published a number of pieces related to televised biology and medicine lectures in the early 1960s. One of these observes that

> Paradoxically, although the purpose of television is dissemination of information to a [large] number of people ... the image of a speaker on the two-dimensional screen ... [creates] a personal relationship with an individual viewer. The most effective television teacher, in effect, speaks to one viewer and uses his personality to communicate with a single individual, however many there are in the total audience. This is a completely different technique from lecturing. (Lawler 1964, p. 174)

This is a technique that requires careful preparation, if not also professional training, as another article from *New Scientist* warns: 'It is well known, and frequently to be observed on normal television, that amateur performances border tremulously on the brink of farce.' One lecture given by several doctors, each speaking in turn, richly illustrates this point:

> The camera then flashes on to [another] doctor. By chance, the doctor is looking particularly vague at that moment. His face lights up only when he begins to speak. He speaks well enough, perhaps, but his audience spends the first few minutes getting used to his eyebrow twitch ... When this no longer seems odd [,] another doctor, by chance, is sitting in his place. Different eyebrows move differently, and are equally absorbing. (Geminus 1960, p. 1290)

The article concludes that those 'who are thinking of using television as a medium for lectures had better take some lessons in television talking' (p. 1290). A very special set of skills is needed to avoid certain eyebrow twitches, or to light up and speak on cue in a television studio as if speaking to a single individual.

These are skills, often seen as inherent qualities, of being televisual, telegenic, and telekinetic. And as Foucault correctly observed, these are the skills of performance or of acting.

Similar concerns arose again in speculation about online learning over the web. One article from the heady days of the year 2000 speculates that it 'wouldn't take much' to post 'video lectures featuring master teachers, or lectures written by textbook authors and presented by trained actors' (Klass 2000, n.p.). It further imagines that such video recordings could 'provide serious competition with even the best lecture hall course.' About one decade later, with the precipitous rise of the MOOC (Massive Online Open Course), the topic of actors replacing professors comes up again. For example, Anant Agarwal, former MIT professor, now CEO of the MOOC consortium EdX, speculated in 2013:

> From what I hear, really good actors can actually teach really well. So just imagine, maybe we get Matt Damon to teach Thévenin's theorem [for electronic circuits] … I think students would enjoy that more than taking it from [me]. (Argwal, as quoted in Young 2013, n.p.)

The lecturer is no longer simply one speaking mouth addressing many listening ears and writing hands, as Nietzsche had said. Thanks to recording and screening technologies – from audio cassettes through TV to YouTube – the lecture now often takes the form of a lecturer, typically speaking in solitude to a camera, giving the appearance of addressing only *one* student's two ears and two eyes. This is the single student or audience member who – regardless of the size of the total audience – is to be addressed as if in an 'intimate and personal' relationship with the speaker. And the lecturer, as both Foucault's and Argwal's characterizations strongly suggest, becomes (or is tacitly expected to be) a kind of 'celebrity.'

Even if most lecturers today are not movie stars or trained actors, we nonetheless live in the age of the academic 'star' lecturer. Consider terminally ill physics professor Randy Pausch, whose 'Last Lecture' has been viewed over 18 million times on YouTube. Other celebrity lecturers include physicist Richard Feynman, whose televised lectures from the early 1960s are now on YouTube and philosopher Slavoj Zizek, who has made a number of documentaries related to his philosophy, and has his own channel on YouTube. In a sense, these academics can be said to have taken on the role of a celebrity, openly and enthusiastically embraced the 'theatricality' of the recorded performance, even if this very often has the character of reality TV rather than a work of consummate cinematic art.

What does it mean that actors can (at least in theory) replace lecturers, authors and researchers? What does it mean that *how* something is spoken becomes more important than what is actually spoken, as Rudolf Arnheim noted? Must the lecturer ultimately become an actor of some kind? In concluding this chapter, I address these questions by comparing the lecture of 1800 to what it has become in the 2000s.

1900–present: the lecture in theory

Might there be some 20th century thinkers who have theorized – as Fichte did in his own time – on the difference between 'spirit and letter' in the lecture, or on the pointlessness of *reciting* what lies printed on the page (or on the PowerPoint slide) for all to see? Strangely, an acute analysis of the 20th century lecture is *not* to be found in the work of figures such as Derrida (2002), Bourdieu (1982), or Foucault himself (1981) – even though *all* of these figures gave lectures explicitly on the lecture itself.[3] It seems to be the case that important aspects of the lecture are obscured rather than illuminated when lecturing is viewed in terms of overarching ontological categories like Foucauldian 'discourse,' Bourdieuian 'production' or Derridian 'arche-writing.' Thus, in order to get an overview of the 20th century lecture as reflected in and through its proliferating media, it is necessary to piece it together from rather scattered observations about academia and lecturing today. Of particular importance in this regard are Canadian sociologist Irving Goffman's comments in his own lecture *On the Lecture*.

Here, Goffman examines the lecture specifically in terms of its media: in terms of speech or oral performance, and the textual techniques that support them. Goffman emphasizes that it is the careful composition of textual media – in his case the typewriter and typewritten word – that allows lecturers to most effectively engage with their audience: 'Your effective speaker is someone who has written his reading text in the spoken register; he has tied himself in advance to his upcoming audience with a typewriter ribbon' (1981, p. 190) It is this 'reading text' and its careful rehearsal that allows the lecturer to achieve the ultimate goal of the lecture, according to Goffman, which is to produce an *illusion*: 'a great number of lectures,' he says, depend on 'a fresh-talk *illusion*.' With 'fresh talk,' the spoken word, Goffman explains, appears to be 'formulated by the [speaker] animator from moment to moment, or at least from clause to clause. This conveys the impression that the formulation is responsive to the current situation in which the words are delivered' (1981, p. 171). Today, of course, Goffman's typewriter and ribbon have given way to a panoply of devices and media technologies intended to keep the speaker's mode of delivery as 'fresh' as possible. These range from word-processors and printers, to PowerPoint slides and their bulleted lists and speaker's notes. In the case of the most sophisticated podcast or videocast presentations, this range of media or bag of tricks has been greatly enlarged to include teleprompters, clever editing and voice-overs – all thanks to ever more flexible and efficacious technologies of the screen. Of course, none of these screen technologies is more ubiquitous and controversial than PowerPoint – whether it is employed live in the lecture hall, shown via YouTube, or mediated in some other way.

Both through its name and in the kind of engagement it engenders, PowerPoint has come to be associated with a certain type of pointing, a type of calling to attention that is pivotal in the lecture. In his book-length analysis of the 'PowerPoint Society' Hubert Knoblauch suggests that the PowerPoint presentation functions as a kind of second order pointing, and that it introduces a kind of circularity in the act of pointing, thus institutionalizing it (2012). The specific '*showing*' or 'pointing' involved in the PowerPoint show is not strictly or directly *dietic* or indexical in nature, according to Knoblauch. It does not point to something immediately contextual. Instead, it is a pointing that involves a selection of something from the realm of information, evidence, or demonstration. It may be an image from the web, from a book or a photo from a lab, museum or archive. In any case, its showing is a technologically and pedagogically significant act. After all, the word 'to teach' has a Germanic root that means to point or show, and is related to the German word for both pointing and showing, *zeigen*. The second order pointing of PowerPoint, which means a highlighting, a representation, something selected and in this sense also simplified, can be seen in many senses as the paradigmatic act of education (see Prange 2012).

It is not coincidental that this is also the essence of the screen – whether it is the projection screen behind the lecturer or the smartphone or tablet screen in one's hand. Phenomenologically, the meaning of the screen, as Introna and Ilharco (2006) tell us, is that it is 'the background that makes relevance and meaning appear' (p. 70). 'Screens,' the authors write, 'function as powerful locations for the possibilities of truth. Truth here,' they further explain, 'is not considered as correspondence of the content of the screen with the world but as an already agreement in our way of living that situates the screen as already meaningful' (Ibid.).

Something similar could be said for the browsers and other windows that frame the lecturer on YouTube. The YouTube lecture, one could also say, finds its exemplary form in the TED Talk, presentations in front of a live audience in which 'speakers are given a maximum of 18 minutes to present their ideas in the most innovative and engaging ways they can' (Wikipedia 2018, n.p.). TED presenters today are advised to cultivate an authentic, even personal connection with the audience to 'deliver the presentation as comfortably as having a conversation with a close friend.' The YouTube lecturer must in other words 'tie' herself to her audience, not only by careful script preparation, but also through rehearsal. TED presenters, for example, are urged to 'practice relentlessly,' and to follow the example of one celebrated TED talker who 'rehearsed her presentation 200 times before she delivered it live' (Gallo 2014, n.p.).

It is also important that in today's academic environment, the lecturing or teaching researcher or philosopher is the *exception* rather than the rule. In the US, for example, the vast majority of those who do university teaching are untenured adjunct faculty, and this recent development represents a clear disaggregation of the integral academic subject or self-envisioned by Humboldt and his Romantic contemporaries. There is no single, unifying, animating soul or spirit that brings together research and teaching, thought and speech, speaker and audience. Instead of 'unconstrained oral communication,' a type of thinking aloud of the kind that might happen in research as much as in teaching, the lecturing teacher today is most often one whose role or function is *only* to lecture and to teach. Instead of the consolidation of spirit, of sparks flying to light fires in other's souls, multiple, fully disaggregated functions and roles, as determined by state funding decisions, are now clearly defined and growing in importance.

When the lecture is regarded as a rehearsed performance – rather than as an authentic expression of the soul – the 'self' or 'selves' that function and are positioned within it also appear rather differently. Certainly, since the early 20th century – if not since Nietzsche's earlier characterizations – the authentic, spontaneous and self-producing self of the Romantic era and its knowledge has been effectively shattered. This applies to the lecturer as well as his or her audience. The lecturing self is reduced to a talking mouth, talking head, or a number of selves or academic roles. 'Unconstrained oral communication to an audience' resulting in 'a significant number of intelligences thinking in unison' has turned into something much closer to a highly coordinated apparatus, a 'curious speaking and hearing procedure' that provides only the *illusion* of the autonomy of thought and action. The many listening ears and writing hands of the audience are thus expected to participate not in the expansion of intellect or reflective self-awareness, but to allow themselves to be momentarily taken in by an *illusion* of unity.

In conclusion, it could be argued that radio, television and their recent permutations on the internet, as well as its manifold 'screenings' all draw attention not to 'what is said' but to '*how* it is spoken' as Rudolph Arnheim noted (1936, p. 36; emphasis in original). In these cases, what is important is clearly *not* ideas, spirit, or intellect, but rather, the precise way that the 'movement in the air which surrounds us,' to use Fichte's words, can be captured and reproduced. Correspondingly, the labor associated with this has become ever more specialized, narrowly focused, and also flexible and precarious.

The academic lecture is being steadily peeled away from the production and circulation of knowledge, from what we might call the substance of teaching and learning. Foucault was surely not the only one to feel like a kind of actor whose recorded performance is more important than any active engagement with the lecturer or what he has said. He is not alone in feeling disappointed and alone. It is the almost certainly the fate of an ever-larger number of teachers who are engaging in a kind of second order or third order showing and also telling, never seeing their web audiences directly or spending time inside of the research lab or library. Regardless, the very persistence of the lecture as a key pedagogical form at a time of the state's embrace of technical and entrepreneurial paradigms for education demonstrates something very important. This is the survival of meanings, experiences and purposes of 'the lecture' as something that comes to us from the past. And these, I believe, are eminently worthy of recognition, investigation and reflection if not also of re-enactment and celebration.

Notes

1 This article is loosely based on chapters 8 and 9 in Friesen, N. (2017). *The Textbook and the Lecture: Education in the Age of New Media*. Baltimore, MA: Johns Hopkins University Press.
2 For example, referencing audio tapes of Foucault's later lectures at the Collège de France, the editors of *Biopolitics* note: 'We have made use of the recordings made by Gilbert Burlet and Jacques Lagrange in particular […] Suspension points [in the text] indicate that the recording is inaudible' (Foucault 2008, pp. xv, xvii).
3 Foucault sees the lecture simply as an instance of (mostly written) 'discourse.' Bourdieu views it in terms of (mostly unwritten) aspects of power, practice, and ritual. Derrida, for his part, sees the lecture as yet another instance of generalized forms of speaking, writing, and even thought – what he labels 'arche-writing.'

References

Agarwal, A. (2013). In J.R. Young, The New Rock-Star Professor: Should celebrities teach online classes? *Slate*, 6. Accessed December 6, 2016. http://www.slate.com/articles/technology/futuretense/2013/11/udacity_courserashouldcelebritiesteachmoocs.html.
Arnheim, R. (1936). *Radio*. London: Faber & Faber.
Bourdieu, P. (1982). A Lecture on the Lecture, in *In Other Words: Essays Toward a Reflexive Sociology*. Stanford, CA: Stanford University Press, pp. 17–19.
Bowman, C. (2017). Johann Gottlieb Fichte (1762–1814). Internet Encyclopedia of Philosophy. Accessed February 6, 2017. http://www.iep.utm.edu/fichtejg/.
Clark, W. (2006). *Academic Charisma and the Origins of the Research University*. Chicago, IL: University of Chicago Press.
Deem, R., Hillyard, S., and Reed, M. (2007). *Knowledge, Higher Education, and the New Managerialism: The Changing Management of UK Universities*. Oxford: Oxford University Press.
Derrida, J. (2002). The University without Condition, in P. Kamuf (Ed.) *Without Alibi*. Stanford, CA: Stanford University Press, pp. 202–280.
Ehrlich, A. (1977). *Fichte als Redner*. [Fichte as a Speaker]. Munich: tuduv-Verlagsgesellschaft.
Fichte, J.G. (1993). Concerning the Difference between the Spirit and the Letter in Philosophy, in D. Breazeale (Ed.) *Fichte: Early Philosophical Writings*. Ithaca, NY: Cornell University Press, pp. 185–216.
FoucaultM. (1970). *Folie, littérature, société*. Interview with T. Shimizu and M. Wantanabe. Accessed February 10, 2017. http://1libertaire.free.fr/MFoucault351.html.
Foucault, M. (1981). The Order of Discourse, in R. Young (Ed.) *Untying the Text: A Post-Structuralist Reader*. London: Routledge, pp. 51–78.
Foucault, M. (2008). *The Birth of Biopolitics: Lectures at the Collège de France, 1978–1979*. New York: Palgrave.
Friesen, N. (2015). Dewey's Cosmic Traffic: Politics and Pedagogy as Communication, in M. Naser-Lather and C. Neubert (Eds.) *Traffic: Media as Infrastructures and Cultural Practices*. Leiden: Brill.
Gallo, C. (2014). 9 Public-Speaking Lessons from the World's Greatest TED Talks. *Forbes*, March 4.https://www.forbes.com/sites/carminegallo/2014/03/04/9-public-speaking-lessons-from-the-worlds-greatest-ted-talks/#2d833b4c4a9d.
Geminus. (1960). It seems to me. *New Scientist*, May 19, 1290.

Goffman, E. (1981). *The Lecture*, in *Forms of Talk*. Philadelphia, PA: University of Pennsylvania Press, pp. 162–195.

Humboldt-Universität zu Berlin (2016). Short History. https://www.hu-berlin.de/en/about/history/huben_html/huben_html.

Ince, R. (2012). Bertrand Russell: The first media academic. Archive on 4. London: BBC Worldwide Limited, 2012. Accessed February 11, 2017. http://www.bbc.co.uk/programmes/b019dzpp.

Introna, L.D. and Ilharco, F.M. (2006). On the Meaning of Screens: Towards a Phenomenological Account of Screenness. *Human Studies, 29(1)*, 57–76.

Karlsohn, T. (2014). On Humboldtian and Contemporary Notions of the Academic Lecture, in T. Karlsohn and P. Josephson (Eds). *The Humboldtian Tradition: Origins and Legacies*. Leiden: Brill, (pp. 44–57).

Kittler, F. (1990). *Discourse Networks: 1800/1900*. Stanford, CA: Stanford University Press.

Kittler, F. (2013). *Philosophien der Literatur: Berliner Vorlesung 2002*. Berlin: Merve Verlag.

Klass, G. (2000). Plato as Distance Education Pioneer: Status and Quality Threats of Internet Education. *First Monday 5(7)*. Accessed February 7, 2017. http://firstmonday.org/ojs/index.php/fm/rt/printerFriendly/775/684.

Knoblauch, H. (2012). *PowerPoint, Communication, and the Knowledge Society*. Cambridge: Cambridge University Press.

Lawler, L.J. (1964). Lecturing by Television. *New Scientist*, July 16, 174.

Nietzsche, F. (2016). *Anti-Education: On the Future of Our Educational Institutions*. New York: New York Review of Books.

Prange, K. (2012). *Die Zeigestruktur der Erziehung: Grundriss der operativen Pädagogik*. Paderborn: Ferdinand Schöningh.

Reisz, M. (2012). Bertrand Russell: The First Media Academic. *Times Higher Education*, January 12. https://www.timeshighereducation.com/features/culture/the-pick-bertrand-russell-the-first-media-academic/418684.article.

von Humboldt, W. (1970). On the Spirit and Organisational Framework of Intellectual Institutions in Berlin. *Minerva 8(2)*, 242–267.

Wikipedia contributors. (2018). TED (conference), July 23. In *Wikipedia, The Free Encyclopedia*. Accessed July 28, 2018. https://en.wikipedia.org/w/index.php?title=TED_(conference)&oldid=851646382.

Young, J.R. (2013). The New Rock-Star Professor: Should celebrities teach online classes? *Slate*. Accessed July 28, 2018. https://slate.com/technology/2013/11/udacity-coursera-should-celebrities-teach-moocs.html.

Chapter 2

Education and world disclosure in the age of the screen
On screens, hands and owning the now

Joris Vlieghe

If education can be defined in terms of a disclosure of the world to the new generation (Arendt 1961), the *technologies* that are used to make this world present make a difference. For a long time, and increasingly so since the rise of Modernity, printed texts have been the dominant medium for bringing into presence the world and making pupils and students attentive to it (Postman 1982; Mollenhauer 2013; Friesen 2017). Up until this day it is very common to believe that in order to become educated one has to read and study books (and that these are, to a certain degree, more important than experiencing the world in a direct, unmediated, manner). As such, it could be said that the book is the *Leitmedium* of modern education (cf. Böhme 2006). It goes without saying that, in principle, an upbringing without books is a possibility (as imagined, for instance, by Rousseau (1979)), but this is the exception to the rule. In view of this, it could be argued that the specific technological characteristics of this medium have decided largely on what modern education looks like. Presenting a content orally is not the same as presenting the same content in a printed way. And the same could be argued when differentiating between disclosing the world with the aid of a book scroll and doing this using the current book format (codex) with bound pages (cf. Vlieghe 2015).

To give just some examples of the importance of technology for our very understanding of education, the notion that there are definite answers to problems, and that an exhaustive theory about the world is possible, or desirable, is dependent on the existence of books – a container of pages that reads from cover to cover, from beginning to end, the content of which, inerasably fixed to paper, never changes.[1] But, also, the very idea that there are exact definitions of concepts, and that a precise formulation matters – an idea that is crucial to what it means to become an educated person today – is dependent on the possibility of fixating our ideas about the world in a printed form (cf. Eisenstein 1979). The idea that in case of a dispute we *just* have to look things up is bound up with the existence of books, the pages of which are univocally numbered, and that preferably have an index – something that was absolutely impossible in an age where scrolls or handwritten texts used to be the dominant cultural medium (Illich 1996; cf. Marin et al. 2018). Moreover, that education is for all and that it is an enterprise that should concern the whole populace would be utterly unthinkable in the era before the invention of the printing press: printing has not only democratized knowledge previously reserved for the elites, it has also made it possible that text is omnipresent and thus that the capacity for reading and writing has become almost a life necessity (Postman 1982).

In that sense, the (printed) book has been a vitally important educational technology. And I mean here technology in a *strong* sense. Following the French philosopher Bernard Stiegler (1998), it could be argued that technologies are not mere instruments at our disposal, in the sense that we could just interchange a dominant technology for a new one without this having enormous consequences for who we are. Technologies not only support but they also shape our subjectivities. They set the limits of what we can, and cannot, say, think, and do. Now, Stiegler goes on to argue, the sense of educational institutions is first and foremost making the young acquainted with the prevailing technologies that structure our access to the world, as well as teaching them to use these technologies in a responsible and critical way. This also means that a shift in the dominant cultural technology has major consequences for what it means both to educate and to be educated.

In view of this, it is important to take stock of a contemporary evolution that seems to threaten the survival, or at least to have a major impact on the preponderance of the book: the transition from what Serge Tisseron (2010) has called the 'culture of the book' to the 'culture of the screen.' By this, he doesn't suggest that we will stop reading or that our digital future will no longer be text based. Rather, the book and the screen are different apparatuses that come with entirely different experiences of what it means to have and gain knowledge, to be an individual, and to live together with others. For instance, in the culture of the book, one can only read one text at the same time, one can only accomplish one reading task at a time, and this task is fulfilled with a care that is uniquely devoted to understanding this one book. In the culture of the screen, by contrast, many screens are staring at their user simultaneously, one can engage in multiple tasks, and these tasks remain always unfinished and provisional. These differences in reading habitus come with different ways in which our relation to reality is structured: we deal with the world in the way we deal with books and screens. Hence, for Tisseron we are witnessing today a transmutation from the 'culture of one' to a 'culture of the multiple.'

Tisseron goes on detecting other related shifts, for instance, the transition from a linear form of thinking (related to the way one traditionally reads through books) to a spatial one (more apt to the networked features of our screen-based devices). He argues, moreover, that the way in which we constitute ourselves as coherent individual beings is rapidly changing. Formerly, processes of identification mirrored the unity and stability of the book – in that we became who we are as the result of repressing of undesired aspects of our lives. As a result, we gained a stable and homogeneous identity. But today,

Tisseron argues, a shift is taking place to identification processes that reflect what we are doing sitting in front of our screens: here, we have multiple identities that we can switch on and off, and between which we can easily change. As such we no longer need to repress parts of our subjectivity, but rely on a kind of splitting of the self. Tisseron's analysis is not far removed from Illich's hypothesis that thanks to reading books we have become *homo textualis*. This involves that, in our self-understanding as human beings, it is crucial that we are 'endowed with a conscience that can be examined as you would consult a book' (Illich 1996, p. 11). This, Illich seems to suggest, completely changes with the advent of *homo digitalis*.

Against this background, I want to focus in this chapter on the impact of the ubiquitous screen, on the way we structure our relation to the world, and how this affects our understanding of education. Again, if education can be defined in terms of world disclosure, it makes all the difference whether this happens via the book or via the screen. More exactly, I argue that the transition to the culture of the screen comes with important *ontological* implications.[2] With this I mean that the most fundamental things, e.g., that there is a meaningful world out there to gain access to, to become attentive for and to care for, change. The world as it appears on the screen has its own characteristic way of being, and this entails that the very meaning of educating and being educated in and for this world transmogrifies. But, rather than developing Tisseron's perspective further, I will turn to the work of Vilém Flusser and the account he gives of the television screen as a perfected window, which comes with a radically new mode of experience of reality.

Understanding the screenness of screens: a reversed genealogical and phenomenological approach

Before doing this, I would like to make a few methodological comments. The argument I develop here is partly historical and partly phenomenological. First, my thoughts are inspired by what Lev Manovich (2001) has called a 'genealogy of the screen.' For Manovich, the screen is a very broad phenomenon and it comprises things we don't always regard as screens, such as paintings or photographs. In his definition, a screen opens 'another virtual space, another three-dimensional world enclosed by a frame and situated inside our normal space. The frame separates two absolutely different spaces that somehow coexist' (p. 99). Now, in order to understand the meaning of the screen as it is more usually understood, we have to move beyond often taken-for-granted views. Often, the meaning of the screen remains unclear to us because we are too close to it given the frequency with which we use it. Hence, it is important to delve into the past and see how particular and contingent events have had a decisive impact on what we know today to be a screen. For instance, it might be instructive to realize that our computer screens go back to radar screens, developed in the Second World War to give real-time information about the location of enemy airplanes. Looking for a manner to avoid the time gap that came with making photographs that could be viewed and analyzed only later, radar technology was the first to establish an instantaneous relation between things that happen in the real world (e.g., an aircraft entering the airspace at a given location) and what happens on the screen. This is decisive for the future of the screen. Older screens can only show past events. With radar, we see for the first time the mass employment (television is founded on the same principle but its mass employment comes later) of a fundamentally new type of screen, the screen which gradually comes to dominate modern visual culture – video monitor, computer screen, instrument display. What is new about such a screen is that its image can change in real time, reflecting changes in the referent, be it the position of an object in space (radar), any alteration in visible reality (live video) or changing data in the computer's memory (computer screen). The image can be continually updated in real time. This is […] the screen of real time' (Manovich 2001 p. 102).

Going further back in time, it appears that the first screens were actually developed out of flat objects that were meant to screen something off (e.g., a fire screen, or a shield to cover the naked body after bathing). Only later does the screen become a projection screen (Huhtamo 2013). The importance of this is that the screen has kept something of its 'original' features, hence we must take this into account when considering what it means to look at a screen today. More concretely, it becomes clear, then, that the screen is not only a means for making something appear. Instead, something can only appear as the result of screening something else off. The screen has the structure of the Heideggerian definition of truth, i.e., in terms of *aletheia* (cf. Introna and Ilharco 2006): the four borders that constitute the screen only allow for drawing attention to what it makes appear by simultaneously hiding particular things (viz., the surroundings). This explains why screens are always *visual*.

Now, the argument I develop differs in one substantial respect from a genealogical approach. I argue that the screen as we know it today, i.e., the interactive digital screen, is not only to be understood based on past events that have shaped (or determined) it. More importantly, the contemporary screen shows us something about all screens – and thus also about all screens past (in the sense Manovich defines them). Older forms of screens, be it paintings, cinema screens, television screens, etc., only imperfectly materialized the possibilities that come with the digital screen. In other words, the digital screen is the screen *par excellence*, a perfected screen that discloses what it *means* to use screen interfaces – it shows what *the* screen is, or has been, all about (inclusive of paintings, cinema screens, television screens, etc.). In that sense, my approach counts as a reversed genealogy of the screen.

Second, my interest in this issue is also phenomenological.[3] That is, I am interested in giving a detailed and rich account of what we experience when we disclose the world through a screen – and how this is different from a world without screens present. Take the analogy of mirrors (cf. Merleau-Ponty 1994, pp. 125, 129): in order to understand what it means that we can see mirror images (and our own mirror image), and to explain why mirrors are so fascinating to look into, it is not sufficient to have an understanding of the laws of optics. Rather, we would have to imagine a world without mirrors (not only without glass mirrors, but also without reflecting water surfaces) and what it entails to live in such a world. Our experience of reality (and of ourselves) would be totally different. I will come back to this later on, as the digital screen is also a mirror (which becomes very apparent when we turn it off). One could even ask the question whether in a world without mirrors screens would ever have come about.[4] The important point to stress for now is *that screens bring about a particular experience of reality*, and that it is important to analyze phenomenologically *what it means* to see things appear on a screen (cf. Carbone 2015)

This entails that I am not so much interested in the content that appears on screens, as I am in the phenomenon of *screening* itself (as Introna and Ilharco (2006) call it). This goes against the bulk of the existing literature on the impact of digital media that focuses on the new ways in which information is available, communication is structured and ideas are created thanks to digital technologies. This is an approach that is most fruitful and justifiable. However, in this chapter, my focus is fully on the use of screens *as such*. As Introna and Ilharco (Ibid.) have argued, regardless of the specific content that appears on the screen, all screens share the *ontological* feature that we already agree that what is to be seen on the screen is relevant and truthful. Screens only work in the way they do because there is what they call an *already agreement*. We must assume that the screen frames whatever appears on it as true and relevant. Of course, we can realize that what is shown on the screen is irrelevant or false, but this always involves the correction of the more original propensity that what we see is what we believe. It is this already agreement that makes the screen into a screen, Introna and Ilharco hold. As hinted at above, when I discussed the Heideggerian truth concept, it is no accident that screens are visual phenomena: it appears that seeing is our means to get access to the world (to the extent that we also use the word seeing to refer to perceiving with other senses – for instance, when we invite someone to feel that a piece of textile that might appear soft actually *feels* rough, and then add 'do you *see*?').

So, in the remaining part of this chapter I want to investigate further the ontological meaning of the screen – not in terms of screen contents, but in terms of the screen as a specific phenomenon that frames reality and that comes with a particular understanding of what reality is. In order to do so, I first turn to the work of media theorist Vilém Flusser, and, more particularly, to his text *Phenomenology of Watching Television* (Flusser 1997) – a most intriguing phenomenological account of how we make sense of the world when we see the world appear on a screen.

Towards an ontology of the screen: television as a perfected window

Although Flusser's text was written before the digital revolution, it is prophetic in many respects. Here, Flusser predicted the rise of the internet as an inevitable consequence of ever more perfected television screens: if we really take seriously the potential television has, this technology simply *has to* become an interactive tool one day, so Flusser envisaged. What interests me more, however, is the opposition he introduces between two fundamental categories under which things appear on screens. These categories are *Vorstellung* and *Darstellung* – which could be translated, albeit not exactly, as representation and presentation. *Darstellung* is, for instance, what we see through a window: when building a house, we leave an open space in the wall in order to see what is out there. As such, the window is a particular *perception form* (*Wahrnehmungsform*): it defines what we can and cannot see (things that are behind the walls are rendered invisible), and it focuses our attention in a particular way (as taken up by Renaissance artists when developing linear perspective). *Vorstellung* is, for instance, what we see when watching an arthouse film: we are well aware that what we see happening in front of our eyes should not be taken as reality. It is solely a representation of a possible reality, but we don't take it to be true. At first, this distinction might not seem helpful, as much of the images we see on television can clearly be categorized as *Vorstellung*. However, so Flusser argues, the power films have to attract our attention is predicated on the more fundamental potential of the screen to present reality (*Darstellung*). Cinema works thanks to a momentary suspension of disbelief, and therefore it is only a flawed application of what television screens render possible.

What Flusser proposes is thus to define, phenomenologically, what watching a television screen is essentially about in terms of a reality effect. It is for that reason that he calls it a perfected window. Now, this analysis is, at first sight, close to Roland Barthes's (1981) account of the effect of non-digital photographic images. When we look at a photo we know that there is a direct causal relation between the thing in front of the camera, the traces left on the photo-receptive filmstrip, and the printed image. Hence, there is an *immediate* sense that what we see on the photograph is real. There is a sense of what Roland Barthes calls 'ça a été.' This reality effect is both unquestionable and direct (our certainty is not the result of an inference, we *just* sense the thing printed on the photo to be real). This explains that the effect photographs have is far more superior than paintings can ever have. Even though a meticulously crafted portrait by Jan Van Eyck is more realistic than a damaged black and white photograph of Baudelaire, the last feels more real, because there is a causal chain between the image and the great poet (the photons that touched the filmstrip, touched Baudelaire's body; cf. Stiegler 2002, p. 76). Something analogous, but in a more improved sense, might apply in the case of the screen.

Education and world disclosure

In spite of the similarities with Barthes' point of view, this is not exactly the point Flusser tries to make.[5] His point is *that the television screen allows us to see things we could never see before, but that are nevertheless real*. We can see things that are too small or too big according to the standards of our ordinary perception, e.g., we can witness chromosomes moving through the cell during cellular growth. We can also see things that we normally cannot perceive because they happen too slowly or too quickly, e.g., we can see a plant moving in the direction of the sunlight, or see the regularities and structures in the movements of the galloping of a horse (as in Muybridge's experiments). We can also take different perspectives on one and the same thing, as the result of travelling, zooming in and out, and other camera techniques.[6] In spite of the fact that we need the screen technology to make these things visible, they are real. Chromosomes and plants really move. What we see on the screen is *Darstellung* – not *Vorstellung*: something is brought into presence, but in such a way that the possibilities offered by traditional perception are surpassed. Hence, so Flusser holds, the television screen is an ameliorated, if not a perfected window.

Like the window, the screen is a technology, but a far more superior one, that discloses the world (*stellt die Welt dar*). The perception form of watching television extends our capacities for making sense of the world *fundamentally*. At this point, Flusser refers to Kant's transcendental aesthetics. For Kant, all perception is structured according to the *a priori* forms of time and space. That is, there are inherent structural properties to time and space that inevitably shape whatever it is we perceive. For instance, we immediately know that an Escher drawing cannot be real, as it goes against the most fundamental conceptions we have about spatiality. When walking up the stairs, we are confident that we will never end up at the beginning of the stairs (as in an Escher drawing). The important thing is that we do not need to think about this: our certainty is not the result of a deduction. Instead, it is *immediately given* in the very act of perceiving reality.

Likewise, we take the chromosome and heliotrope movements we see on the screen as real – immediately and without the need for deduction. In this regard, there is no difference with what happens when we look through a window. However, this would not have been possible in Kant's day and age.[7] So, what Flusser is arguing for is that, because of the invention of television screens, we are witnessing today a *radical* shift in perception forms. This is not merely a matter of a change in cognitive or affective structures, but more essentially *a transmogrification of our whole sense of what counts as real*. And so, Flusser does not shy away from claiming that the fact that the world can be disclosed through screens and that we take what we see for real has turned us into a new kind of human being.

In conclusion, the screen, as a perfected window, can be seen as a framing apparatus that makes things appear in ways that were inconceivable in the past. It frames differently what it means that the world appears to us, not only cognitively and affectively, but also *qua reality*. That there is a world outside, that something counts as real, that something is real enough to be worthy of our attention, etc. thus gets a completely new meaning.[8] As such a major ontological shift has taken place. In the next section, I will develop further what could be called, in Flusser's spirit, an ontology of the screen. At the same time, I will also challenge Flusser's ideas. Obviously, my interest lies in the digital screen and not the television screen. I will hold that it is the *digital* screen that brings about this ontological shift – and, as indicated – that this has always been what screens are essentially about: a particular *Darstellung* of the world. Hence, it is not the case that the (television) screen is the perfected window, so much as that the digital screen is the perfected screen. Understanding the meaning of the digital screen entails an understanding of the screen *as such*.

The perfected screen: tactile vision and to own the now

As I just said, I have serious doubts that the window is an accurate metaphor for understanding the screen ontologically – i.e., for articulating that what appears on screen is framed as *Darstellung*. In fact, a whole series of alternative metaphors have been suggested: as I said earlier on, the screen could be regarded as a mirror, but others have also intimated that the screen is a face (Wellner 2014, inspired by Levinas), skin (Dalmasso 2013, inspired by Merleau-Ponty), a wall (rather than as a window (Virilio 1994)). Even toilets have been considered as adequate descriptions of what screens essentially are.[9] Anyway, as Mauro Carbone (2013) suggests, the window is a metaphysical apparatus that installs a split between two realms. It sets apart and opposes two spaces: there is a 'here' and a 'there.' The window produces a space where someone sees without being seen herself as opposed to a space of full visibility on the other side.

Hence, the basic operation related to windows is 'seeing-through' or 'seeing-beyond': we move from one realm to the other. The screen, by way of contrast, is not a transparent medium (cf. Dalmasso 2013). As indicated at the beginning of the text, the screen hides (screens off), and as such it is an opaque medium. However, this opacity does not constitute an impediment: as Carbone (2013) argues, it is exactly thanks to this opacity that we can see things and events on a screen (in the sense that Merleau-Ponty also claims that we have the capacity to see not in spite, but thanks to our bodies (Ibid.)). More exactly, when watching a screen we do not see through it, or beyond it, being transported towards another realm. Rather, we are thrown back onto ourselves, in the sense that we have an embodied experience that reverberates with what is to be seen on the screen. We look at the screen and the screen looks back.[10]

I don't want to make too much out of Carbone's speculations here, since they might apply to what we experience when watching a film, but they do not apply to screens in general. Nevertheless, I follow him in his critical analysis that the window is not a suitable metaphor.[11] This is especially so if we consider what we experience when we watch the screen of our handheld devices. We hold our smartphone in the palm of our hands, but it is not as if we stare through our hand into a realm on the other side. Instead, what we see immediately fuses with our tactile experience of holding our device in our hand. Cooley (2004) refers to this synesthetic mode of perception as *tactile vision*. We simultaneously see and hold the world in our hand. Rather than being a metaphysical apparatus, the screen of our mobile screenic device is a radically immanent apparatus. There is nothing 'beyond' what we seize by our very hand that has relevance and counts as real.

This explains why people can visit an art museum, not in a traditional contemplative manner (e.g., finding the right position before the painting and then slowly contemplating it), but simply by staring at the screen of their smartphone while shooting or filming art objects. What counts as relevant and real is that the art works in question are now somewhere stored in their screen-based device. Consider also the transition in the meaning of shooting photographs. Whereas this practice used to consist of *making* pictures, i.e., using the camera in order to produce a printed photograph that existed separately from the machine with the aid of which it has been produced, smartphone photography is literally *taking* pictures: the photograph remains in the machine, as it is the same screen that we use to generate and to look at the picture.

What is at stake is that the things that appear on the smartphone screen, thanks to the merging of the visual and the tactile, appear at the same time as real (in Flusser's sense of *Darstellung) and* as something I possess here and now: they are real because they are the only things that are relevant and that matter; and they are our own possession as looking at what appears on the screen coincides with the experience of grasping and owning. In that sense, the best metaphor for the screen is perhaps the mirror. When something appears on the screen it appears as 'our own' – something that we ourselves own. But, on a basic phenomenological level, this case can be made harder. I refer here to the famous experiments of Henri Wallon about how infants and apes respond to the reflection in a mirror.[12] The gist of Wallon's work is that animals don't show a particular interest in what appears on the screen and start looking behind the mirror, whereas children are completely captivated by the phenomenon of self-reflection itself. It seems that they are fascinated by the fact that on a flat reflective surface (be it a glass mirror or the water of the lake) things can appear. Confronted with reflections on mirrors we cannot *not* look. And that is probably not different from our relation to screens.

The argument I want to make is, first, that this experience we can have with the screen of our smartphones teaches us something about the ontological meaning of *the* screen, of all screens. Suggesting here a reversed genealogy, it could be argued that paintings, photographs, television screens, etc. are all about the experience of holding, or trying to grasp the world (in one's hand). It is the smartphone that brings this into full actualization. Second, in the age of the digital screen we witness a radical transformation of what counts as real and relevant. Realness and relevancy seem to be defined by what appears on the screen of our smartphone.[13] This entails that our relation to the world becomes an entirely immanent affair.

This dovetails with the analysis Michel Serres (2012) has presented in his essay on the new, digital generation, *Petite Poucette* – which, to my knowledge, has not been translated into English, but which, referring to the Dutch translation (*De wereld onder de duim*), could be rendered as *The World under our Thumb*. This text, interestingly, has very concrete implications for thinking about what education is all about. This small text could be read as a critique of the transmission model of education, i.e., that in an age in which we have constant online access to all available knowledge, we should no longer demand of the new generation to memorize learning contents. Instead we should take this previously unknown situation as a fantastic opportunity and as a liberation from mind-numbing study practices. Instead of learning things by heart, it is more important now to learn how to deal critically and responsibly with the streams of information we have at our disposal.

Serres suggests all this, but I don't think that this is the most interesting point he is making. After all, this merely speaks to an age-old discussion between teacher-centered and student-centered models of education. This is a discussion that fully remains within the parameters of what we take education to be. What Serres hints at is that, with the advent of screen-based technologies, the very notion of education might change altogether. As suggested in the beginning of this chapter, education could be seen as being essentially about disclosing the world to the new generation. In a culture of the book, this means something radically different as compared to this happening in a culture of the screen. The main difference, so I have tried to argue in this text, is that world disclosure used to be a matter of transcendence, whereas today, or in the near future, it becomes fully a matter of immediacy: what counts as relevant and real, is that which I can grasp in my hand, here and now.[14]

Or, to use another terminology Serres relies on a lot: the condition under which the generation of digital natives grows up is one of '*maintenant*'. This French word signifies both 'now' and 'holding in one's hand' (*main-tenant*). What matters is thus *that we own the now*. If this analysis is correct, it has major implications for educational theory and philosophy. If we want to think about how to give shape to future education, and about how to bring the world into presence to the new generation, we have to take into account that the experience of disclosing the world has undergone a radical shift in meaning. This is, we will have to respond to conditions that are hitherto unforeseen. This, of course, entails much more than accepting or stimulating the use of handheld devices in schools, but will require that we conceive of education in a new, fully immanent key.

Notes

1 This, at least is a thesis defended by Michel Melot (2004) who elaborates Panofsky's famous contention that linear perspective is not just a technological invention but a 'symbolic form'. This is a form that expresses a whole world view and that defines a way of thinking. For Melot the book is the symbolic form *par excellence* of western civilization.

2 Throughout this article I will use the terms *ontology* and *ontological* in a strictly phenomenological sense: reality *as it appears to us* changes substantially. The way I use these words also relates to the Foucaultian project of a historical ontology: throughout time the conditions of what counts as real shift (Cf. Hacking 2004 and footnote 7).
3 The approach I develop here could also be called post-phenomenological in the sense of the work of Don Ihde (2010), who tries to integrate phenomenological analysis with an interest in the historical conditions of technological objects in their full materiality.
4 In his genealogical endeavours to understand 'new media,' Manovich (2001) argues that digital media originated in the contingent event of coupling two already existing technologies, viz., the calculator and the screen. I would argue that this coupling is not enough, and we also have to add mirror technology as a precondition for digital media to come about.
5 In another text, Flusser (2000) actually criticizes the so-called reality effect that comes with photography. Too often we forget that the photo camera is a machine that takes a lot of decisions for us. It is a 'black box' that operates autonomously: the photographer only decides to press the button at a given moment, but she has no knowledge of the mechanical and optical processes that makes the image appear on the lens (whereas we can much more easily imagine how a painting is constructed).
6 In that sense, Dziga Vertov's experimental film *Man with a Movie Camera* would be a very good illustration of the point Flusser is making: the many different positions the camera can take discloses the world in new and unforeseen ways, substituting our natural eyes with a 'kino-eye' (cf. Manovich 2001). This is of course most ironical, as it are the techniques we owe to the invention of cinema (*Vorstellung*) that made possible the effects Flusser makes so much of (*Darstellung*).
7 In this respect, Flusser is close to Michel Foucault's (2003) idea of the *historical a priori*: there are conceptual structures that, *a priori*, shape how the world appears, but these structures themselves change throughout history. Different eras come with different subjectification forms.
8 A good illustration of this last point, moving on from television to digital screens, is what we experience when we communicate with friends and family using Skype-like technology, for instance, when we have moved house to a far-away country. In this case, it is not uncommon for digital natives to experience the meeting as a *real* encounter. It seems that conditions that used to be vital, such as physical presence or the possibility of touching one another, have become meaningless for them. The so-called virtual encounter doesn't feel in any way less meaningful and less real. Furthermore, it would make sense to claim that during such a conversation, one is literally in the presence of one's loved ones. This would go completely against any traditional notion of spatiality as articulated in Kant's philosophy. For Kant, being in space *means* being at point x and hence not being at any other location. One cannot be in two places at the same time. However, due to the invention of interactive screens it has become *possible* to *experience* exactly this. As a consequence, fundamental notions regarding what it means to be at home and to be abroad have radically changed – or, more exactly: they have become meaningless, they are no longer perceived as real (cf. Godart 2016).
9 This is suggested by Zizek in the documentary *The Pervert's Guide to Cinema* (2006). Commenting on the famous scene in *The Conversation* (1974) where the surveillance expert tries to find out what is happening in the hotel room next door, when the toilet overflows with the blood of the victim of the killers he is trailing. This is a most unpleasant experience, Zizek holds, as our expectation is that what we flush away doesn't return. Zizek then goes on to argue that this is exactly what cinema does: repressing something that nevertheless can return.

10 As Wellner (2014) argues, screen-based devices always appear as closely intertwined with our own bodies, in the sense that they address us as a face (or, more exactly, as a quasi-face). For instance, '[t]he screen of the cell phone, like a facade of a home, represents an exteriority which hides an interiority. The screen acts like a face that requires a response' (Ibid., p. 311). Therefore, in order to understand our rapports to the digital, we need to take into consideration bodily and emotional qualities that relate to the screen that always appears as something other (alterity) in the strong sense of that word.
11 In a sense, this has been corroborated by the designers of the graphical operating systems of our computers. For a long time, the most popular of these was indeed called Windows (cf. Carbone 2013). However, for our smartphones we use now an interface that is fully based on touching virtual buttons. And indeed, the most recent versions of Microsoft Windows Software have started to imitate touch-based smartphone interfaces.
12 This, of course, has been taken up by Lacan in his formulation of the mirror stage (Lacan 1953).
13 Against this, it could be brought in that we do not know how our digital technologies will look like in, say, 30 years. Maybe they will become integrated in our bodies to such an extent that they can no longer be called convincingly screens in a phenomenological sense. Nonetheless, if we try to make a representation of what this entails, it is difficult to get around the screen, as is shown in Keiichi Matsuda's project of a hyper-realist view of the future (https://www.youtube.com/watch?v=YJg02ivYzSs).
14 Cf. the work of Till Heilmann (2010) on the digital. Loosely inspired by McLuhan, Heilmann holds that we have to understand the digital as a new cultural technique that is based on hitting keys with our fingers.

References

Arendt, H. (1961). The Crisis in Education, in *Between Past and Future: Eight Exercises in Political Thought*. New York: Viking Press.

Barthes, R. (1981). *Camera Lucida*, translated by Richard Howard. New York: Hill & Wang.

Böhme, J. (2006). *Schule am Ende der Buchkultur. Medientheoretische Begründungen schulischer Bildungsarchitekturen*. Bad Heilbrunn: Klinkhardt.

Carbone, M. (2013). La vie mouvementée des écrans. *Écrans*, 1(3), 21–33.

Carbone, M. (2015). *The Flesh of Images. Merleau-Ponty between Painting and Cinema*, translated by M. Nijhuis. New York: SUNY.

Cooley, H. (2004). It's All About the Fit: The Hand, the Mobile Screenic Device and Tactile Vision. *Journal of Visual Culture*, 3(2), 133–155.

Dalmasso, C. (2013) Voir selon l'écran. Autour d'une rencontre entre visibilité et théorie filmique, in M. Carbone (Ed.) *L'empreinte du visuel*. Les Acacias: Metis-Presses, pp. 107–125.

Eisenstein, E. (1979). *The Printing Press as an Agent of Change: Communications and cultural transformations in early modern Europe* (2 vols.). Cambridge: Cambridge University Press.

Flusser, V. (2000). *Towards a Philosophy of Photography*, translated by Anthony Mathews. London: Reaktion Books.

Flusser, V. (1997). Für eine Phänomenologie des Fernsehens, in S. Bollmann (Ed.) *Medienkultur*, = ftb 13386. Frankfurt am Main: Fischer Taschenbuch Verlag, pp. 103–123.

Foucault, M. (2003). *Archaeology of Knowledge*, translated by. A.M. Sheridan Smith. London: Routledge.

Friesen, N. (2017). *The Textbook and the Lecture. Education in the Age of New Media*. Baltimore, MA: Johns Hopkins University Press.

Godart, E. (2016). *Je selfie donc je suis. Les métamorphoses du moi à l'ère du virtuel*. Paris: Albin Michel.

Hacking, I. (2004). *Historical Ontology*. Cambridge, MA: Harvard University Press.

Heilmann, T. (2010). Digitalität als Taktilität. McLuhan, der Computer und die Taste. *Zeitschrift für Medienwissenschaft, 2*, 125–134.

Huhtamo, E. (2013). *Illusions in Motion. Media Archaeology of the Moving Panorama and Related Spectacles*. Cambridge, MA: MIT Press.

Ihde, D. (2010). *Heidegger's Technologies: Postphenomenological Perspectives*. New York: Fordham University Press.

Illich, I. (1996). Text and University. On the idea and history of a unique institution. Accessed May 29, 2018. http://www.davidtinapple.com/illich/1991_text_and_university.PDF.

Introna, L. and Ilharco, F. (2006). On the Meaning of Screens: Towards a Phenomenological Account of Screenness. *Human Studies, 29(1)*, 57–76.

Lacan, J. (1953). Some Reflections on the Ego. *The International Journal of Psycho-Analysis, 34(1)*, 11–17.

Manovich, L. (2001). *The Language of New Media*. Cambridge, MA: MIT Press.

Marin, L., Masschelein, J., and Simons, M. (2018). Page, Text and Screen in the University: Revisiting the Illich hypothesis. *Educational Philosophy and Theory, 50(1)*, 49–60.

Melot, M. (2004). Le Livre comme forme symbolique. Conférence tenue dans le cadre de l'Ecole de l'Institut d'histoire du livre. Accessed May 29, 2018. http://ihl.enssib.fr/le-livre-comme-forme-symbolique.

Merleau-Ponty, M. (1994). Eye and Mind, in A.G. Johnson (Ed.), translated by M.B. Smith. *The Merleau-Ponty Aesthetics Reader*. Evanston, IL: Northwestern University Press, pp. 121–149.

Mollenhauer, K. (2013). *Forgotten Connections: On Culture and Upbringing*, translated by N. Friesen. London: Routledge.

Postman, N. (1982). *The Disappearance of Childhood*. New York: Vintage Books.

Rousseau, J.J. (1979). *Emile, or On Education*, translated by Allan Bloom. New York: Basic Books.

Tisseron, S. (2010). *Cultures du livre et des écrans. La cohabitation indispensable*. Le Carnet PSY, *144*.

Serres, M. (2012). *Petite Poucette*. Paris: Editions le Pommier.

Sobchack, V. (2004). *Carnal Thoughts: Embodiment and Moving Image Culture*. Berkeley, CA: University of California Press.

Stiegler, B. (1998). *Technics and Time, 1*, translated by Richard Beardsworth and George Collins. Stanford, CA: Stanford University Press.

Stiegler, B. (2002). The Discrete Image, in *Echographies of Television: Filmed Interviews*, translated by Jennifer Bajorek. Cambridge: Polity Press.

Virilio, P. (1994). *The Vision Machine*, translated by Julie Rose. Bloomington, IN: Indiana University Press.

Vlieghe, J. (2015). A Technosomatic Account of Education in Digital Times. Neil Postman's views on literacy and the screen revisited. *Studies in Philosophy and Education, 35(2)*, 163–179.

Wellner, G. (2014). The Quasi-Face of the *Cell*Phone: Rethinking alterity and screens. *Human Studies, 37(3)*, 299–316.

Chapter 3

Screening the classic: A case of re-mediation?
The new chronotope and some possible educational consequences

Stefano Oliverio

Introduction

The aim of this chapter is to contribute to the inquiry into 'schooling at the end of the book-culture' (Böhme 2006). In this phrasing, there are at least two assumptions: not only is the school, as the agency that 'organizes intergenerational relations' (Stiegler 2008, p. 127), to be studied in the light of *hypomnemata* – i.e., the set of technologies that are the condition of possibility for these relations to happen, in the form of the ushering in and sharing of a heritage – but the book has represented the main medium of the school as a specific educational institution and, therefore, its demise (in favor of the screen) implies either a dismantling of schooling or, at least, its overhaul.

Without being able to map out and discuss in this context all the theoretical positions addressing this issue, we could identify, with a grain of simplification, the two extremes of the gamut: on the one hand, there is the appeal to a homeostatic approach, in the wake of the pioneering studies of Neil Postman (1979). Dovetailing the ideas of Marshal McLuhan with the studies of Eric Havelock, Postman identified in timely fashion that a major process was going on in education with the transition from the book culture (promoting what he called the 'typographic mind' (Postman 1985)) to a screen culture (that, at the time in which Postman wrote, was represented by television: for an insightful reassessment of some of Postman's tenets, see Vlieghe 2016). He saw in this process a (possibly calamitous) threat to the kind of cognitive abilities that the school, as the institution of the book culture, had been able to ensure and advocated a sort of resistance to any attempt to make the school more convergent with the new techno-experiential constellation. In this view, the value of the school consists precisely in offering a context in which, 'homeostatically,' those abilities are to be cultivated that are at risk of disappearance on account of the new technologies and the kind of *forma mentis* that they promote (Postman 1979).

On the other hand, there is the appeal to (a sort of) *de*schooling, as the school would be a belated educational form in the age of the web. To illustrate this stance, I will refer to a work that does not engage with the question of the end of the book culture (being, instead, in many respects, also an extraordinary intellectual travel through many fundamental books of the Western tradition), insofar as it follows a completely different argumentative path, by creatively revisiting some nodes of Western philosophy in order to overcome modern schooling: I mean Robbie McClintock's (2012) superb *Enough. A Pedagogic Speculation*. However, McClintock's views, appropriated idiosyncratically here, are instrumental in advancing the present reflection, because, on the one hand, at the level of his explicit argumentation, he examines the modern school system as a case of a logic of the 'enclosure' (Ibid., ch. 2) that establishes boundaries in space (e.g., classrooms in school buildings), time (e.g., the succession of school grades according to the age of the children or the rigid division of the school hours), and curriculum (the compartimentalization of disciplines). The logic of the enclosure works as a device to distinguish between what lies within the boundaries and what without. On the other hand, at the level of the textual fabric of his volume, McClintock builds a kind of hypertext, thus problematizing and deconstructing the book form.

By combining these two dimensions – as aforementioned in an idiosyncratic move – we could argue that the book may be viewed as the technological correlate of the school as the site of the enclosure. McClintock's endeavour is to disengage education from its conflation with schooling and this requires replacing the logic of the enclosure (resulting from an 'area mapping' [Ibid., p. 31], which assigns to each element its definitive position) with the deployment of a 'place mapping,' which, instead, 'schematize[s] what potentially could take place by showing locations and the channels of interactions between them' (Ibid., p. 47). This move could be considered as coextensive with an overthrow of the book form in favor of the incessant building of connections on the web.[1] Indeed, to draw on Hans Blumenberg's (1986) conceptuality, we could argue that the book is a manifestation of area mapping insofar as it is the phenomenon of the construction of a unified totality out of what is 'disparate, set widely apart, contrasting' (pp. 17–18). As the 'weakening of the authenticity of experience' (Ibid., p. 17), replaced with 'the written and ultimately printed tradition' (Ibidem), the book is accomplice with the school as a site of enclosure and, by contrast, the screen could open up a new space of experience, possibly resulting in the complete demise of the school in favor of new disseminated and diffuse forms of education.

In the following I will address the question of the school as suspended between the (possibly declining) book era and the emerging screen era by focusing on the notions of the 'historical tradition' and the 'classic,' which are arguably pivotal in the school as an institution connected to the book culture. After investigating the educational significance of the phenomenon of the 'detraditionalization,' as an outcome of the emergence of new media (§ 1), I will zoom in on the idea of 'the classic' and on the specific historicist inflection of this notion, and I will explore whether and how it should be revisited in the light of the new technological constellation dominated by the screen.

Schooling and detraditionalization: the beheaded and the *'maintenants'*

I will take my cue from an insightful fragment from Novalis: 'Bücher sind eine moderne Gattung historischer Wesen, aber eine höchstbedeutende. Sie sind vielleicht an die Stelle der Traditionen getreten.' [Books are a modern kind of historical being, however a supremely significant one. They have perhaps taken the place of traditions.]

In its apothegmatic conciseness, this maxim gathers a wealth of meanings, all of which would be relevant for the present discussion. I will confine myself to highlighting only two points: first, the saying establishes a close connection between the notions of 'book,' 'modern,' and 'historical being.' We could venture to rephrase it as follows: in modernity the historical way of being that characterizes human beings comes to the fore through the book form; this is accordingly the vehicle of a *conscious* appropriation of the emergence of a *specific* kind of historicity. In this perspective, second, introducing it with a bit of hesitation ('perhaps'), Novalis seems to insinuate that traditions could have ceded to books, that is, that recently (= etymologically *modo*, 'modernly') the phenomenon of the handing down of the past to the new generations happens within and through books. The book names the place of a re-articulation and a redefinition of the relation to and with the past and, therefore, of the intergenerational relations to which education essentially amounts.

By developing this train of argumentation, we could say that the book form, as the specific inflection that the historical way of being receives in modern times, is the correlate of the school, understood as the modern educational institution *par excellence*. To explore this matching of the book culture and the school, I will draw on some tenets of the French philosopher Marcel Gauchet (2010), who, while noting that tradition (understood as the process of the transmission of what a society considers as valuable) cannot but play a pivotal role in schooling, highlights that the (modern) school has had an ambivalent relationship with it: 'On the one hand, it builds itself against tradition. It appeals to the method and to the reasoned transmission against the way of appropriation through impregnation [...] On the other it is based, in its everyday workings, upon that dimension of tradition that in principle it rejects' (p. 71).

To play on the vocabulary of Blumenberg introduced in the previous section, we could say that the 'reasoned and methodical transmission' is the act that brings to a conceptual unity what is disparate, that is, widespread in a form of life; it 'collects' this heritage in a rational form, by thus making it 'readable.' The Latin etymology (*legere*), which resonates both in the words of collecting and in lecture/lesson and clusters together the ideas of 'gathering' and of 'reading,' would be, then, more than an erudite curiosity but rather it would point to an important dimension of the 'scholastic' device and its 'bookish' character and would signalize the intimate co-belonging of the book and the (modern) school.

Against this backdrop, we could interpret some of Gauchet's concerns, when he highlights the impact of detraditionalization on education. As he notes, '[t]here is [...] tradition whenever it continues to be recognized tacitly that there exists in the past a reserve of perpetual present upon which we do not cease to draw' (Ibid., p. 70). As a consequence, by detraditionalization he understands 'the dissolution of tradition as an effecting social form' (Ibidem). In Gauchet's view, part of our contemporary educational predicament is that students are 'beings who, spontaneously, are contemporary with no past. We are the first in history for whom there is nothing but a dead and mute past' (Ibid., p. 73).

Gauchet does not refer specifically to the question of the disappearance of the book culture but some reflections of his about the 'externalization of knowledge' could be profitably appropriated in this context. Indeed, information and communication technology cause an *'objectification* of knowledge [*savoirs*],' which is turned into an *'environment at one's disposal*, providing many technical prostheses' (Ibid., p. 85; emphasis in the original). The upshot is that knowledge 'becomes something that is fundamentally outside itself' (Ibidem) and, accordingly, manageable and manipulable. The idea that knowledge is outside the individual brings with it the demise of that notion of a 'well-made head,' which is pivotal in modern education and refers precisely to a mind that has the tools of internalizing and, thus, organizing knowledge (Ibidem).

Since Edgar Morin's (1999) homonymous work, Montaigne's notion of the 'well-made head' as opposed to the 'well-filled head' has been a recurring theme of the recent French philosophical-educational reflection. To understand Gauchet's specific appropriation of this *topos*, it could be helpful to compare it with its most recent occurrence in the French debate. Michel Serres (2012) introduces this notion by significantly highlighting how it emerged in Montaigne as the symptom of major transformations of *hypomnemata*: 'Through writing and printing memory changed up to the point that Montaigne wanted a well-made head instead of a well-filled one' (Ibid., p. 22; see also p. 31). However, the new technological constellation completely alters the scenario: now it is no longer a question of a head well-filled or well-made, because the new generations are happily beheaded beings who have displaced their knowledge into the new devices in which it is 'objective, collected, collective, connected, freely accessible' (Ibid., p. 31). In the place of the head, there is an exhilarating void for the 'inventive intelligence' and 'the authentic cognitive subjectivity' of youth (Ibidem).

The new technology externalizes knowledge but the transition to a new educational condition is still in progress. Indeed, the electronic media have not freed themselves from the book, 'although [they should] imply a totally different thing from the book, totally different thing from the transhistorical form of the page' (Ibid., p. 34). In the long run, 'the new technology [will] oblige us to depart from the spatial format implied by the book and the page' (p. 35), but at present 'the *page* dominates and leads us. *And the screen reproduces it*' (Ibid., p. 33; emphasis added). Moreover, our 'pedagogy' and its architectural correlates ('[t]he same disposition, the same classrooms and corridors: *always the format inspired by the page*' [p. 35; emphasis added]) have not been adequately revamped yet.

Serres does not indicate in detail what a screen disengaged from the page could look like and how an 'unbooked' screen could match the educational aspirations of the youth finally beheaded and, thus, set free from the pendulum between well-filled and well-made heads. Indeed, there is rather a continuity than an opposition between these last two statuses, in Serres' view: 'If Montaigne had explained the ways through which a head could be perfectly made, he would have depicted, in fact, a box to fill and the well-filled head would have been back' (Ibid. p. 36). The only real overcoming is the void left behind by the beheading as the abandonment of the question of the filling and/or making of the head through the downloading of knowledge into the memory of electronic devices and the possibility of its constant retrieval and visualization on the screen.

Is it the proliferation of screens that will break the format of the page? Pierced by the screens that the youth keep in their hands, will the walls of the classrooms be finally torn down, that is, will thus the youth overcome the margins of the page format and come into their 'authentic cognitive subjectivity'?

By playing with the French word for 'now' [*maintenant*: literally, holding in the hand], Serres has spoken of smartphones and their screens as the real '*maintenant*' for youth.[2] What Gauchet laments in terms of detraditionalization and of the 'being contemporary with no past' is perhaps the replacement of the continuity of history with a forcefield of '*maintenants*,' never containable within the margins of the page. Drawing on Serres allows us to better elicit some dimensions of meaning of the position of Gauchet. While sharing some points with Serres, Gauchet gives them diametrically opposed evaluative connotations: for him the contrast between well-filled and well-made heads is the opposition between the mere absorbing required by tradition operating by means of impregnation and the rational appropriation of tradition which postulates, therefore, the student as 'a rational subject' (Gauchet 2010, p. 72), actively involved in her/his learning. To refer to the Novalis dictum: the meaning of books as a replacement of traditions is that, on the one hand, they give a rational organization to the knowledge deposited in tradition and, on the other, they invoke the 'intelligence' (literally, the *intus-legere*, the reading-into) of youth as students, their 'mastery of the rational principles of knowledge' (Ibidem). This intelligence is also a form of 'collecting inside': when valorizing the knowledge of the well-made head and highlighting that it is put at risk by the contemporary externalization, Gauchet's view, as I have been reconstructing it, is that the book appeals to an internal appropriation of knowledge: knowledge is a kind of re-collecting, of *Er-innerung* of the historical heritage, through the medium of that rational arrangement that is the book as the condition of 'intelligibility.'

John Dewey (1988) has noted that '[m]ankind likes to think in terms of extreme opposites. It is given to formulating its beliefs in terms of Either-Ors, between which it recognizes no intermediate possibilities. [...] Educational philosophy is no exception' (p. 5). Should the dialogue established between Gauchet and Serres fall within this dichotomous stance? Should we be doomed to face the choice between Serres's 'inventive intelligence' and intelligence as the internalization of the historical heritage?[3] Is the maintenance of cultural heritage definitely alien to the '*maintenants*,' the beheaded now-beings with screens in their hands? Or, as 'perhaps' books have taken the place of tradition as the way of our historical being, can we anticipate that somehow screens will take the place of books not as the denial of the historical being but precisely as a new instance of it?

Post-history, the new chronotope, and the re-mediation of the classic

A positive answer to the last question seems to be excluded by the influential theories of Vilém Flusser, who highlighted the connection between writing and history: 'Only one who writes lines can think logically, calculate, criticize, pursue knowledge, philosophize—and conduct himself appropriately. Before that, one turned in circles. And the longer one writes lines, the more historically one can think and act. The gesture of writing produces historical consciousness, which becomes stronger and penetrates more deeply with more writing, in turn making writing steadily stronger and denser' (Flusser 2011, p. 11). And with defining clarity: 'Writing consciousness should be referred to as historical consciousness. […] History is a function of writing and the consciousness that expresses itself in writing' (Ibid., pp.7, 8). In the epoch of '[t]he informatic revolution […] print, the alphabet, and [their] kind of thought [are rendered] superfluous' (Ibid,. p. 54). In the age of universal programming, dominated by propositional calculus (and by if-then propositions) '[h]istory, and the mode of thought that produces history, is over' (Ibid,. p. 59).

A Flusserian view radicalizes the Gauchetian perspective: not only are we to face a phenomenon of detraditionalization but we are entering a phase of post-history, as the kind of consciousness that produces history is intimately linked with writing and, therefore, doomed to disappear along with writing. The book would represent, accordingly, the last manifestation of the 'historical being' of human beings and the screen, whose operations are made possible by programming, would not take up its baton but would inaugurate a different era in which 'nonlinguistic thought (mathematical and pictorial, and presumably completely new ones as well) will expand in ways we cannot yet anticipate' (Ibid., p. 63).

The educational implications of this revolution could be described in Serresian terms, as he portrays the youth manipulating their smartphones and thus deploying 'the cognitive field […] which can be called procedural' and cultivating an '*algorithmic* thought' (Serres 2012, p. 76; emphasis in the original) that would replace the historical thought – Serres, however, does not draw explicitly this conclusion. This kind of thought would represent the revenge of youth against 'the geometer Socrates,' who had humiliated the young Meno as a mere manipulator of procedures (Ibid., p. 78) and had established the superiority of a kind of thought sustained by that very writing that he seemed to contrast.

If we followed a Flusserian-Serresian trajectory, we should think of pedagogical practices that take into account the reversal of historical thought in favor of algorithmic and procedural thought, focusing on 'series of gestures and manners of proceeding' (Serres 2012, p. 76). In another context, Flusser (1995, p. 230 ff.) has invited us to think of a philosophy of gestures as that which substitutes philosophy of history in the epoch of post-history. Developing autonomously this insight, it could be suggested that, at the level of educational theory, this paradigm shift could consist in abandoning the vocabulary of growth or development or becoming in favor of a focus on the gestures through which, by manipulating our devices, we navigate a post-historical world. Education would not be the history of the process through which one takes her/his own form, thanks to a familiarization with and an internalization of the heritage of the past, but the unanticipated ways in which one marshals her/his inventive intelligence, sustained by the use of algorithms. We would be experiencing, accordingly, a caesura, not simply the replacement of one manifestation of our historical being with another.

There is, however, a trifling stumbling block, perhaps no more than a case of homonymy, which could give us pause: in starting to spell out the new cognitive algorithmic landscape, Serres introduces the concept of code, as 'the set of correspondences between two systems to be translated into one another' (Serres 2012, p. 79), and he reminds us of its etymology: the Latin *codex*. This is precisely the name for the ancestor of the book, which 'introduce[d] something absolutely new [...]: the page. [...] the page as a discontinuous and self-sufficient unity separates at each turn an element of the text from the others, which our gaze perceives as an isolated whole' (Agamben 2017, p. 101).

As aforementioned, it could be merely a case of homonymy, which, while striking people intoxicated by language and unable to imagine any 'nonlinguistic thought' (Flusser 2011, p. 63), would have no real meaning. However, it could also be a trigger for an exploration of the page and the procedural figures as two sides of one and the same phenomenon and, thus, for the abandonment of both the image of the relay race (in which one kind of *hypomnemata* replaces the previous one) and that of the caesura. We should rather think of a horizontal rearrangement of techno-cultural forms[4] and learn both to see the book dimension of the screen not merely as the remnant of a past age in the expectation of a full disengagement of the latter from the former, and to navigate the book through the experience of the screen.

In order tentatively to indicate what this could mean, I want, first, to introduce some tenets of Hans Ulrich Gumbrecht, who highlighted 'the idea that the configuration of time that developed in the early nineteenth century has, for about half a century now (and with effects that become clearer every day), been succeeded by another configuration for which no name as yet exists. The title conferred upon the now obsolete chronotope [is] "historical thought/consciousness"' (Gumbrecht 2014, p. xii). For Gumbrecht, too, then, the historical chronotope has been disappearing and a new, still unnamed, one has been emerging, which presents the 'problem [...] that we are no longer able to bequeath anything to posterity' (Ibid., p. xiii). However, he does not seem scared, like Gauchet, by this process of 'detraditionalization,' in which he views, instead, the opportunity of recovering a sense of our body and presence in space as the form of human self-reference, by abandoning the domination of the Cartesian privilege for subjectivity and its process of meaning making and world interpretation (interpretation of meanings always implying a going beyond the physical substance towards the 'spiritual' signification).

Without being allowed to reconstruct here the sophisticated argumentation that Gumbrecht (2004) elaborated about the crisis of 'historical thought' understood as the 19th century radicalization of Cartesian subjectivity, I will confine myself to pinpointing a couple of aspects and bending – and even twisting – them towards an idiosyncratic educational interpretation. First, Gumbrecht interprets the phenomenon of the demise of the historical consciousness in terms of 'pasts flood[ing] our present; automated, electronic systems of memory play a central role in the process. Between the pasts that engulf us and the menacing future, the present has turned into a dimension of expanding simultaneities' (Gumbrecht 2014, p. xiii). Can his idea of a 'broad present' help us to escape the dichotomy between history and post-history and to identify a domain in which, while the historicist mold is broken, we are not left only with gestures of algorithmic procedures but can maintain some (new) form of historical thought? In other words, without ceding to Gauchet's pessimistic worries, can we make some sense of them by inhabiting the broad present?

In this perspective – and this is my second point – I want to refer to Gumbrecht's concept of 'presentification.' By this notion, Gumbrecht understands 'our eagerness to fill up the ever-broadening present with artifacts from the past' (Gumbrecht 2004, p. 121), which are approached less as objects to interpret in their meaning (that is, according to the pattern of historical consciousness) than as an opportunity for present experience: 'The desire for presence makes us imagine how we would have related, intellectually and with our bodies, to certain objects (rather than ask what those objects "mean") if we had encountered them in their own historical everyday worlds. Once we feel how this play of our historical imagination can be appealing and contagious, once we lure other persons into the same intellectual process, we have produced the very situation to which we are referring when we say that somebody is capable of "conjuring up the past"' (Ibid., p. 124).

In the case of texts (in the humanities, for instance), paradoxically, at least in some respect, this could be furthered by the screen,[5] although Gumbrecht does not draw this conclusion and seems rather to think of the pedagogical use of the new media mainly in terms of online courses, adequate for transmitting standard knowledge (Ibid., p. 130), which will allow us to reserve classroom interactions for stimulating and challenging discussions and for the exposure of students to complexity.

To briefly illustrate my point, I will refer to some pedagogical tips of one of the most prominent experts of Italian literature, Claudio Giunta (2017). In a class on Petrarch, instead of beginning the lesson directly with the anthologized text in a book (in order to *interpret* it, Gumbrecht would say, by going beyond the physical appearance towards its meanings), Giunta suggests starting from the autograph pages, which are now at the disposal of each and every person using the web (a positive outcome of the externalization of knowledge, which Gauchet seems to underestimate and which, instead of making us contemporary of no past, could grant us new forms of access to the past). The autograph of Petrarch, as presented through the screen, may represent a kind of presentification both in the aforementioned sense (= a way of 'fill[ing] up the ever-broadening present with artifacts from the past' (Gumbrecht 2004, p. 121)) and because it triggers 'presence effects,' in Gumbrecht's vocabulary, that is, the text is not primarily there in order to be an object of interpretation (according to the typical hermeneutical stance) but rather in order to be experienced in its 'superficial' and 'aesthetic' otherness. While the notion of 'surface' has enjoyed bad press within the hermeneutical chronotope (as the meaning is precisely what is disclosed by going in depth, under the surface), new technologies could bring us 'somehow'[6] into the presence of ancient texts and enable us to experience at least part of their 'materialities' (in the mentioned case, for instance, the peculiar handwriting of the poet, the way in which he organized the page, etc.). Obviously, significant epistemological questions arise: to what extent could we speak of 'materiality' in the case of a manuscript accessed through the screen? Is it legitimate to speak of an 'aesthetic' experience of the text once the latter is mediated through the surface of the screen? Are we not confronted with a quasi-Platonic nightmare of a double surface (the surface of the 'presence effects' accessed, moreover, through the surface of the screen)? I cannot explore this issue in detail here but it is to ask whether this anxiety of the double surface does not derive from a view of the 'aesthetic dimension' of experience already mortgaged by the hermeneutical chronotope and whether our educational engagement with screens could help us to deconstruct and reconstruct what counts as materiality, presence and aesthetic experience: perhaps screens do not (only?) dismantle and dissolve the physical but they (also?) enable us to access the 'physical' dimension through new paths.

The pedagogical move suggested by Giunta could be fruitful in many respects:[7] first, it would offer an experience of presentification in that pupils would see the handwriting of the poet and could be invited to decipher it etc. (this deciphering occurring at a double level, insofar as it regards not only the 'personal' peculiarities of Petrarch's handwriting, that is, the 'material' reverberation of his hand on paper, but also the spelling of most words, which is different in comparison with the form currently adopted: see the example below); second, pupils would discover that the composition within the page in Petrarch is different from that which we find in contemporary books. This could stimulate a dialogue on the reasons for these differences (essentially linked to the need to exploit as fully as possible the medium – paper or parchment in the case of Petrarch) and could represent an opportunity to reflect on the specificity of our ways of understanding a typical page. However – and this is the key point in the present argument – this 'presentifying' strategy, appealing also to the aesthetic dimensions of the text and to its 'presence effects', does not work counter to the 'historical being' but could represent an enrichment of it (in this respect, I part company with Gumbrecht's stance). Indeed, to give just one example, there are significant rewards also at the level of interpretation of the poem and of its historical contextualization (however, they are not attained primarily through the hermeneutical work on the meanings of the text, but rather thanks to its 'presence effects'). To stick to Giunta's example, let's take the sonnet *Amor piangeva, ed io con lui talvolta*. In an anthology we will find it written this way:

> Amor piangeva, et io con lui talvolta,
> dal qual miei passi non fur mai lontani,
> mirando per gli effecti acerbi et strani
> l'anima vostra dei suoi nodi sciolta.
> Or ch'al dritto camin l'à Dio rivolta,
> col cor levando al cielo ambe le mani
> ringratio lui che' giusti preghi humani
> benignamente, sua mercede, ascolta.
> Et se tornando a l'amorosa vita,
> per farvi al bel desio volger le spalle,
> trovaste per la via fossati o poggi,
> fu per mostrar quanto è spinoso calle,
> et quanto alpestra et dura la salita,
> onde al vero valor conven ch'uom poggi.

In his autograph page, Petrarch, instead, couples the verses in this way:

Amor piangeua & io cō lui tal u uolta	Dal qual miei passi nō fur mai lontani
Mirando per gli effecti acerbi & strani	Lanima uostra de suoi nodi sciolta
Or chal dritto camin ladio riuolta	Col cor leuando al cielo ābe le mani
Ringratio lui che giusti preghi humani	Benignamēte sua mercede ascolta
Et se tornando a lamorosa uita	Per farui al bel desio uolger le spalle
Trouaste per la uia fossati o poggi	Fu per mostrar quāto e spinoso calle
Et quāto alpestra et dura la salita	Onde al uero ualor cōuen chuom poggi

Along with the 'presence effects' (connected with the differences in writing, spelling and morphology, which could be used also to reflect on the very act of writing, in different contexts and with different media), there are also 'meaning effects,' for instance the discovery of the acrostic AMORE [love] in the first five verses on the left column. What is important, however, is that this meaning element is intimately related to the way in which Petrarch materially wrote his poem. By disengaging the poem from the 'book page' and accessing it through the webpage, which allows us to navigate through some of the materialities of the text (e.g., by magnifying a detail of the poet's writing), we are not only exposed to a 'broad presence' of the text but we are also enabled to get in contact with historical and hermeneutical levels not always accessible through the book format (e.g., the way in which Petrarch composed his works or in which he used the page or in which he built meaning effects, like the acrostic AMORE etc.).

I cannot proceed further with an exploration of the wealth of pedagogical possibilities granted by a similar approach but I will confine myself to noting that they are connected a) with the resources provided by the new media and with the externalization of knowledge; and b) with the forms of navigation of the text that they offer. A classic like Petrarch's poem thus screened does not screen us off from the experience of the text but enables us to screen dimensions of the text (and more generally of book culture) that would otherwise remain concealed. Instead of lapsing us into the drift of detraditionalization, the screen could help us to promote 'a new historical culture corresponding to [the] new chronotope' (Gumbrecht 2004, p. 122). This is what I have tentatively defined as a horizontal rearrangement of *hypomnemata*.

I would propose, for this move, the phrase 're-mediation of the classic', by idiosyncratically appropriating Bolter and Grusin's (2000) notion. While the aforementioned pedagogical treatment of Petrarch's sonnet could somehow testify also to the dialectic of hypermediacy and the search for immediacy, which is at the core of their concept of remediation (p. 5), I would like to use the concept of re-mediation to capture two aspects: first, the shuttling between and the interweaving of different media as a vehicle to inhabit our broad present and cultivate a historical imagination attuned to the new chronotope; and, second, the opposition to the 'remediating' appeal to the classics and the canon merely as a way of compensating for the losses engendered by detraditionalization (this is the usual educationally and culturally conservative response).

In this perspective, on the one hand, I would suggest walking in Gumbrecht's footsteps, when he highlights that 'our encounters with classics [have become] more relaxed because their power to speak to us directly is no longer threatened—nor is it peculiarly theirs. *In the new chronotope the documents of the past are present with truly confusing variety and require not so much preservation from amnesia as infiltration*' (Gumbrecht 2014, p. 56; emphasis added). In particular, he detects a shift towards 'an *existential* perspective' as 'we relate [the classics] to the manifold eventualities and challenges encountered in individual lives' (Ibid., p. 57).

On the other hand, I would advocate moving a step further forwards (or, better, sideways) by valorizing the possibility of the new media in our engagement with the classics and by taking into account some of the concerns about the perils of detraditionalization without yielding, however, to any apocalyptic (Eco, 1964) tones. Thus, we could perhaps even (and eventually) describe the screen not as the gravedigger of historical thought but as an unprecedented manifestation of it.

Notes

1. It is hardly necessary to specify that, if this interpretation uses McClintock's volume as a source of inspiration, it cannot in any way be considered as the outcome of McClintock's argument.
2. Serres made this word play in an interview in which he presents his book. I am grateful to Dr. Joris Vlieghe for having drawn my attention to this interview.
3. I should specify that Gauchet does not use the word 'intelligence,' but I have found it helpful to maintain it, by exploring its etymological deposits through a Gauchetian lens, because it establishes an immediate relation to Serres.
4. Elsewhere (Oliverio, 2015), I used the expression 'convergence culture,' by readapting it from media studies (see Jenkins, 2006). I am grateful to Dr. Piotr Zamojski (University of Gdansk) for having drawn my attention to the fact that the phrase could risk smacking of Hegelianism, as if there were a sort of *Aufhebung* or synthesis of old and new media. I have to postpone until another occasion a more developed discussion of the many deep and insightful remarks that Dr. Zamojski has made about the question of convergence culture.
5. Due to space constraints, I cannot develop here in more detail this argumentative trajectory, in which I would appropriate some refined analyses of the Italian philosopher Mauro Carbone (2016), who has plausibly argued how the screen should not be read in terms of a 'window,' according to a metaphor that could be traced back to Leon Battista Alberti and refers to a space of 'representation' predicated on the subject/object separation and on the reference to a '*metaphysical "beyond"*' (in this sense the 'window' is the trope for Cartesian subjectivity and its search for meaning in Gumbrecht's sense). The screen, instead, inaugurates the domain of a '*mythical "elsewhere"*' (p. 115; emphasis in the original). It could be argued that this 'mythical elsewhere' could also be the site of presentification.
6. It is hardly necessary to highlight that a relevant epistemological challenge is implied in this 'somehow.'
7. It is appropriate to specify that I will reappropriate in an autonomous way and expand – in the wake of the argument of this paper – Giunta's remarks.

References

Agamben, G. (2017). *The Fire and the Tale*. Stanford, CA: Stanford University Press.
Blumenberg, H. (1986). *Die Lesbarkeit der Welt*. Frankfurt am Main: Suhrkamp.
Böhme, J. (2006). *Schule am Ende der Buchkultur*. Bad Heilbrunn: Julius Klinkhardt.
Bolter, J. D. and Grusin, R. (2000). *Remediation. Understanding New Media*. Cambridge, MA: MIT Press.
Carbone, M. (2016). *Filosofia-schermi. Dal cinema alla rivoluzione digitale*. Milano: Raffaello Cortina editore.

Dewey, J. (1988). Experience and Education, in J.A. Boydston (Ed.) *The Later Works of John Dewey, 1925–1953, vol. 13*. Carbondale and Edwardsville, IL: Southern Illinois University Press, pp. 1–62.

Eco, U. (1964). *Apocalittici e integrati*. Milano: Bompiani.

Flusser, V. (1995). *Gesten. Versuch einer Phänomenologie*. Frankfurt am Main: Fischer.

Flusser, V. (2011). *Does Writing Have a Future?*Minneapolis, MN: University of Minnesota Press.

Gauchet, M. (2010). Des savoirs privés de sens?, in M.-C. Blais, M. Gauchet, D. Ottavi, *Conditions de l'éducation*. Paris: Pluriel/Fayard, pp. 63–92.

Giunta, C. (2017). *E se non fosse la buona battaglia? Sul futuro dell'istruzione umanistica*. Bologna: il Mulino.

Gumbrecht, H.U. (2004). *Production of Presence: What Meaning Cannot Convey*. Stanford, CA: Stanford University Press.

Gumbrecht, H.U. (2014). *Our Broad Present. Time and Contemporary Culture*. New York, NY: Columbia University Press.

Jenkins, H. (2006), *Convergence Culture: Where Old and New Media Collide*. New York, NY: New York University Press.

McClintock, R. (2012). *Enough. A Pedagogic Speculation*. New York, NY: The Reflective Commons.

Morin, E. (1999). *La tête bien faite. Repenser la réforme, réformer la pensée*. Paris: Le Seuil.

Oliverio, S. (2015). The Need for 'Connectedness in Growth'. Experience and education and the new technological culture. *Education & Culture 31(2)*, 55–68.

Postman, N. (1979). *Teaching as a Conserving Activity*. New York, NY: Dell.

Postman, N. (1985). *Amusing Ourselves to Death: Public Discourse in the Age of Show Business*. New York, NY: Viking Penguin.

Serres, M. (2012). *Petite Poucette*. Paris: Manifestes Le Pommier.

Stiegler, B. (2008), *Prendre Soin: Tome 1, De la jeunesse et des générations*. Paris: Flammarion.

Vlieghe, J. (2016). A Material and Practical Account of Education in Digital Times: Neil Postman's views on literacy and the screen revisited. *Studies in Philosophy and Education 35(2)*, 163–179.

Section 2

Mappings

Chapter 4

Classroom spaces in the making: a sociomaterial account of digital screens in BYOD schools

Samira Ali Reza Beigi and Mathias Decuypere

[*scene 1*] The teacher is sitting in front of the classroom when he loudly asks one student to turn off the lights and pull down all the window blinds. The video on the interactive whiteboard starts immediately after the class goes dark and silent. Students are all facing the big screen, most of them have their laptops open in front of them. On the big screen, a man in the middle of a desert points to a windmill behind him. As he talks about different inventions of the golden Islamic age, such as algebra, an online game interface pops up on the laptop screen of one pupil who is seated in the front row. His fingers move on the touchpad silently and his body is aligned with the borders of the screen as he guides an animated worm that crawls in the space and eats others to get larger. His gaze shifts constantly from the laptop screen to the big screen. It doesn't take long before another laptop screen displays the same game from a row behind. The class is quiet – only the voice of the man talking about the history of algebra breaks the silence. On the spur of the moment, the teacher stands up and walks to the back of the class. With each step, finger strokes switch the screen back to the course material (a PDF file). Sitting behind all the students now, the teacher can see what appears on the pupils' personal screens. One of them, seated on the last row, bends the screen and aligns her body with the edges of the screen. She turns her back every few minutes to see in which direction the teacher is looking.

[*scene 2*] There are not so many voices in the classroom, and everyone is gazing at their personal laptop. One pupil opens her laptop's browser and types 'gothic churches in Paris' in the search bar. Her earbuds are in her ears, and her phone is on the desk. She doesn't wait to see what the search results are. Instead, she turns away her gaze to select another music track on her phone. Her gaze turns back to the search window and she clicks on the few first links. A notification abruptly pops up in the corner of her laptop, and she scans through the message she received on WhatsApp. Afterwards, she turns her eyes back to the search results and skims the contents of the websites that have been opened. She takes her earbuds out and asks the teacher to come to her desk. The teacher walks to her desk and stands behind her to be able to see the screen, which they continuously look at when talking.

Bring Your Own Device to school

Personal digital devices such as laptops and tablets were introduced in schools around a decade ago, thereby integrating formal school education with digital and web technologies. The Bring Your Own Device (BYOD) model is one of the clearest manifestations of how personal digital devices are present in today's schools. This model refers to 'the technology model where students bring a personally owned mobile device with various apps and embedded features to use anywhere, anytime for the purpose of learning' (Song, 2014, p. 52). While the most common objects in the 20th century classroom consisted of slates, boards, pens, sheets of paper, chairs and desks, personal digital devices have become central objects in today's BYOD schools.

One of the main characteristics of deploying computers at school in general, is the one-to-one interaction of the pupils or the teachers with these devices. However, the specific element of the BYOD model is that it involves the use of devices that are *owned* by students. They bring their personal stuff, stored onto these devices, to school (Carvalho et al. 2016). This includes music playlists, pictures, and social contacts. By bringing personal devices (and therefore one's personal stuff) to school, it could be argued that, to a certain extent, the classroom journeys to multiple (e.g., gaming, music) places that cannot, all of them, be situated within the physical confines of the classroom itself. Nevertheless, the immediate physical environment is directly affected by these journeys, as the two vignettes with which this chapter opened demonstrate. The space of the classroom is changed by the presence of personal devices, and by activities performed on these devices, which are not related to the lesson instructed by the teacher (e.g., playing online games, and scrolling through social media feeds and personal contacts). The question is now what happens when such activities are becoming dominant in the classroom, and how precisely then? We investigate which sorts of space are enacted in such a BYOD classroom, and what happens to the role of the teacher and students in such spatial enactments? This is the issue that is central in this chapter. More exactly, we aim at exploring the emerging spaces of the classroom during formal lesson hours by means of an ethnographic observation inside one BYOD school (Belgium).

A sociomaterial approach to space

To pursue our research question, we adopt a sociomaterial lens that enables us to scrutinize the different actors in the classroom that are constituting space in a specific way. Sociomaterial approaches allow for disentangling the construction of various classrooms in a symmetrical vein, thereby focusing on different spatialities that are enacted in and through the various relations being established between human and nonhuman (e.g., digital) actors. This feature of sociomaterial approaches implies that the focus of the researcher is not merely directed towards students, teachers, and their interactions in the classroom. Rather, the materiality of the classroom, including the blackboard, the desks, the textbook, and the devices equally plays an active role in the construction of classroom space. These things and humans are called *actors*. 'Actor' refers here to 'anything that does modify a state of affairs by making a difference' (Latour 2005, p. 71). Put differently, through a sociomaterial lens, classroom settings are observed and investigated by identifying the different actors (both human and nonhuman) that populate these settings, and that actively contribute to their spatial composition (Decuypere and Simons 2014). In this regard, Fenwick (2014) elucidates the principle of symmetry in sociomaterial approach:

> Instead of examining only human actors, their individual skills and their social inter-relationships, a sociomaterial view treats the social and material elements of knowledge practices as entangled and mutually constitutive. (p. 258)

Approaching actors present in BYOD schools in a symmetrical vein means that digital devices are not considered to be passive objects that remain in the background, fulfilling (or not) particular human expectations. Rather, by implementing them at school, they actively co-constitute different (sorts of) spaces at school.

A prime characteristic of sociomaterial approaches is that actors are not considered in isolation, but rather in view of the *relations* they establish with one another (Law 2007). Focusing on the specific types of relation that are established between different actors allows sociomaterial researchers to discern the particular *effects* that this relational interplay brings about in the setting. This relational interplay suggests an understanding of space that is not pre-given, or absolute. In this sense, space does not exist prior to the actors and their relations, and it does not take a singular and fixed (e.g., Cartesian or Euclidean) form. Rather, space is a product of 'relations which are necessarily embedded material practices which have to be carried out, it is always in the process of being made' (Massey 2005, p. 9). The relational approach to space stresses that space is always being constructed, and hence, that different *types* of space are constantly in the process of being enacted (Law 2002).

Although sociomaterial approaches stress the situated enactment of space (and time), the different *types* of space that come into being are not often subject of fine-grained analysis (Decuypere and Simons 2016a), we have argued that social topology offers a complementary yet more specific perspective in order to account for different *types* of time and space being enacted through such relational compositions.

The origins of topological thinking are to be situated within the mathematical field of topology. In mathematical topological thinking, the form and size of actors is never pre-given or absolute. Rather, actors can be deformed. The same applies to practices as a whole: depending on the relations established between actors, a practice might change (or keep) shape (Law 2002). Inspired by such reasoning, the field of social topology adopts a similar argument with respect to space, and concretely analyzes the multiplicity and complexity of specific spaces that are generated in and through the relational composition of a particular educational practice. For instance, within one and the same setting, different spatialities such as regional, network, and fluid ones might be enacted and manifest themselves (Mol and Law 1994; Law 2002).

Sociomaterial and sociotopological studies of space in educational research

In previous years, there have been several sociomaterial explorations of how space is being relationally constituted in educational settings (e.g., Nespor 1994, 2002; McGregor 2003, 2004; Paechter 2004; Rißler et al. 2014). All these studies show in a concrete manner how the spatiality of educational institutions, such as schools and universities, is not confined to their physical walls. Rather, these studies have shown that relations established between a variety of educational actors such as the curriculum, policy actors, specific educational objects, or the physical environment all enact different spaces. The sociomaterial and sociotopological studies of space have found new grounds of exploration with the introduction of information and communication technologies (ICT) to educational settings. These technologies raise the issues of virtual vs. physical, presence vs. absence, cyberspace vs. immediate physical space in educational studies of space (for an overview on sociomaterial spatialities, see Fenwick et al. 2011).

However, the number of studies that explore these new topological accounts of space are limited. As an example of such approach, and drawing on the concepts of regions and networks, Sørensen (2009) observes how the blackboard creates two homogenous and clearly separated spatial regions. First, the region in front of the blackboard to which everyone's attention is drawn. This region acts as the proverbial 'home' for the teacher, and students can only be invited (by the teacher) to go there. As such, they are the 'guests' in front of the spatial 'blackboard' region. A second region being enacted is the 'pupil' region, where the pupils take seats and from where they look at the blackboard.

Sørensen argues that these two distinct (and physically situatable) spaces become more fluid in a virtual learning environment. Students constantly edit stuff and add elements to the virtual space, through which they overcome the physical distance that used to exist between them and the blackboard. In a similar vein, Decuypere and Simons (2016b) draw attention to the roles the screen plays in academic practices. They describe how specific ways of relating with the screen enact different spatial and temporal relations (such as the space of the big screen as a 'common reference space', or the time 'before' the presentation), and demonstrate that the screen is an active informer that performs specific operations in educational settings.

This chapter is situated within this context of sociomaterial and topological studies in educational sciences, with a specific interest in the enactment of different spatialities, and it does so by focusing on the role of digital devices as active contributors to and (co-) constructors of various classroom spaces in a BYOD school.

Towards the sociotopologies of BYOD classrooms

Our ethnographic study took place over two periods of time (2016–2018). For this study we observed what happens in classrooms as well as in the library, cafeteria, and the hallways. Our classroom observations included various lessons in secondary and high school grades. We observed these settings with a specific attention for various actors present in the classroom, and particularly for how these actors relate with each other.

In the school where our ethnographic study took place, there is a classroom for each teacher of a subject matter, which has its own specific class design (wall decorations with pictures, quotes, diagrams, and maps). Thus, students and their devices are the actors that have to move and change classes every lesson, whereas the teacher remains in his/her own classroom space.

With regard to digital devices, a first thing to note is the diversity of these devices present in each classroom. During a formal lesson, what is manifestly present are student laptops (on their personal desks), the interactive whiteboard (on the wall), and the teacher's laptop (personal desk up front). On a closer look, however, smartwatches here and there (on the wrists) and smartphones (in pupils' pockets on or under their desks) can equally be discerned.

Attached to these digital actors, we can often see personal decorations in the form of stickers, printed pictures with friends, or colorful cases. Personal devices are thus further personalized – both on their front sides (the screen, which regularly contains personal content) and on their backsides (because of the stickers and other personal decoration).

In the remainder of this chapter, we proceed by first taking into account the physical *arrangement* of desks and whiteboards, which vary based on the size of the class and the decision of the teacher. We will describe the main classroom arrangements of the school under investigation and highlight the *spatial relations* that actors establish within each arrangement. Second, we focus on the *physical features* of digital devices, such as horizontality and verticality of the screens, and their size and shape. Finally, we combine both perspectives in order to discuss the spatial relations that are enacted in the BYOD classroom. In investigating these spatial relations, attention is paid to the various relations between different actors, namely between digital devices, body formations and specific positioning and movements of actors. In this study, the topological lens helps us to scrutinize the spatial enactments in their multiplicity. Concepts such as *zones* and *regions* will aid us in identifying these differences. We adopt the notion of *zone* to demarcate the areas that have no strict and clear cut borders. *Regions*, however, are homogenous areas with divided boundaries (Sørensen 2009).

Before describing these classroom arrangements, it is important to note that we refrain from an in-depth analysis of specific digital actors (e.g., WhatsApp messages, personal pictures or emails) (see, e.g., Stevens 2017) and limit ourselves to highlighting the relations that come about between the arrangements and the physical features in the formation of space.

Classroom arrangements

In this section, we analyze how different classrooms are physically arranged and how the *physical* space of the classroom is filled with chairs, desks, whiteboards, students, and teacher. Additionally, we identify the spatial relations enacted in each arrangement. The term arrangement refers to the interconnected order of things and humans in the classroom. Among the observed classes, three different arrangements can be distinguished.

The first arrangement (see Figure 4.1) is what we could call the 'traditional' classroom setting. In this arrangement, the whiteboard and the interactive whiteboard (smart board) are placed next to one another. The teacher's desk is

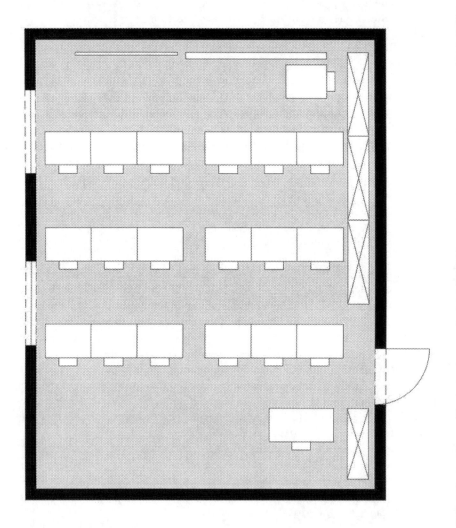

right in front of the interactive board and all the desks and chairs form rows that face both boards. Thus, the arrangement of desks and boards constitutes *a very specific spatialization of the classroom*: a directional space that has a front and a back, in which the wall that holds the board is considered as being 'up front,' at which all (pupils') gazes are directed. The teacher's laptop sits on the desk in front of the board and it is mainly used when the interactive board *together* with the teacher present something to the students. These are the moments when a text, an image or a PowerPoint presentation is displayed on the board. In these situations, the teacher sits and/or stands next to the board, for what is being displayed on the board requires explanation, or instruction.

An additional desk is situated at the opposite side of the classroom, where the teacher's paperwork and a desktop computer are to be found. This double positioning of desks, one empty at the front and one full of papers and office accessories at the back, stabilizes the spatial regions where the teacher can and is allowed to operate. The teacher is sitting at the back during those moments that the interactive board is operating while presenting content to the students *by itself*, e.g., a YouTube video about the degree of freedom in biology class, or a documentary about different oceanic planes in geography class.

While standing or sitting in the front, the teacher is either the *starter* of computer programs (pushing the start button of the video, displaying images), when the device is presenting something itself, or the *assistant* of the interactive board. In the last case, (s)he annotates (commenting on the text, adding a few sentences to the slides, or giving instructions) what is being displayed on the board. Hence, when the teacher is in front of the board, and is not explaining something herself, it can be said that (s)he acts as the *spokesperson* of the screen. As soon as her assistance is no longer required, the teacher can move to the back, where all of her *stuff* is placed. The next scene (scene 3) is typical for this arrangement: the teacher is sitting in *front* of the class to *play a video*. She moves then to the back of the class a couple of minutes after the start of the video.

[*scene 3*] The interactive whiteboard presents the definition of innovation on a PowerPoint slide. 'Don't bother with writing, the slides are shared with you on Managebac'[1] the teacher says, moving away from his desk. Immediately, the students open the file on their devices. The teacher reads the definition out loud, when Olon, a pupil sitting at the back of the class raises his voice to Gabi who is sitting in front of him: 'You are texting, Gabi!'

The pupils' personal screens in this arrangement have the same orientation as the interactive board: towards the front of the physical classroom. This signifies that looking at the board or the teacher requires the same body posture as looking at the laptop screen. The direction of the blackboard and the screens creates the possibility for the students to simultaneously perform multiple actions, such as typing a message on the laptop, searching on Google, looking at the board, and listening to the teacher, without shifting their body. Moreover, in this arrangement, *the position of each student in relation to the rest of the class* becomes important, for rows of students make the screen content visible for those who are positioned behind others. Scene 3 demonstrates how one student can notice what is happening on the other pupil's screen, while this is not apparent at all for the teacher, since the teacher's movement is restricted to go from the front to the back and not in between the rows.

The second arrangement is the most common one in this school (see Figure 4.2). In this arrangement, the whiteboard and the interactive board are placed on opposite sides of the classroom. The desks are grouped together and spread out over the room. Unlike the previous arrangement, no desks are facing any of the boards. Instead, desks face each other, which implies that the pupils' gazes can meet. Hence, in this arrangement, the orientation of individual

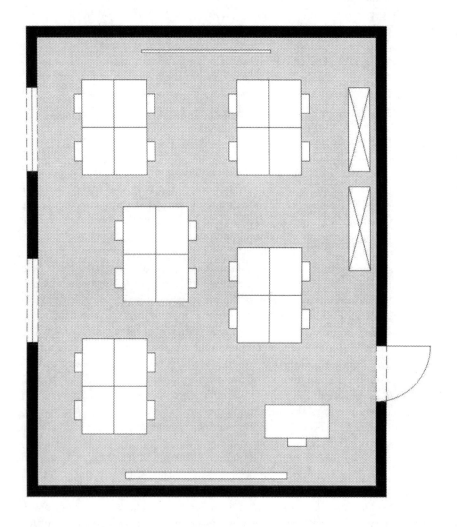

laptop screens and both whiteboards are not the same. This necessitates *a shifting of the gaze and the body* to attend to any of the boards when they are active. This is in contrast with the first setting, in which pupils could gaze at each other's' screens while looking at the big boards.

This characteristic, together with the positioning of the two boards on different sides, does not afford a singular orientation for the class, in terms of front and back. Instead, the personal screen and the boards are interlacing, which implies that *one can only attend to one of them at a time*. Although in this arrangement the teacher can better notice when the personal device is active and the pupil's body is tuned to it compared to the first arrangement, the pupils can perform multiple actions on the screen (e.g., texting and annotating a poem) at the same time. The teacher's access is still limited, however, and requires his/her constant mobility. Nevertheless, the possibilities for the teacher's mobility is increased: the teacher can walk between the pupils' seats and in several directions in the classroom. This possibility allows her/him to observe some personal screens, even when he/she is seated at her desk.

The third arrangement is an uncommon setup that was only implemented towards the end of our ethnographic observations. This setup was proposed by one of the teachers as a response to the previous arrangements. Whereas in the two abovementioned arrangements the teacher's space of mobility was limited to different degrees, in this arrangement, the empty center of the room provides a space for the teacher to reach any of the students' desks. The desks here are placed in two main rows that all face the wall. The two boards at the two sides of the room are behind the students. As shown in Figure 4.3, two desks are designed for the teacher: one close to the interactive board and the other close to the whiteboard. In this arrangement, when something is presented on any of the boards, both bodies and chairs need to be (fully) turned and change direction. The classroom does not have a collectively pre-defined back or front. Moreover, sitting at the desk, the gaze of the students is only directed towards the personal screen and the wall. Establishing any relation (with regard to the physical space) other than towards the screen requires the movement of the body, which means that, in and through this arrangement, *only one thing can be done at any given time*. This could be working on individual tasks (where everyone is facing their screens), giving presentations (where all the chairs are turned towards the screen), or having class discussions (where all the chairs are turned and create a big circle). Unique for this circular setting is that the content of each pupil's individual screen is (very explicitly) rendered visible for the teacher (and not for other pupils, as was the case in the second arrangement), who can move around the room and observe what everyone is doing.

Tracing the vertical and horizontal screens

In this section, we take a closer look at the features of the physical surfaces in the classroom (traditional 'surfaces' such as blackboards and notebooks, as well as digital surfaces such as screens) and categorize these surfaces in terms of their verticality and horizontality.

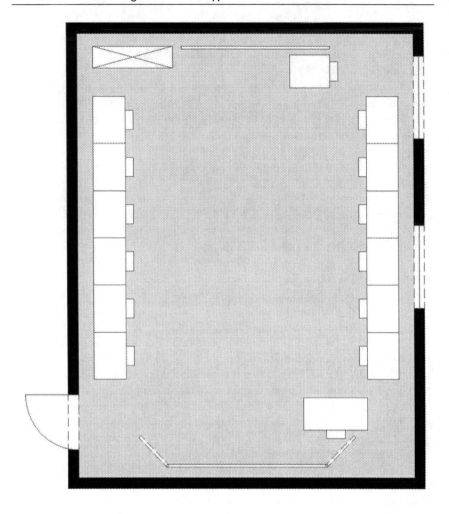

1 Verticality

In traditional classroom arrangements, the blackboard is a flat surface hung vertically on the wall that engages with the gaze at the eye level. The blackboard, thus, is a public *vertical* surface positioned to capture attention, to demonstrate knowledge and to claim authority (Sørensen 2009; Roehl 2012). Hence, body gestures are formed for the public encounter between knowledge and students. In contrast to the blackboard, paper notebooks are *horizontal* surfaces situated on desks to engage with privately displayed knowledge through an individual, horizontal, and active engagement. As such, when engaging with knowledge, for instance, to solve mathematic equations, bodily gestured are closed.

In the case of digital surfaces, however, smaller devices such as tablets and smartphones can be positioned both vertically *and* horizontally, depending on the situation. Laptop screens and the interactive board, in turn, are necessarily always positioned vertically. The verticality *and* horizontality of digital screens establish specific relations with other actors, such as course materials, gaming platforms, and pupils' bodies. Consequently they enact – as we will argue – different sorts of space in the classroom. This is clear from the next scene.

[*scene 4*] A word document is open on Kevin's laptop and the words appear hesitantly. The interactive board displays a world map divided into different regions indicated by different colors. The teacher is standing in front of the interactive board and is pointing to the legend of the map. "Can you look at the key [legend], what does it say?," he asks. All the laptops are open on the small group desks and the sound of typing fills the class occasionally. Only three laptop screens are visible to the teacher. He walks to the other side of the class, where he can notice some other laptop screens. One pupil moves her laptop to the opposite corner, bends its screen and covers the screen with her body, thereby foreclosing the teacher's gaze. While the map is displayed on the interactive board, Rory touches the keypad and scrolls through a PDF document, of which the map is one component. Jolie's desktop shifts as her finger slides on the touchpad. WhatsApp messages, PowerPoint slides, a photo album, and Spotify are rapidly shifting with a stroke. With slow steps, the teacher walks to other side of the class and takes a look at other screens as he talks. 'Global hectares,' he says as he draws a square on the whiteboard. 'It is the area,' he adds. The teacher, the slide on the board and the laptop screen are the three main actors that are presenting something and therefore the gazes switch mainly between them.

Although the laptop screen is a vertical plane, just as the blackboard, it does not enact similar relations. The vertical surface of the interactive and whiteboard is mostly static and non-personal. Things appear and disappear depending on what the teacher does, but there is no constant motion of things. The interactive board that projects the screen of the teacher's laptop is put on *freeze* mode (the freeze button on the remote controller), when the teacher is working individually.

On personal laptop screens, however, things are constantly moving. On each laptop screen, there are multiple *desktops* that can be switched with a finger swipe to the left or right (horizontal movement). Moreover, on each desktop, webpages and documents are scrolled up and down rapidly, allowing another dimension of movement (vertical movement).

As argued by Sørensen (2009), the blackboard materializes the centrality of knowledge, by demonstrating it publicly, whereas the one-to-one engagement with the personal screen decentralizes knowledge, and enables a more fluid relation. The vertical laptop screen does demonstrate the knowledge in the way the blackboard does, but not publicly. The verticality of the laptop screen in the setting of a formal lesson enables a personal and private interaction with the laptop. However, through the verticality of the screen, the content on the screen is potentially exposed. As indicated in the first and the fourth scenes, the body aligns itself occasionally with the edges of the device *to screen the screen*. The body as such is enacted as a component that is devised by and through the device. The spatial effect of the one-to-one interaction with the vertical screen, and the protecting of the screen with the body, configures a semi-private space in the classroom. This stands opposed to the whiteboard as a space where the centralized knowledge appears on a public screen.

Additionally, not only the body acts as an actor that screens the screen, but the laptop itself equally acts as a *vertical wall*. On one side, the laptop screen on the front emits light and captures the attention through what appears on it. Yet, nothing can pass through its other (personalized and decorated back) side. Hence, the back of the screen operates as a wall here, which separates and creates different types of actor, i.e., actor(s) in front of the laptop vs. the teacher and other pupils on the backside, to whom the screen is not visible.

Through the verticality of the personal screen, the described class arrangements enact specific spatial relations. In the first classroom arrangement discussed earlier, the laptop screen acts as a wall between the teacher and the students. As long as the teacher is in front, she finds herself in what could be called a *zone of exclusion*: she is excluded from the flow of content on the pupils' personal screens. This is to be distinguished from pupils, who are in a *zone of glancing*, which includes both their own screens and that of other pupils. As the first scene shows, the worm game contagiously spreads in the class.

In the second arrangement, however, the direction of attention is clearly signaled. As discussed, this arrangement requires redirections of the gaze and the body between the personal screen and the interactive board. The third arrangement enacts opposite relations between the devices, teacher and students. Here, the teacher is the one who is operating in the zone of glancing, whereas the students are restricted to the walls and thus operating in a zone of exclusion themselves.

2 Horizontality

[*scene 5*] The smartphone is in Thomas' pocket, and his gaze is on the Padlet document that is open on his laptop. The Padlet document of all the laptops is shared on the interactive board. In this way, the words that appear on each Padlet are communally displayed on the board. Thomas takes his phone out and moves closer to the laptop screen. His finger moves on the screen until it goes back to his pocket after three minutes, and goes back to typing words on the Padlet.

Adams and Thompson (2016) argue that the size of digital devices is a decisive factor in using them in public spaces. Similarly, during a lesson in a classroom, the size of the device, next to the horizontality and verticality of the screen, plays an important role. The smartphone screen flickers under the desk, or is used while being protected by the laptop screen. Irrespective of whether or not smartphones are an active part of the classroom (meaning that they are being used as part of the lesson plan), they can be detected here and there. Likewise, smartwatches silently vibrate on wrists and attract the (individual) gaze.

Now, although smartphones, tablets and smartwatches can be positioned both horizontally and vertically in the classroom, these devices are mainly positioned horizontally. Unlike the eye-level gaze characteristic for working on a laptop, the top-down gaze on the horizontal screen cancels out the immediate environment. While interacting with the laptop screen, pupils can still notice their immediate environment, whereas the horizontal screen of the smartphone significantly limits the visible physical space. The effect of this relation is the stronger coupling of the body with the device, and, more particularly, with the content displayed on the screen.

One of the other distinctions between horizontal and vertical screen surfaces is that the horizontal screen does not expose the content the way the vertical screen does. The horizontality of the screen diminishes the possibility of exposure, and hence renders the space around the device a more enclosed and private one as compared to the verticality of laptops. In sum, the horizontal surfaces enact a more intimate and private surrounding space. Here, the student can enter an *immersive space*.

The space of the classroom

In this section, we will draw on the abovementioned class arrangements to trace the relational spaces of vertical and horizontal screens with regard to the classroom setting. In the first arrangement, the class has a spatial direction towards the large boards. This physical feature of this arrangement enacts a space that is *multifunctional* (Decuypere and Simons 2016b), meaning that several functions can take place in this arrangement while maintaining the same body posture, e.g., looking at the board, playing the worm game, messaging on WhatsApp and taking notes.

The teacher populates the frontal *region* of the class and, hence, is confronted with many vertical walls (the backs of the open laptops). This means that each personal laptop enacts two regions: a 'behind' and a 'front' of the screen. On the one hand, the region of the front of the screen is where the content is exposed to the actors, and it equally enacts the zone of glancing. The 'front' region is equally where the body itself is being enacted as a 'screen' (i.e., as a wall that screens off). This happens when the content should be protected (from e.g., the teacher's gaze). On the other hand, the 'back' region of the laptop is enacted when the screen acts as a wall, preventing any interaction with the content that appears on the screen, hence situating the teacher in a zone of exclusion.

If the teacher continues to keep the front of the class as her/his 'home region', her/his interaction with personal screens and pupils remains limited, as (s)he is then dwelling in the zone of exclusion. Yet, it can very often be noted that vertical walls *mobilize* the teacher to the back of the class, where (s)he can have a better access to the screens. In doing so, the teacher leaves the zone of exclusion in order to be able to enter the spatial zone of glancing that is enacted by these vertical walls.

In the second arrangement, there is no fixed spatial center to the class. Rather, the class is decentralized: there is no front to the class, since the two boards are placed in two opposite sides of classroom. Additionally, bodies are not directed to any of the boards when seated at the desks. Instead, the laptop screens and the boards enact an *interlacing* space. In the second arrangement, the mentioned activities (chatting, looking at a presentation displayed on the board, note taking, glancing at others' screens) cannot take place in the same space and with the same body posture. Each of these activities necessitates an embodied *tuning in* to space by the pupils. Through this specific arrangement, the teacher is never totally in the zone of exclusion: she can always tune in or out as well. Likewise, there are always some laptop screens that are in the zone of glancing in this arrangement. This implies that, in this arrangement, the space of the classroom endows the teacher with a substantial amount of authority: the arrangement makes that s/he can very easily tune in or out (especially when compared with the first arrangement).

The third arrangement has been created to maximize the teacher's presence (and hence her authority) in the zone of glancing. In this arrangement, all the laptop screens are rendered visible to the teacher, as (s)he is mostly in the region *in front* of the laptops. Equally, all pupils' bodies face the wall, which indicates other students to be mostly in the zone of exclusion. This arrangement enacts a space of *mutual exclusivity* for the pupils: this arrangement configures the classroom space in such a way that all activities are completely separated spatially. Precisely through the minimization of the zone of exclusion for the teacher, the screen is constantly exposed to the teacher, and therefore actions such as chatting or gaming are not likely to happen on the laptop screen.

The space of mutual exclusivity for pupils specifies the physical configurations of the class in relation to different class performances. For instance, an independent work with devices such as annotating a poem, or making a presentation is performed in a *space of isolation*: all pupils are faced to the wall, with their vertical screen visible to the teacher. This way, the students are detached from the here and now of the classroom, and other actors present in the class. Yet, at the same time, they are *drawn into* the space enacted by their personal screen. In contrast to this space of isolation, where bodies face the wall, and students are situated in one another's zone of exclusion, collective activities require a different physical reconfiguration. In the third arrangement, a collective space is *only* enacted when all the chairs and bodies turn and all gazes intersect. Whenever the voice is given to the board (i.e., when the big screen starts to 'speak' through the audiovisual displaying of information), or when a discussion that addresses the group as a collective starts, the chairs and the bodies turn and form a circle, leaving the laptop screens on the background.

With regard to the horizontal screens, the first arrangement contributes to the creation of *private* spaces that can easily be uncoupled from the immediate environment. These horizontal screens create *in-visible* spaces that are only visible for the individual looking at them. These spaces exist parallel to the collective space of the lesson. In the third arrangement, however, these private spaces are flagged easily, as the individual, private space in front of each desk is exposed to the teacher.

Fenwick et al. (2011) argue that with the presence of mobile technologies in the classroom, the authoritative role of the teacher as the only bearer of meaning is blurred, since meanings are not in possession of the teacher. Instead, meanings are negotiated by participants through collaboration. Hence, cyberspaces can spatially reconfigure the forms of knowing, sociality and subjectivity enacted through educational encounters (pp. 156–157).

As demonstrated throughout this chapter, the notion of authority is constantly enacted through different spatial configurations. The third arrangement, in this regard, was a willful intervention of a teacher being confronted with how she constantly had to compete with personal devices to maintain authority. The device as such exerts authority, not only on the physical space, but equally on other spatialities, enacted by embodied practices (pupils being constantly tuned in with different device programs) and by the actors' movements through this classroom space (e.g., the teacher's movements). Therefore, different enactments of space, as being in constant emergence, are intimately related to issues of authority and to the question who can (and is allowed to) perform particular activities.

Concluding thoughts

Advocates of the presence of digital devices at schools argue that these devices encourage individualized learning, i.e., that learning is increasingly personalized, based on the pace and interests of students. Accordingly, it is often argued that this would help them to be autonomous, self-imposed, and self-monitored learners (Fenwick et al. 2011). Personalized and individualized learning is argued to allow students to regulate their own learning rhythm, and style. However, as illustrated in this chapter, different spatial configurations enacted in BYOD classrooms are not unambiguous, and are furthermore often in conflict with one another. This has important consequences for how we can consider 'personalization' and 'individualization' in digitally saturated classrooms.

On the one hand, the student is in a certain sense *given responsibility* to *navigate* these different spaces smoothly. However, navigating through the *in-visible, private*, and *collective* spaces, and, at the same time, being in the zone of *glancing* can be a difficult task to handle during a lesson. Personal learning, hence, is a matter of being able to smoothly navigate the different sorts of space that are enacted in a collective classroom setting, which are often in conflict and/or in tension with each another. On the other hand, this chapter equally shows that individualization and personalization only stretch so far, and are always co-dependent on the figure of the teacher and the other pupils present in the classroom. As such, the teacher acts as the *monitor* of spaces, who has to mobilize herself in order to keep track of the class practices. However, as it is also noted by Mifsud (2014), through these variously enacted spatial configurations, the teacher's authority is sometimes equally challenged through the enactment of zones of exclusion. Whereas the regular discourses of personalization mainly focus on customized (online) learning processes, this chapter sheds a light on how personalization and individualization concretely 'take place' at BYOD schools.

This chapter showed how the spatial aspects of classroom activities reveal hybrid patterns and relations between heterogeneous actors. It furthermore showed the importance of understanding to what extent contemporary classroom spatialities are tied to digital devices, sociomaterial networks and the infrastructure that make these technologies work. It seems that the strengths of these elements are so forceful that imagining the disappearing of one of these ties will completely change the spatiality of the classroom.

This research was funded by KU Leuven Internal Funds, grant number STG/17/029.

Note

1 The school's learning management system.

References

Adams, C. and Thompson, T.L. (2016). *Researching a Posthuman World: Interviews with Digital Objects.* Springer Nature. https://doi.org/DOI 10.1057/978-1-137-57162-5.

Carvalho, L., Goodyear, P., and de Laat, M. (2016). *Place-Based Spaces for Networked Learning.* https://doi.org/10.4324/9781315724485.

Decuypere, M. and Simons, M. (2014). On the Composition of Academic Work in Digital Times. *European Educational Research Journal* 13(1), 89–106. https://doi.org/10.2304/eerj.2014.13.1.89.

Decuypere, M. and Simons, M. (2016a). Relational Thinking in Education: Topology, sociomaterial studies, and figures. *Pedagogy, Culture and Society* 24(3), 371–386. https://doi.org/10.1080/14681366.2016.1166150.

Decuypere, M.Simons, M. (2016b). What Screens Do: The role(s) of the screen in academic work. *European Educational Research Journal* 15(1), 132–151. https://doi.org/10.1177/1474904115610335.

Fenwick, T. (2011). Reading Educational Reform with Actor Network Theory: Fluid spaces, otherings, and ambivalences. *Educational Philosophy and Theory* 43(SUPPL. 1), 114–134. https://doi.org/10.1111/j.1469-5812.2009.00609.x.

Fenwick, T. (2014). Knowledge Circulations in Inter-para/professional Practice: A sociomaterial enquiry. *Journal of Vocational Education & Training* 66(3), 264–280. https://doi.org/10.1080/13636820.2014.917695.

Fenwick, T., Edwards, R., and Sawchuk, P. (2011). Emerging Approaches to Educational Research: Tracing the socio-material. *Emerging Approaches to Educational Research: Tracing the Sociomaterial*, 232. https://doi.org/doi:10.4324/9780203817582

Latour, B. (2005). *Reassembling the Social: An Introduction to Actor-Network-Theory.* Oxford: Oxford University Press.

Law, J. (2002). Objects and Spaces. *Theory, Culture & Society* 19(5–6),91–105. https://doi.org/10.1177/026327602761899165.
Law, J. (2007). Making a Mess with Method. *Centre for Science Studies* March, 1–12. https://doi.org/http://dx.doi.org/10.4135/9781848607958.n33.
Massey, D. (2005). For Space. *America*. https://doi.org/10.1016/j.futures.2009.04.019
McGregor, J. (2003). Making Spaces: Teacher workplace topologies. *Pedagogy, Culture and Society* 11(3), 353–377. https://doi.org/10.1080/14681360300200179.
McGregor, J. (2004). Spatiality and the Place of the Material in Schools. *Pedagogy, Culture & Society* 12(3), 347–372. https://doi.org/10.1080/14681360400200207.
Mifsud, L. (2014). Mobile Learning and the Socio-materiality of Classroom Practices. *Learning, Media and Technology* 39(1), 142–149. https://doi.org/10.1080/17439884.2013.817420.
Mol, A. and Law, J. (1994). Regions, Networks, and Fluids: Anaema and social Topology. *Social Studies of Science* 24, 641–671.
Nespor, J. (1994). *Knowledge in Motion – Space, Time and Curriculum in Undergraduate Physics and Management. Knowledge the Identity and School Life*, vol. 2. https://doi.org/10.1017/CBO9781107415324.004
Nespor, J. (2002). Studying the Spatialities of Schooling. *Pedagogy, Culture and Society* 10(3), 483–491. https://doi.org/10.1080/14681360200200155.
Paechter, C. (2004). Metaphors of Space in Educational Theory and Practice. *Pedagogy, Culture and Society*, 12(3), 449–466. https://doi.org/10.1080/14681360400200202
Rißler, G., Bossen, A., and Blasse, N. (2014). School as Space: Spatial alterations, teaching, social motives, and practices. *Studia Paedagogica* 19(4), 145–160. https://doi.org/10.5817/SP2014-4-7.
Roehl, T. (2012). From Witnessing to Recording – Material objects and the epistemic configuration of science classes. *Pedagogy, Culture and Society* 20(1), 49–70. https://doi.org/10.1080/14681366.2012.649415.
Song, Y. (2014). 'Bring Your Own Device (BYOD)' for Seamless Science Inquiry in a Primary School. *Computers and Education* 74, 50–60. https://doi.org/10.1016/j.compedu.2014.01.005.
Sørensen, E. (2009). *The Materiality of Learning: Technology and Knowledge in Educational Practice*. Cambridge: Cambridge University Press.
Stevens, T. (2017). *Blending Learning and Technology: Degree Studies at Vocational Training College as a Case in Point*. Melbourne Graduate School of Education. Retrieved from https://minerva-access.unimelb.edu.au/handle/11343/194878.

Chapter 5

Beyond the Screen: Hatsune Miku in the Context of Post-Digital Culture

Annemarie Hahn and Kristin Klein

> Computers as we know them today will a) be boring, and b) disappear into things that are first and foremost something else: smart nails, self-cleaning shirts, driverless cars, therapeutic Barbie dolls, intelligent doorknobs that let the Federal Express man in and Fido out, but not 10 other dogs back in. Computers will be a sweeping yet invisible part of our everyday lives: We'll live in them, wear them, even eat them. (Negroponte 1998)

What Negroponte prognosed rather boldly 20 years ago might have sounded like science fiction back then, but seems far less unrealistic today. Computational devices, and with them screens, have become omnipresent and are integrated into our everyday practices. The ways we relate to the networked screen, how we contribute to (internet) culture, and how we interact with others through the screen is in constant movement. In a digitally networked society, screens are no longer primarily relevant as single devices but it is their connection to other screens that fundamentally changes their meaning compared to screens before the internet. They are part of a complex socioeconomic and technological network. If, following Negroponte, computers and screens are increasingly merging with our surroundings, we need to look beyond the screen and focus more closely on the structures that it is embedded in. What are the relevant shifts in screen culture and how do they affect the conditions of education today? Regarding screens as parts of larger networks, the question arises, who acts and is able to act within these networks. These new constellations bring about new power relations and thus imply questions of capacity and power to act.

By using the case of the virtual character Hatsune Miku, we want to analyze in the following how cultural production and social interaction have changed in the age of interconnected screens. Starting from a phenomenological perspective, we question structural characteristics that are relevant for the description of subjectivation processes in current media culture. Thereby we focus not only on the screen itself but on the networks, on the *making* of screen culture and on the screen as a technology of subjectivation. Looking at processes of collective production and consumption enabled by – and at the same time constituting – networked screen culture, we define the screen as a dispersed communal space. Moreover, we suggest an even broader definition of the screen, as being constantly performed. The structures beyond the visible screen, and this is our main argument, are a fundamental part of it. In the following, we pursue the question of how Hatsune Miku can be described with regard to educational theory and what insights can be derived from this about ways of subjectivation in the current post-digital culture.

Post-digital culture

The term *post-digital* in connection with culture refers not merely to digital tools, but to the ubiquity and pervasiveness of the networked infrastructure that constitutes cultures (Leeker et al. 2017). Following Stalder, culture should be understood as a condition by which 'the processes of social meaning – that is, the normative dimension of existence – are explicitly or implicitly negotiated and realized by means of singular and collective activity' (Stalder 2018, p. 7). Hence, culture is not to be taken as a simple superstructure. Rather, it is guiding action and shaping society by condensing practices that produce meaning in artefacts, institutions and living conditions (Stalder 2018, p. 8). According to Baecker, the dominant media technologies have significant impact on societal structures and cultural forms. He compares the potential of computer technology with the extent of social and cultural transformation the printing press has brought about, for example, new cultural techniques such as reading and writing, and the emergence of new institutions like schools (cf. Baecker 2007, p. 102f). Therefore, the changes caused by digital innovations have to be taken into account on a broader scale, especially with regard to the understanding of culture in the sense Stalder describes it.

Since the early 1990s, processes of digitalization have found their way into our daily lives, even where we cannot see it. For instance, because of digital navigation systems, the rapid availability of information, and the fact that now images and videos can be shared in real time we move about and communicate differently. Online platforms influence the way we consume news and influence political landscapes more than ever before.[1]

The term *digital* might just refer to electronic computers, to digital technologies and devices. This understanding of the digital, however, is insufficient. From a technological point of view, Cramer remarks that:

> 'Digital' simply means that something is divided into discrete, countable units […] whether zeroes and ones, decimal numbers, tally marks on a scrap of paper or the fingers (digits) of one's hand – which is where the word 'digital' comes from in the first place […] Conversely, 'analog'

means that the information has not been chopped up into discrete, countable units, but instead consists of one or more signals which vary on a continuous scale, such as the sound wave, a light wave, a magnetic field. (Cramer 2015)

Hence, digital does not necessarily stand for 'computational', and analogue is not just simply the opposite of digital. There are analogue computers as Cramer points out 'using water and two measuring cups to compute additions and subtractions – of quantities that can't be counted exactly' (Cramer 2015). However, we look at digital transformations in a much broader sense, and ask how they are embedded in cultural practices. According to Stalder, digital then signifies 'the set of relations that, on the infrastructural basis of digital networks, is realized today in the production, use, and transformation of material and immaterial goods, and in the constitution and coordination of personal and collective activity' (Stalder 2018, p. 8). He focuses thus more on the relational aspects and social transformations of digitality than on the binary opposition between *digital* and *analogue, material* and *immaterial* (cf. Ibid., p. 9).

This concept of the digital as defined by Stalder is close to the notion of the *post-digital*, as it has been used by other authors (Cascone 2000; Berry and Dieter 2015; Cramer 2015) to describe social and structural changes related to the technological shifts of the last decades. The post-digital can be understood as a critical response to techno-utopian aesthetics and the economic and political perspectives associated with them (cf. Stalder 2018, p. 9f). The prefix *post* puts emphasis on the fact that the disruption brought about by digital information technology has already happened. It is a marker for a new quality of digitality referring to a continuation and – maybe less visible – change of the digital into new power structures (Cramer 2015). The 'post-digital is represented by and indicative of a moment when the computational has become hegemonic' (Berry 2014). There are a large number of practices, especially in the field of art and cultural production, that explore how digital technology and its effects become increasingly present in visual phenomena (cf. Contreras-Koterbay and Mirocha 2016, p. 9). For instance, the *New Aesthetic*[2] is a term coined by Bridle as well as a Tumblr blog that documents and at the same time critically examines the pervasion of digital technologies at social, cultural and political levels. The collection depicts and creates a visible layer of social changes intertwined with technology, e.g., visualized GPS tracks of joggers or AI software generating *believable fake photos* of people. In the words of Bridle:

> It is impossible [...] not to look at these images and immediately start to think about not what they look like, but how they came to be and what they become: the processes of capture, storage, and distribution: the actions of filters, codes, algorithms, processes, databases, and transfer

protocols; the weights of datacenters, servers, satellites, cables, routers, switches, modems. Infrastructures physical and virtual; and the biases and articulations of disposition and intent encoded in all of these things, and our comprehension of them. (Bridle 2013)

Similarly, in the phenomenon of the screen, complex techno-political issues culminate (Bosma 2013). This diagnosis asks for a new mode of thinking about the screen and emphasizes the necessity to invent strategies to see beyond it. In the following, we want to show how aspects of post-digital culture are related to the screen by examining the example of Hatsune Miku.

Prosuming Hatsune Miku

Originating in Japan, but now present worldwide, Hatsune Miku is a virtual character that appears as a teenage girl in school uniform with two long turquoise-coloured pigtails. She is presented with certain human attributes. Following Wikipedia, she is 16 years old, 158 cm in height and weighs 42 kg. The pronoun the figure is associated with is 'she' and *she* is portrayed as a childlike and joyous personality.[3] Her name can be translated as *first sound from the future*. Hatsune Miku appears on different screens. Most famously, she is projected, via 3D hologram techniques, life sized on an almost translucent surface during concerts. Furthermore, she is the protagonist of hundreds of thousands of YouTube videos. Various companies promote their products with her in television and cinema advertising formats. There is also an augmented reality app that lets her appear in any place one can think of.

Initially designed to market *Vocaloid2*, a vocal-synthesizing computer software released by *Crypton Media* in 2007, the anime character has become today the subject of numerous fan art projects such as songs, dances, and animations. The character is shaped by many participants and articulated in many different forms, which are produced, disseminated, and perceived via screens. In magazines about pop culture, such as *The Verge*, Hatsune Miku is often described as an *open source celebrity*[4] and promoted as *the first truly crowd-created virtual talent*.[5] Her image is produced in the same way the image as that of a human pop star, i.e., by going on tour and being advertised in late night shows.

Hatsune Miku's songs are composed by a large community. The actress Saki Fujita lends the anime character her voice, which is recorded in short samples and stored in the database of the software, so that songwriters and producers can make use of them. In this way, Hatsune Miku was able to release over 100,000 songs and remixes. This is, in fact, a commercialized activity from which, among others, big industry profits. Performing in ads for brands including Domino's and Toyota, Hatsune Miku is an attention hub for many, but a money maker for only a few. Nevertheless, the pictures and songs of the anime character can be used freely for non-commercial purposes. More specifically, *Crypton Media* launched the website *Piapro*[6] accompanying the software to support peer production.

Hatsune Miku is a globally dispersed example of *prosumerism*. The term prosumer was first coined by Toffler in 1980 to describe individuals who are both consumers and producers, creating and designing a product or service for personal use (cf. Toffler 1980). Today, the term refers more generally to peer production in the context of user-generated content. This has become a basic principle of web-based practice. The phenomenon Hatsune Miku exemplarily joins the formerly separate states of cultural production and reception, which are no longer distinguishable. Screen culture undergoes today a fundamental shift: production and reception take place simultaneously and both actions are potentially attributed to one and the same actor.

Collective (post-)production

Now, with more and more people having access to the same tools and taking advantage of the possibilities characteristic of networked digital cultures, modes of collaboration have changed as well. This shift becomes evident by looking at the phenomenon of Hatsune Miku. Not all participants need to possess all skills necessary in order to contribute to the elaboration of the character. If someone wants to write lyrics, for instance, but does not know how to program Hatsune Miku's voice or how to play an instrument, he can easily find someone on the *Piapro* platform to collaborate with. Fans contribute to the creative success of the figure by producing and sharing new songs whenever they want and without having to wait for official releases. They can also direct music videos, choreograph a Miku dance or translate a song into another language.

Collaborative production profoundly changes how culture is shaped. Not only is the number of people creating and distributing their ideas growing but, if we are to assume that different skills enable to participate in and contribute to post-digital society, the information, tools and software we can access change as well. Producing Hatsune Miku is not about creating something entirely new, but about making use of, reassembling and varying existing material, in order to add to Hatsune's character. Hence, a basic principle of creative production is the practice of 'working with objects that are already in circulation on the cultural market, which is to say, objects already informed by other objects' (Bourriaud 2002, p. 13). Bourriaud uses the term *postproduction*, formerly a rather technical term for editing processes in television, film, and video such as 'montage, the inclusion of other visual or audio sources, subtitling, voice-overs, and special effects' (Ibid.). More than 15 years later, the modalities of production have become much more normalized with the proliferation of computational devices and the internet.

Remixing, sampling, copying, editing and distributing information have become collective practices of post-digital culture. Cultural artefacts, in turn, are predominantly consumed, produced and distributed online. New ideas can go viral almost in real time, and there is an enormous variety of these ideas due to the recombination of existing ideas that are often appropriated while ignoring intellectual property (Cramer 2015). What is more, in post-digital culture, an idea needs to be changeable. Otherwise it can't be further circulated and stay alive. In the case of Hatsune Miku, new versions are constantly being created within a common frame of reference. As a result, the multitude of stories in the formation of Hatsune Miku consequently needs to be addressed in terms of collective authorship.

The screen as communal space

The increasing rate at which content is produced and distributed today is based on and results in constant data streams. This information abundance leads to permanent negotiations of meanings. New collective frames are needed to establish shared references, to define options for action and to make resources available, and thus to re-evaluate our understanding of communality (cf. Stalder 2018, p. 79f).

Today, communal cultural production, even in real time, is not only restricted to coming together in physical space. Rather it extends to individual, separate devices that are connected to each other and that connect each other, independent of a specific location. For the artist Seth Price, changes in media culture entail that collective experience is now based on 'simultaneous private experiences, distributed across the field of media culture, knit together by ongoing debate, publicity, promotion, and discussion' (Price 2002, n.p.). Access to culture does not need to be inevitably physical anymore. Now that we make most of our cultural experiences online, the screen can be considered as communal space (Vierkant 2010), the internet as a new neighbourhood (cf. Rainie and Wellmann 2012, p. 13).

Rainie and Wellmann, who coined the term *networked individualism*, define new ways of coming together today by delineating a *Social Network Revolution*, which has 'afforded more diversity in relationships and social worlds – as well as bridges to reach these worlds and maneuverability to move among them' (Ibid., p. 11f). These changes are described on a structural level as the *new social operating systems*. Following this logic, the key actor in social constitution is the *networked individualist*. This means – also with regard to communal cultural production – that 'people function more as connected individuals and less as embedded group members' (Ibid., p. 12). The Hatsune Miku phenomenon is only one example for individuals working together temporarily or meeting for a Hatsune Miku-related event.

The idea of *networked individualism* raises the question of *how* people are integrated into larger contexts and *how* processes of exchange are organized today (cf. Stalder

2018, p. 89). Communality, as Stalder argues, is a fundamental characteristic of digitality, for the actual subject of cultural production is 'under the conditions of digitality not the individual but the next larger unit' (Ibid., p. 79). The new communal spaces, however, are fragmented and spread all over the world. Platforms like Facebook, Instagram or YouTube that connect individuals therefore play a central role. They are providing important infrastructures for exchange and coming together, while deciding about social and moral rules and laws according to which this interaction is structured (cf. Seemann 2018).

Performing the screen

The question of how communal processes are organized in post-digital culture has ramifications for the constitution of subjectivity in general and for creative production in particular. The subject described here is no longer a singular one. We can again refer here to the example of Hatsune Miku. The participating actors are, as we have seen, manifold, as the virtual character exists on many levels: first, she is a projection as a hologram on an almost invisible screen during concerts, but she also exists as a figure animated by software written by software engineers, made audible via a sound database and a voice-giving actress. Her songs are written or postproduced by many authors and she is brought onto stage by sound and visual technicians and distributed via various globally connected platforms. Hence, the attempt to understand Hatsune Miku as a single subject does not adequately grasp the phenomenon. Instead, the subject appearing as the figure Hatsune Miku is a *communal* one. It is constantly produced in performative acts of creating, sharing, computing, rendering, collaborating, using software, impersonating. Its infrastructure is not only designed by humans but it is fundamentally based on interactions between humans and technology. Therefore, Hatsune Miku cannot be sufficiently described as an anime, but should be regarded as a new form 'of "intra-action" between what is usually considered to be either human or machinic agency' (Leeker et al. 2017, p. 9).

In her concerts, Hatsune Miku is performing in front of an audience that often sings along, cheering at the end of every song as if there were a 'real' human being on stage who is able to interact with the crowd. The concert situation is almost a usual live event, but what seems to be a live situation evoking strong emotions, is nonetheless a program in the literal sense of that word. 'Live,' in this context, means people coming together to see the anime character, to be with her, but, even more so, to be together, to share common knowledge and affection. The act of coming together and engaging in the collective situation in front of the screen also allows, as Pazzini argues, for assuring oneself via the screen that there exists a collectively supported reference framework (cf. Pazzini 2015, p. 71).

In addition, the community members associated with Hatsune Miku invent themselves *in front of the screen* but also *beyond it*: they define themselves through their practice, i.e., by producing and consuming and thus embodying the narrative. In creating variations of the character and publicly displaying their work, they not only contribute to a meta-narrative, but receive feedback for their individual work which constantly transfers into a collective one. As Hatsune Miku is permanently (re)produced by her audience, her constitution changes every second. However, her age or basic appearance as an animated human never changes over the years; instead, she appears as an entity that maintains a consistent image. Being translated into different forms, from digital formats to realizations in physical space and back, the screen in its function as display links these different materialities of Hatsune Miku's appearance. Therefore, Hatsune Miku shows how the virtual and the physical space are always already intertwined.

The multiple ways in which Hatsune Miku appears are not produced linearly, but created constantly and simultaneously. Digitality implies much more complex media emergences performed by networks almost in real time. These networks, as mentioned before, not only consist of human actors, neither are they only screen based or exclusively bound to computational devices. What appears as Hatsune Miku on screen is rather to be described as a 'relation of performativity' (cf. Leeker et al. 2017, p. 11), in which agency is permanently produced by the interaction of human and nonhuman actors: 'digital devices and infrastructures perform, and they make humans (and non-humans) perform. "Smart things" profile and categorize, foresee and predict, propose and delete, charm and become dubious' (Ibid.). It is important to note, especially in connection to Hatsune Miku, that these attributions are no longer seen as dubious anthropomorphization but are now commonly used to describe technological objects and software (Ibid.).

Zahn uses the image of nodes of media cultural milieus to depict the new conditions of networked screens, as *'environmental agency*, which is neither dominated by people nor by technologies alone'[7] (Zahn 2017, p. 78). The screen in its disposition as interface may suggest that humans are in control of digital technology. However, the entire process of how the screen evolves can be understood and described as joint performative action by a wide variety of actors. While we certainly have to pay attention to how technology and its infrastructures are designed, the screen understood as device is only one node of a large network in which only a minority of all nodes is accessible or even visible. If we acknowledge that digital technologies are now widely and fundamentally participating in the 'making' of culture (Leeker et al. 2017, p. 11) then we need to think of the screen as an actor in itself.

Beyond the screen

While the word screen (from Old French *escran*: a screen that protects against heat) can have many diverging and converging definitions, varying from divider, buffer and protector, display and mask, surface and storage to transmitter and translator, and can be applied to different contexts – as objects of protection (e.g. shield, curtain, net) or means of enclosure among others (see Bravo 2003) – in the context of post-digital culture we want to suggest another, even broader definition of the screen.

Screens can now be seen as part of a translation of collective narratives, affects and artefacts. Today, they exceed the function of devices as 'nodes of a globally networked, digital media culture'[8] (Zahn 2017, p. 74). Screens are thus part of a larger infrastructure, a larger cultural framework that is not perceivable (by humans) in its entirety. In this way, the materiality of screens can be described as tangible parts of an in some respect invisible system consisting of software, data and code, as well as social and economic layers. The various screens Hatsune Miku appears on are in motion, never in a fixed state, as what is being shown on them is created by many and further is an initiator for the production of new forms of interaction. The screen is, in this sense, always situated in certain dynamics and it dissolves into and re-establishes from non-visible structures. It therefore is an aid to presentation but is in itself a presentation and above all a commentary contribution to discourse (cf. von Bismarck 2008, p. 71) and hence a contribution to a constant production of post-digital culture.

Screens no longer appear and have effect exclusively as standalone devices. They are always connected to other screens, to cultural production and consumption and therefore each screen participates in the making of post-digital culture. An understanding of the screen in its relational framework, even more so as constantly being deconstructed and reinstated in globally connected performative acts, shifts the focus from single devices to underlying techno-political issues.

Education beyond the screen

In the context of education, it is necessary not only to think about ways humans can access and influence digital technology but, at the same time, to take into account the relevance of structural changes that have an enormous influence on educational settings. Digitally networked screens are both the result and facilitator of production within changing cultural environments, which are characterized by, as described above, prosumerism, communal (post-)production and new communal constellations among others. How then can these characteristics be considered and also enabled in educational settings?

We propose to change the perspective on education in the context of constantly changing media environments. We need to focus not on the single screen that has impact on subjectivation processes of human beings anymore. Rather, we must concentrate on the structures and relationships that determine our actions within a culture that can no longer be distinguished from its mediality. In other words, we need to address questions of mediality and subjectivity to increase our understanding of education today.

If it is true that changed mediality leads to changed subjectivity (Jörissen and Meyer 2015, p. 7), we must examine the networked screen for its possibilities of subjectivation. The screen in its network structure challenges us to regard education as interaction and mutual influence of the involved actors. The screen itself is one of them. The screen as actor then becomes part of a collective subject, involved in digital network structures and thus digital technologies of subjectivation.

Following these thoughts, we must negotiate the role of individual humans in their relation to themselves and to other human beings and how this affects their relation to the world. In the same manner, we have to rethink collective subjects, constituted by human and nonhuman actors on a structural level. Furthermore, we must not lose sight of new power structures within arising platform dynamics in order to locate agency.

So, what can we learn from the example of Hatsune Miku in this respect? Our analysis indicated that cultural production in post-digital culture can no longer be described under the same premises as before in terms of what we consider as subject. Accepting these changes means that we have to take the implications for self-world-relations with regard to screens seriously: prosumerism, as a constitutive part of post-digital culture, changes the self-conception of the individual respecting its relations within a network. It changes the possibilities and the customs to contribute and to make use of existing ideas and materials. Collective (post-)production also requires a redefinition of skills the individual needs for participating in society. If in post-digital culture, with the networked individual in mind, certain skills are no longer to be thought exclusively in the context of individuals but also shared in between and across them, they need to be addressed at an infrastructural level both in virtual as well as in physical space. Similarly, if in post-digital culture the infrastructure behind the screen gains in importance, more attention must be paid to specific settings of education in order to enable new forms of communality in addition to the ones already enabled by common platforms.

Screens under the current collapse of physical space in networked culture (cf. Vierkant 2010) and the *cyberspace turned inside out* (cf. Meyer 2015, p. 218) are always in movement, dispersed and in many ways de- and reterritorialized. Ideas are in circulation until they become visual, they are performed and manifest themselves in physical space. If we were to follow the thesis from the beginning, stating that screens in the near future will be inseparable from our surroundings, even from our own bodies, we need to find different ways of describing post-digital culture in its progression. As Lovink writes, referring to digital technologies, 'the challenge will not be the internet's omnipresence but its very invisibility' (Lovink 2016, p. 10).

We therefore need to develop ways to see beyond the screen, even beyond detached discussions of metadata, algorithmic governance and platform politics to make underlying structures and fundamental techno-political issues visible, to come to a greater understanding of what shapes art, culture and education.

Notes

1. See the latest case of Cambridge Analytica and its potential to influence people based on their collected data.
2. http://new-aesthetic.tumblr.com/.
3. The design of the character Hatsune Miku plays into Japanese gender stereotypes, and thus mirror a certain image of girls and women in Japan. This article cannot shed any further light on this problem at this point, but wants to point out that Yuji Sone explores this more closely (cf. Sone 2017).
4. https://www.theverge.com/2014/10/9/6951375/david-letterman-hatsune-miku-anime.
5. http://mikuexpo.com/.
6. http://piapro.net/intl/en.html.
7. Translated from German by the authors: 'Medien werden in dem skizzierten ökologischen Sinne als Infrastrukturen von Wahrnehmungen, Affekten, Handlungen von sowohl menschlichen als auch nichtmenschlichen Akteuren thematisch. Sie ermöglichen, erzwingen und verschließen Verbindungen, Relationen auf vielen Ebenen, wie beispielsweise auf bio- und soziotechnologischer Ebene, zugleich werden Wahrnehmungs- und Handlungsmöglichkeiten auf die an diesen Prozessen beteiligten Akteure verteilt und man spricht von einer *environmental agency*, die weder von Menschen noch von Technologien allein dominiert wird' (Zahn 2017, p. 78).
8. Translated from German by the authors: 'Bildschirme als "Knoten" einer weltweit vernetzten, digitalen Medienkultur' (Zahn 2017, p. 74).

References

Baecker, D. (2007). *Studien zur nächsten Gesellschaft*. Berlin: Suhrkamp Verlag.
Berry, D. (2014). Post-Digital Humanities. Computation and cultural critique in the arts and humanities. *Educause Review*. Accessed April 30, 2018: https://er.educause.edu/articles/2014/5/postdigital-humanities-computation-and-cultural-critique-in-the-arts-and-humanities.
Berry, D. and Dieter, M. (2015). *Post-Digital Aesthetics. Art, Computation and Design*. New York, NY: Palgrave Macmillan.
Bosma, J. (2013). Post-Digital is Post-Screen: Arnheim's visual thinking applied to art in the expanded digital media field. *A peer reviewed journal about (Aprja)*. Accessed September 28, 2017. http://www.aprja.net/post-digital-is-post-screen-arnheims-visual-thinking-applied-to-art-in-the-expanded-digital-media-field/.
Bourriaud, N. (2002). *Postproduction. Culture as Screenplay: How Art Reprograms the World*. New York, NY: Lucas & Sternberg.
Bravo, D. (2003). *Screen (1)*. Accessed April 30, 2018. https://lucian.uchicago.edu/blogs/mediatheory/keywords/screen-1/.
Bridle, James (2013). *The New Aesthetic and its Politics*. Accessed April 30, 2018. http://booktwo.org/notebook/new-aesthetic-politics/.
Cascone, K. (2000). The Aesthetics of Failure: 'Post-digital' tendencies in contemporary computer music. *Computer Music Journal* 24(4), 12–18.

Cramer, F. (2015). *What Is Post-Digital? A peer-reviewed journal about (Aprja)*. Accessed March 17, 2018. http://www.aprja.net/what-is-post-digital/.

Contreras-Koterbay, S. and Mirocha, Ł. (2016). The New Aesthetic and Art: Constellations of the postdigital. Institute of Network Cultures. *Theory on Demand, 20*. Accessed April, 30, 2018. http://networkcultures.org/wp-content/uploads/2016/07/TOD20-final.pdf.

Jörissen, B. and Meyer, T. (Eds.) (2015). *Subjekt Medium Bildung (Medienbildung und Gesellschaft 28)*. Wiesbaden: SpringerVS.

Leeker, M., Schipper, I., and Beyes, T. (2017). Performativity, Performance Studies and Digital Cultures, in M. Leeker, I. Schipper, and T. Beyes (Eds.) *Performing the Digital. Performativity and Performance Studies in Digital Cultures*. Bielefeld: Transcript Verlag, pp. 9–20.

Lovink, G. (2016). *Social Media Abyss: Critical Internet Cultures and the Force of Negation*. Cambridge: Polity Press.

Meyer, T. (2015). Next Art Education. 9 essential theses. In T. Meyer and G. Kolb (Eds.). *What's Next? Band II: Art Education*. Munich: Kopaed.

Negroponte, N. (1998). Beyond Digital. *Wired (December)*. Accessed April 30, 2018. http://www.wired.com/wired/orchive/6.12/negroponte.html.

Pazzini, K.-J. (2015). *Bildung vor Bildern. Kunst – Pädagogik – Psychoanalyse*. Bielefeld: Transcript Verlag.

Price, S. (2002). *Dispersion*. Accessed May 1, 2018. http://www.distributedhistory.com/Disperzone.html.

Rainie, L.and Wellman, B.(2012). *Networked: The New Social Operating System*. Cambridge, MA:MIT Press.

Seemann, M. (2018). *What Is Platform Politics? Foundations of a New Form of Political Power*. Accessed April 30, 2018: http://www.ctrl-verlust.net/what-is-platform-politics-foundations-of-a-new-form-of-political-power/.

Sone, Y. (2017). *Japanese Robot Culture: Performance, Imagination, and Modernity*. New York, NY: Palgrave Macmillan.

Stalder, F. (2018). *The Digital Condition*. Cambridge: Polity Press.

Toffler, A. (1980). *The Third Wave*. London: Collins.

Vierkant, A. (2010). The Image Object Post-Internet. Accessed April 30, 2018. http://jstchillin.org/artie/pdf/The_Image_Object_Post-Internet_us.pdf.

von Bismarck, B. (2008). Display/Displacement. Zur Politik des Präsentierens, in J. John, D. Richter, and S. Schade (Eds.) *Re-Visionen des Displays. Ausstellungs-Szenarien, ihre Lektüren und ihr Publikum*. Zurich: JRP Ringier Kunstverlag, pp. 69–82.

Zahn, M. (2017). Bildschirme. Medienökologische Perspektiven auf das (in)dividuelle Phantasma in der aktuellen Medienkultur, in T. Meyer, A. Sabisch, O. Wollberg, and M. Zahn (Eds.). *Übertrag. Schriftenreihe Kunst Medien Bildung, vol. 2*. Munich: kopaed, pp. 73–81.

Chapter 6

Beyond digital screens – media ecological perspectives on artistic practices in the digital media culture

Manuel Zahn

We live in a screen culture: screens of all sizes and technical shapes determine our everyday life. With steadily increasing digitization they have even multiplied themselves. These days, they face us everywhere, and we carry them around with us, some of them in intimate relationship close to our bodies. This development does not even stop in front of the school or the classroom: the teacher has to compete with other onscreen media of knowledge transfer such as the blackboard, the projector and the screens of the smartboards, laptops, tablets, and students' smartphones.

In a first step, I would like to explore the term screen itself, i.e., its multiple levels of meaning against the background of today's digital media culture. In a second step, I will take a media-ecological perspective and thematise screens as 'nodes' of a globally networked digital media culture, and, at the same time, shift the theoretical view from the individual to the *dividual*, i.e., a multiple distributed and divided/shared subjectivity. In this process, the term of individualization loses the prominent position it has had for a theory of aesthetic education and it is no longer an orientation for research, or for pedagogical practice. Moreover, it could be suspected that clinging to this term causes a misunderstanding of our actual conditions and the complex interdependencies in pedagogical practice. Therefore, I will focus more on (material, physical, social, and media-technological) milieus in which dividual processes are taking place.

As a last step, I return to contemporary artists, as well as to artistic practices of so-called *post-internet art*. These artists are no longer investigating the aesthetics of the digital screen. Instead, they pay attention to what is *beyond* the screen, to the digital infrastructure, and to its impact on our culture and our perception, affection, and thought processes. Moreover, not only the reflection on digitized perception is a central concern of artistic practices, but also the redesign and transformation of a digitized culture itself. According to this format, the first objective of my analysis is to provide a general perspective with regard to the digitization of culture and its effects. Second, I aim at opening a new perspective for thinking about aesthetic education.

Current media culture as screen culture

It seems to be intuitive knowledge that screens can be understood, first of all, as tangible, technical, and technological objects that people have been using for a very long time, as storage, presentation, and communication media. This is also the perspective on the screen – understood as a flat, rectangular surface that is positioned at some distance from a perceiving subject – which Lev Manovich takes up in his book *The Language of New Media* (2001). In the chapter *The Screen and the User* (Ibid., p. 99) he outlines a historical trace of today's screen culture that ranges from the first paintings he calls 'classic screens' to the 'dynamic screens' of cinema and television to today's computer screens in all sizes and shapes. While the basic form of the screen in a structural sense remains relatively stable in spite of the historical development, its materialization is subject to fundamental changes in temporal, spatial, and material-technical perspective.[1] Paintings and photographs remain immobilized representations and inscriptions of visual reality, whereas the images of the cinema screen became movable, being the result of a sight that had been mobilized via the film camera. According to Manovich, the computer screen, which is dominating today's media culture, produces a third type of screen on which digital information is transformed in real time (Manovich 2001, p. 101). These digital real-time screens are constantly circulating and distributing a stream of data and information that structures our societal, political, and institutional relations, as well as our individual relations towards the world, ourselves, and others. Consequently, Manovich dedicates the second half of his essay to the visual relationships between screens and the people who use them.

Following Manovich, we can speak of the current existing screens in media culture as elements of an apparatus (*dispositive*), in the sense of Michel Foucault (1978) or Giorgio Agamben (2009), who, in my view, outlined one of the most general, simplest, and, at the same time, most beautiful formulations for the apparatus:

> Further expanding the already large class of Foucauldian apparatuses, I shall call an apparatus literally anything that has in some way the capacity to capture, orient, determine, intercept, model, control, or secure the gestures, behaviors, opinions or discourses of living beings. (Agamben 2009, p. 14)

For Agamben, the term apparatus is not only limited to prisons, psychiatric institutions, factories, universities, schools, confessions, or, more broadly, any kind of juridical and political measure or discipline (where the connection with power is in a certain sense evident). It also comprises language, painting, writing, literature, photography, the cigarette, shipping, computers, mobile phones, and many more (Ibid.). It would be easy to name examples of how much the digital, networked screen media and, as it were, the global *technosphere* of the *world wide web* has captured and changed our attention, our perception and senses, our modes of communication, our culture of memory, as well as the formats of storage and presentation of information for a long time. And it is urgently necessary to investigate to what extent humankind has undergone transformations with and through the digital images of these screens, and to expand the so far exclusively language-based educational theories towards theories of visual education (see also Zahn 2012, 2015). But, at this point, I would like to add another layer of meaning to the screen. Therefore I turn to the work of Jacques Lacan.

L'écran: the term 'screen' as used by Lacan

According to Agamben, there are two large ontological categories in the world: living beings and apparatuses. Processes of subjectification or individual subjects, then, arise from the relationship between living beings and apparatuses. Apparatuses specify more or less concrete forms of subjectification. In this respect, one and the same living being can be involved in manifold processes of subjectification, such as being subjectified as television viewer, gardener, curator, tango dancer, photographer, painter, bodybuilder, jogger, teacher, smoker, moviegoer, internet user, etc.

With Jacques Lacan, this relationship between living beings and apparatuses can be thought of as even stronger from a human perspective than with Agamben. Lacan's attention shifts from the technological apparatuses and the subject forms that they provide, towards human beings as users of onscreen media. For humans, the onscreen media are not just technical stuff and instruments, but their content and symbolizations, combined with imaginations, interests, demands, and wishes, matters. These, in turn, help to structure the relations between them and the apparatuses. Lacan describes the *foundation* and *frame* of these imaginations, pictures, and objects of desire as a *phantasm* (see Lacan 1987, p. 66). He sees the *phantasm* – in difference to fantasy and imagination – as a kind of intersubjective *screen that one cannot actually see oneself*, but in which all perceptible signs, pictures, and other representations are inscribed. To be clear: this screen is *not* exclusively formed by the imagination of one single, individual subject; since a *phantasm* is always shaped by the cultural other, it has a symbolic side, which stretches out in between a subject and other subjects, as well as objects in the world, in a way that at the same time separates and connects. According to Lacan, the screen thus offers the possibility of bridging the gap between the individual subject and its foreign counterpart, by offering it the opportunity to take in different subject positions and simultaneously a path into intersubjectivity. Karl Josef Pazzini's understanding of the screen is very close to that of Lacan, and more precisely, when he writes in *Die Angst, die Waffen abzugeben* (2015), that screens represent the desire of subjects to assure a shared perception:

Nevertheless, this resonates [in every subjective perception, MZ] in a wish: to assure one's own perception as one common to all. [...]. This longing still corresponds to the visible projection surface in almost every classroom, the blackboards and the (medieval) panel, later the canvas and the screen contribute to the exhibition of works of art in a public context. They demand the formation of a common body of perception.[2] (Pazzini 2015, p. 71)

In summary, Lacan's understanding of the screen can be seen as the basis of cultural symbolic orders, which makes individual experience understandable and communicable, and which thus structures individuals as desiring subjects. Thereby the screen is the *interface* of subjective perception, thought, and action, as well as an element of an apparatus, as connections between heterogeneous elements such as discourses, practices, techniques, artefacts, architectures, and many more, in and with which people act. In that sense, we can think of digital screens as 'nodes' in the complex network of these heterogeneous elements. These 'nodes' tie together symbolic, aesthetic, and imaginary dimensions of perception, experience, and communication with a material dimension of an imperceptible digitized technological infrastructure.

To use another metaphor: we can think of the digital network as a mycelium. The actual organism consists of a large invisible subterranean network. And what we used to call a 'mushroom' is merely a visible fruit body of the mycelium. In analogy to the mycelium metaphor we can say: what seems to be an object in digital culture – e.g., digital gadget, a screen or something on this screen – is a secondary manifestation, a 'node' of an underlying, extremely complex technological infrastructure. This technological infrastructure connects heterogeneous actors, humans, and nonhumans like machines, cables, satellites, software, algorithms, protocols, codes, data, interfaces, RFID and GPS transmitter, countless mobile devices.

Networked screens as 'nodes' of media-cultural milieus

How can digital media culture be described, understood as a manifold of apparatuses in the sense of Foucault and Agamben, in which people are been subjectified when they are for example using digital screen technologies? This is one of the main questions of the media-ecological take on culture, a school of thought within the landscape of media studies that is becoming ever more important (see Löffler and Sprenger 2016). Media-ecological thinking goes hand in hand with a media concept that no longer only covers individual media, but that is particularly interested in media ensembles, entire networks of media-technological connections. In the ecologic sense outlined, media are to be thematized as infrastructures of perceptions, affects, actions of both human and nonhuman actors. They enable, enforce and close connections/relations on many levels, e.g., on a biotechnological and socio-technological level. At the same time, possibilities of perception and action are distributed among the actors involved in these relational processes. Therefore one has to speak about an *environmental agency*, which is dominated neither by humans nor by technologies alone. However, this distributed subjectivity and agency does not first come about with the advent of computer technology. One can easily name a whole list of theoretical positions (e.g., Gilles Deleuze, Felix Guattari, Erich Hörl, Bruno Latour, Bernard Stiegler) that convincingly show that people have always become subjects in relation to techniques and technologies. But what is unique about today's global, digitally networked 'technosphere' is that we become fully aware of these subjectivizing processes of division and participation (see Hörl 2016, p. 42).

Furthermore, we must reckon with the fact that there is the desire of many actors to control the networked, digital screen media in their favor. According to the French philosopher Bernard Stiegler (2008), the current media culture is more than ever pervaded by an economic logic and an instrumental reason. The creative, participative, and emancipatory possibilities of the *social web*, which have been conjured up again and again, are opposed by the fact that the currently convergent media systems of network culture and social media are dependent on a calculating, finance capitalist economy and its marketing, that are geared to the consumption of novelty and principles such as usability, acceleration, individualization as well as excellence, effectiveness, and efficiency. The different subject forms of contemporary media culture described by Agamben thus converge in the *phantasm* of an entrepreneurial subject, who willingly conforms to the aforementioned economic principles, who understands itself as a bundle of competences, and who undertakes the most varied efforts of self-optimization.

At the same time, the only apparently individual (undivided, self-contained) inhabitant of contemporary digital media culture is opened to the other, i.e., the others in its environment. He is divided in manifold ways, e.g., he communicates with others in a symbolic way and at the same time he is always being addressed physically and sensually, as the philosopher Michaela Ott explicates in her latest book *Dividuationen. Theorien der Teilhabe* (2015). Following, among others, writings by Gilles Deleuze and Felix Guattari, she develops theoretical possibilities of describing the contemporary being-in-the-world of humankind. The guiding concept of her descriptions is the 'dividuum.' The human being as a dividuum is still recognizable as a single body, but it is not completed, not undivided, just not individuated in the world, but more or less consciously embedded in manifold references, participation, and division processes of various magnitudes, which, in turn, incessantly inform and subjectivize it. In this double figure of participation and division, the technological apparatuses of digital media culture not only support us in our possible relations to the world and to our self, but they also unwillingly affect, condition, and subjectivize us, far below the threshold of our consciousness. This is because the sensorial system of digital devices not only affects our body. They also connect to our perception, feeling, and thinking, and determine them to a certain extent (see also Perniola 2009; Hörl 2011, 2013).

In this perspective, human subjectivity appears as a distributed reality, co-constituted by a variety of others, as it is embedded in media-technological apparatuses that are partly unknown to it. Human subjectivity, as understood by media-ecological theories, is only one of many other interconnected subjectivities. In this sense, a media-ecology approach differs fundamentally from other theories that think of human subjectivity in terms of integration and of the internalization of external factors (such as socialization processes, cultural techniques, and symbolic practices). The theoretical framework of media ecology not only broadens our thinking about subjectivity to not yet accounted aspects, it also brings to the fore the fact that humans have never been individuals, but rather have to be thought of as *manifolds* in the sense of Gilles Deleuze. Media scientist Mark B.N. Hansen explains:

> Literally enveloped in a multiscale and distributed sensory environment, our subjectivity does not attain a higher order of its power because it absorbs and processes what is outside, but rather through its immediate participation or involvement in the polyvalent agency of innumerable subjectivities. Our distinctly human subjectivity therefore operates as a multi-valued structure of variable-sized microsubjectivities, each of which functioning in a different way, but with considerable intersections.[3] (Hansen 2011, p. 370)

In the outlined media ecological perspective on the world, the dividuum is related in manifold physical, sensory, technical, and social references to an exterior (to others, to an environment or a milieu). Hence, a more complex theory is needed that can describe the dynamics, situatedness, materiality, and mediality of present processes of dividuation (as a contemporary form of *Bildung*). To me, the term apparatus (*dispositive*) introduced above with Agamben seems to be suitable to think alongside media-theoretical, praxeological, and educational perspectives (see Zahn 2015). Media-ecological analyses of pedagogical situations in the context of aesthetic education could deal, for example, with the sensory effects of materials, artistic techniques and practices, and media technologies on human beings in a profound manner, as suggested by Mario Perniola (2009) in his *Sensology*. According to Perniola, artefacts, e.g., media of all kinds, not only represent meanings and discourses: they have an effect through the use of the senses, which they train and thus form.

In view of this, aesthetic education (*Bildung*) should be theoretically reformulated. More exactly, it should be regarded as a practice of the dividuum in different situational, material, medial, social relationships, interdependencies, and transmissions within which it has formed itself and continues to develop – in search of other, new options of perception, articulation, and action, as well as new modes of use in complex media technology environments. Here, connections can be made with the media-ecological position of Katja Rothe (2016), who proposes to critically investigate the use of media in a praxeological and ethical-aesthetic perspective, and, moreover, to consider the design and the use of media, following Foucault, as an ethical project in which one forms an attitude, a style of dealing with the world, others and one's own life. From the perspective of media ecology, the creative practice of existential forms or lifestyles shifts from the anthropological question of the successful or happy life of the individual to media anthropological questions of a dividuum that 'explore the possibilities of "concern for oneself"' (Ibid., p. 51) on the basis of technical-human coexistence.

MP3 – the meaning of a format and its cultural impact

This last idea also speaks to questions of power. In this regard, it is interesting to turn to the field of computational aesthetics and its relation to human perception. I am thinking here, as one example among many others, of the reconfiguration of our perception through digital psychoacoustics and psycho-visualistics in form of compression algorithms like .mp3, .jpg, or .mpg4/h.264.

It is no exaggeration to think of them as the most significant transformations of our perceptual practices in digital media culture. Jonathan Sterne (2012) speaks in his extensive study on the audio compression format .mp3 of a 'perceptual capital,' or rather of an 'imperceptual capital.' In his work, he draws attention to the crucial role of compression software in the development of modern media and sound culture. Sterne also hints towards several powerful economic rationalities that have guided the construction of .mp3. Key among these insights is the incorporation of the human body within a scientific understanding of technical systems. In order to engineer an efficient technical system, the capacities and limits of how we interact with (or serve as parts of) these systems must be taken into account. Sterne refers to this mode of engineering as 'perceptual technics.' The most important technique is called 'perceptual coding.' It's built around a mathematical model of the gaps and absences within the audible spectrum of human hearing. Through this mathematical model the .mp3 encoder compares the content of the audio to what it 'knows' about human hearing and removes what it 'thinks' its user won't hear. Finally, the .mp3 encoder also does some things to the stereo image, based on assumptions about where people do and don't need to hear stereo, and it cuts off some of the very highest frequencies, assuming (correctly) that most adults don't hear well above 16 kilohertz thresholds. So, the success of .mp3 is based on the fact that thanks to the previous drafted compression algorithms a piece of music can be reduced to one-tenth of its data, which means a tenth of the transfer costs over the telephone network. Big suppliers like Telekom or AT&T thus save about 90 percent of the cost of data delivery.

It also follows from this that psycho-acoustics is nothing more than a decision about what people do not necessarily have to listen to. This is clearly informed by, let us call it, a business model: to control the senses and to accustom consumers to standardized formats. Similar computational processes happened (and still happen) to digital images and digital videos. This entails that educational research should not only focus on digital screens and interfaces, but that we also have to find out more about their technological environment, i.e., the digital infrastructure that is shaping our aesthetic milieus.

The challenge for pedagogy – and in particular of aesthetic education – is, on the one hand, to deal with technological gadgets (e.g., smartphones) and media phenomena (e.g., advertising). But, on the other hand, it also consists in addressing something that systematically withdraws from visibility and objectivity: the infrastructures of digital technology, its conditions, and its effects. But how to do this? In the following, I would like to suggest one possible way to take, and more specifically in relation to artistic practice.

Beyond digital screens: art and artistic practices as motors of aesthetic reflexions on digital culture

I turn to art because it can be understood as a form of critical approach through which aesthetic potential and social impact of 'new' technologies, of our 'technological condition,' to put it with the German media scholar Erich Hörl (2011), can be explored. More precisely, contemporary artists pay attention to what is *beyond* screens, the digital infrastructure, and to its impact on our culture, our perception, our affective life, and our thought processes. Before I discuss two examples of such contemporary artistic practices, I would like to explain how I understand criticism in this context.

Artistic/aesthetic practice understood as critical practice does not (or at least not always) directly criticize something; neither does it not make explicitly critical judgments about something. Rather, it suspends judgment: it leads, in other words, to a crisis of judgment. This brief definition refers to the concept of criticism, as Michel Foucault develops it in his lecture *What is Criticism?* (1992, p. 17). For Foucault, criticism leads to an art or a technique, on which it is also based: 'the art of not being so governed' (Ibid., p. 12). (This is also the reason why criticism as a resistant practice is or should be of great importance for aesthetic education in particular and for educational science in general.) But which practice constitutes art, this technique of critique? As I have written above with Foucault, we can understand criticism, over and against the everyday use of this term, as a practice that suspends judgment. Instead of judging or condemning, critique just suspends the judgment and surrenders itself to the objects, situations, and phenomena. But criticism also goes beyond suspending judgment and opens up different practices and thus different possibilities for perception, thought and action. One result of this is that the dominating discursive order of evaluation becomes addressable.

In other words, a critical practice in relation to technologically, politically, culturally regulated, and normalized modes of knowledge can only succeed if it is anchored in these modes of knowledge and at the same time pursues the goal of going beyond them. Critique seeks to question certainties and orders of which the critic him or herself must make use in the very act of criticism.

The critical practice outlined here resembles structurally what I understand by aesthetic practice/experience, viz., a practice that is characterized by devotion to (objects in) the world (Horkheimer 1952), which one wants to explore and ultimately understand, by sensitization at all levels of experience, and, ultimately also by resistance. In aesthetic experience, we are no longer solely oriented in our perception and imagination by how we judge a situation from an economic point of view. We resist an economic logic, and evaluate an event or a situation by putting between brackets the goals and purposes we pursue in it or what we hope to achieve in this situation. Rather we also pay attention to perceptions, sensations, and imaginations that are otherwise excluded by the aforementioned reductive mechanism.

Aesthetic practice as critical practice would therefore also be a criticism of aesthetics: it begins with modes of perception and action that have become self-evident, with discursive normalizations and norms as well as with hegemonic aesthetic orders and dispositives that make something perceptible in a very specific way. I am thinking of aesthetic and artistic practices that use strategies of destabilization and subversion, to make (usually invisible) existing orders and norms 'visible,' or at least thinkable. I discuss now two examples of this.

'Breaking up': glitch aesthetics and datamoshing

In the last years a few music videos were produced, such as Chairlift's *Evident Utensil* (2009), Kanye West's *Welcome to Heartbreak* (2009), Wastefellow's *Wonder* (2016), or Calvin Harris music video *My Way* (2017), in which glitches became the aesthetic principle. Glitch refers to the compressed video image in its ambivalent structure: as an algorithmic data structure (calculated in real time) and as an optical surface (see Briz et al. 2011; Menkman 2011). All these videos show color shifts, streaks, pixilations, defigurations, and other disturbances of the surface of the photographic image, which suddenly recover figurative qualities, only to be defigured again by the movement of another image.

These videos play with the aesthetic difference between digital video imagery and the traditional aesthetic paradigms of photo- and videographic appearances. The 'glitch aesthetic' of digital video is based on datamoshing. The term datamoshing has become an idiom of artistic expression, an abbreviation for hacking into the compression algorithms of digital video.

When digital videos are compressed, the compression and transformation program analyzes the video material and determines frames (the so-called keyframes) in which a lot of movement takes place. The following frames (the so-called deltaframes) then describe 'only' the motions of the pixels based on the keyframe. In other words, the subordinate deltaframes contain something like a catalogue of pure differentiality and movement data. A 'hack' of the digital video in the sense of datamoshing exists when one removes the keyframes and replaces them with keyframes from another video. In the computed mixed image of the keyframes of another video and the reference deltaframes, the 'memory' of a motion differential is realized.

The aesthetic strategy of these videos has shown and exposed the digital image as a technological aesthetic 'hybrid.' In other words: through the artist's interventions, the usually invisible, dynamic data structure of the digital images becomes visible in the photographic surface as traces of the hacked compression code.

'Bad ass motherfucker' (Roth USA 2005 to present)

The business card of Evan Roth shows the start page of Google and the search bar stating the words 'bad ass motherfucker.' The mouse pointer is on the button 'I'm Feeling Lucky,' which brings the searcher directly to the website of the first hit. If you follow these 'instructions' on the card, you get to Evan Roth's website. The background is, of course, that Roth has optimized his website for the Google search algorithms, so that this search term refers directly to him. Through this detour, he appropriates the term 'bad ass motherfucker' in an indirect, but most effective way.

Roth shows at the same time how the public is changing in a digital culture. The attribution 'bad ass motherfucker' is not given by Roth himself, but by a number of search queries. The search query generates not only a results page on the Google servers but it shapes various URLs/links into a context, which is only presented by this search. This context is like a 'history,' a structure that gives identity. Identity in digital media culture is still the result of recorded events, but it is also (and above all) a node in the network of different attributes and search queries.

Aesthetic education as aesthetic reflexion of digital culture

When the digital appears as a hegemonic actor, artistic reflections of the digital receive an emancipative function. Therefore, in digital culture, not only the reflection of digitized perception is a central concern for artistic practices, but also the redesign and transformation of the digital culture itself. The first aim of aesthetic education (in relation to contemporary artistic practices) is to provide an analytical media-aesthetic perspective with regard to the digitization of culture and its effects. Second, it aims at the development of a pedagogical perspective.

Taking such a perspective we can ask: what is the aesthetic scope for the intended use of an interface or a piece of software? And which forms of subjectification as users are inscribed in software? But also: which free spaces, critical practices, or new relations can arise from the digital, especially spaces and practices that grant the possibility of non-affirmative articulations (as described using the example of datamoshing/glitch)?

These questions can be discussed aesthetically, but also more explicitly in pedagogical contexts. Since aesthetic articulations in pedagogical contexts always entail the possibility of detaching oneself from the implicit logics of the digital media culture, things such as our being governed by the dictate of digitally mediated creativity, but also productivity and networking ideologies can become objects of aesthetic reflexion and of thinking about counter-strategies (e.g., decontextualization, misappropriation, resignification, modding, hacking). So aesthetic milieus, and forms of digital culture, can be reflexively put at use in a pedagogical perspective. They then become possibilities for aesthetic articulation. This entails an open and attentive attitude towards digital culture, which at the same time can reflect its normative implications and, if necessary, (at least) tries to subvert them.

Videos

Evident Utensil – Chairlift (Dir.: Ray Tintori, 2009); https://www.youtube.com/watch?v=mvqakws0CeU.
 Welcome to Heartbreak – Kanye West (Dir.: Nabil, 2009); https://www.youtube.com/watch?v=wMH0e8kIZtE.
 Wonder – Wastefellow (Dir.: Conor Donoghue, 2016): https://www.youtube.com/watch?v=10mUJTmd9Jk.
 My May – Calvin Harris (Dir.: Emil Nava, 2017): https://www.youtube.com/watch?v=b4Bj7Zb-YD4.

Notes

1 From a structural point of view the basic form of a screen also can be understood in concepts like 'frame' or 'framing,' which delimits and emphasizes an image from the visual field of perception (see Mersch 2014, p. 23).
2 '"Dennoch schwingt das [in jeder subjektiven Wahrnehmung, MZ] als Wunsch mit: sich der eigenen Wahrnehmung versichern als einer, die allen gemeinsam wäre. […] Dieser Sehnsucht entspricht noch die in fast allen Unterrichtsräumen vorhandene, von allen sichtbare Projektionsfläche, die Tafel – Tafeln sowie das (mittelalterliche) Tafelbild, später die Leinwand und der Bildschirm tragen zur Ausstellung von Kunstwerken in einem öffentlichen Kontext bei. Sie fordern zur Bildung eines gemeinsamen Wahrnehmungsbestandes heraus.'
3 'Buchstäblich in ein multiskalares und verteiltes sensorisches Umfeld eingehüllt, erlangt unsere Subjektivität höherer Ordnung ihre Macht nicht, weil sie das, was außen ist, aufnimmt und verarbeitet, sondern vielmehr durch ihre unmittelbare Mitteilhabe oder Beteiligung an der polyvalenten Handlungsmacht unzähliger Subjektivitäten. Unsere ausgesprochen menschliche Subjektivität operiert demnach als mehrwertiges Gefüge größenvariabler Mikrosubjektivitäten, die je unterschiedlich, doch mit erheblichen Überschneidungen funktionieren.'

References

Agamben, G. (2009). *What is an Apparatus? and Other Essays*. Stanford, CA: Stanford University Press.
Briz, N., Meaney, E., Menkman, R., Robertson, W., Satrom J., and Westbrook, J. (Eds.) (2011). GLI.TC/H READER[ROR].20111. Tokyo: Unsorted Books.
Foucault, M. (1978). Das Dispositiv, in *Dispositive der Macht. Michel Foucault über Sexualität, Wissen und Wahrheit*. Berlin: Merve, pp. 119–125.

Foucault, M. (1992). *Was ist Kritik?* Berlin: Merve.
Hansen, M.B.N. (2011) Medien des 21. Jahrhunderts, technisches Empfinden und unsere originäre Umweltbedingung, in E. Hörl (Ed.) *Die technologische Bedingung*. Frankfurt am Main: Suhrkamp, pp. 365–410.
Horkheimer, M. (1952/1985). Begriff der Bildung, in *Gesammelte Schriften*, vol. 8. Frankfurt am Main: Fischer, pp. 409–419.
Hörl, E. (Ed.) (2011). *Die technologische Bedingung*. Frankfurt am Main: Suhrkamp.
Hörl, E.H. (2016). Die Ökologisierung des Denkens, in P. Löffler and F. Sprenger (Eds.) *Medienökologien. Zeitschrift für Medienwissenschaft 14*. Zurich, Berlin: Diaphanes.
Hörl, E.H. and Hansen, M.B.N. (2013). Medienästhetik. *Zeitschrift für Medienwissenschaft 8*. Zurich, Berlin: Diaphanes.
Lacan, J. (1987). *Die vier Grundbegriffe der Psychoanalyse*, Seminar XI (3rd ed.), Berlin: Weinheim.
Lacan, J. (2006). *Die Bildungen des Unbewussten*, Seminar V (1957–1958). Vienna: Turia & Kant.
Löffler, P. and Sprenger, F. (Ed.) (2016). *Medienökologien, Zeitschrift für Medienwissenschaft 14*. Zurich, Berlin: Diaphanes.
Manovich, L. (2001). *The Language of New Media*. Cambridge, MA: MIT Press.
Menkman, R. (2011). *Institute of Network Cultures | No. 04: The Glitch Moment(um)*. Amsterdam: Institute of Network Cultures. Accessed June 15, 2018. http://networkcultures.org/blog/publication/no-04-the-glitch-momentum-rosa-menkman/.
Mersch, D. (2014). Sichtbarkeit/Sichtbarmachung. Was heißt 'Denken im Visuellen'?, in F. Goppelsröder and M. Beck (Eds.). *Sichtbarkeiten 2: Präsentifizieren. Zeigen zwischen Körper, Bild und Sprache*. Berlin, Zurich: Diaphanes, pp. 19–71.
Pazzini, K.-J. (2015). *Bildung vor Bildern. Kunst – Pädagogik – Psychoanalyse*. Bielefeld: Transcript Verlag.
Ott, M. (2015). *Dividuationen. Theorien der Teilhabe*. Berlin: b_books.
Perniola, M. (2009). *Über das Fühlen*. Berlin: Merve.
Rothe, K. (2016) Medienökologie – Zu einer Ethik des Mediengebrauchs, in L. Sprenger (Ed.) *Medienökologien, Zeitschrift für Medienwissenschaft 14*, 46–57.
Sterne, J. (2012). *MP3. The Meaning of a Format*. Durham, NC, London: Duke University Press.
Stiegler, B. (2008). *Die Logik der Sorge. Verlust der Aufklärung durch die Technik und Medien*. Frankfurt am Main: Suhrkamp.
Zahn, M. (2012). *Ästhetische Film-Bildung. Studien zur Medialität und Materialität filmischer Bildungsprozesse* (Theorie bilden). Bielefeld: Transcript Verlag.
Zahn, M. (2015). Das Subjekt des Kinos, in B. Jörissen and T. Meyer (Eds.) *Subjekt Medium Bildung* (Medienbildung und Gesellschaft 28). Wiesbaden: SpringerVS, pp. 77–92.

Chapter 7

Next school's art education[1]

Torsten Meyer

The background of this chapter is the assumption that hardly anything is as important for the structures of a society and the form of a culture than the dominant media of dissemination in that society. This assumption is shared by a lot of authors from very different disciplines. Not only Marshall McLuhan, Manuel Castells, Niklas Luhmann, and Régis Debray, but also the sociologist and cultural theorist Dirk Baecker states in his *Studies on the Next Society* that the extent to which the introduction of the computer will impact society can only be compared to the introduction of language, writing, and the printing press before it (see Baecker 2007). Following management philosopher Peter F. Drucker, Baecker calls the society that is based on computers as the leading media technology the *next society*. The *next society* produces a next economy, a next politics, a next science, a next humanity, a next university, a next museum, a next school, a next architecture, and a next art.

This chapter is an attempt to address the assumptions by the media and cultural theorists just discussed. I do so by seeking how the field of art education can adequately respond to this new situation. More exactly, I will sketch a new idea of school which could be the school of the *next society*.

Scope

Next art education and *next school*: these terms might sound somewhat brisk, perhaps even slightly visionary. But that is precisely how they are meant to sound. I am concerned here with a number of basic considerations that gnaw at me when, against the backdrop of my profession, which involves training art teachers, and which is hence very much concerned with the next generation (of teachers, of pupils, of schools), I think about 'what's next' in art and about the education of the future (and about the future of education).

To begin with, let us note that schools – and anyone who has attended one will know this – have a problem with the new. In principle, the new is not a matter for schools, at least it is not the subject of teaching. A school has other functions. A school is one of those places whose explicit purpose it is to keep the communication process going, allowing the information contained within the memories of one generation to be transmitted to the memories of the next. What we refer to as *paideia* or what we call *culture* is maintained by institutions such as the school. It is about passing on content regarded as culturally significant, the tradition of what has proved culturally important, and what is therefore considered worthy of preservation. Cultures can use their schools to prove and preserve themselves.

There is another preliminary remark I have to add here: school has a great deal to do with future, even with science fiction. In principle. School is fundamentally connected with the new – with the uncertain, the unforeseeable, with the possible. To begin with, the new generation, the new *subjects* are rather *projects*. If we do not learn – and teach – for school but for life, the educational efforts of teachers must aim to qualify pupils to participate in a society that does not yet even exist.

What I mean by this, and this is what I like to tell my students right at the beginning of their studies at the art teacher training department, is a simple calculation. I ask them for how long do they think they will have an impact into the future? For example, if you are a student born in 1993 and are now 25 years old, and will begin your teaching career, then you will be working with pupils until you retire – that will be about 40 years later, so in the year 2058. In the final year you spend working, you may be teaching 10-year-old pupils, whom you will be required to prepare for their own futures. Assuming life expectancy is the same as today, the lives of these pupils, born in 2048, will end around 70 years later, so in the year 2128. So, in the final year of your career, your education efforts should aim to ensure that your pupils will still be able to participate competently in the society of the year 2128. And I could view my own work as a university teacher as requiring me to aim *now* to enable you to do this.

That is a giant leap into the future (110 years). Of course, I have overdramatized things here for clarity. But even if we are a little more realistic and simply assume that when you are around 50, if you want to pass something on to a 10-year-old pupil that will be of benefit to them when they themselves are 50 years old, then we are already talking about the year 2080.

The dimensions of this leap in time become clear if we consider the same period in the other direction. In the more dramatic version, this means we are back in 1901. The art of Classic Modernism is just around the corner. This was the year when, in Germany, the first *Kunsterziehungstag*, or art education day, was held in Dresden, marking the beginning of the (modern, and, as such, true) intellectual history of art education. We can soon look forward to the 'new media' of (silent) film and radio. We will still have to wait almost an entire human lifetime until the invention and spread of the television. The more realistic version takes us back to 1958. Approximately 10 years before the television became a mass medium and a cultural revolution turned the whole world upside down, a fourth-semester teacher training student is concerned with what he, as a 50 year old in 1975, will have to offer a 10-year-old pupil so that they in turn will be able to master life as a 50 year old, on the cusp of the next society, in 2018 – a good 20 years after web 1.0 and almost 10 years since web 2.0.

1. *This would be the general starting point for next art education: just like any educational theory, it must be radically based on the future. It is concerned with becoming, not with being. This is best achieved by seriously focusing on 'the now.'*

Crisis

When talking about next art, more is meant than announcing the next hype in the art world, which is 'out' again just as quickly as it was 'in.' Next art is thought of in a broader context. It is about the consequences of large-scale processes of change in media culture. The background to this is the basic assumption, which stems from the epistemological tradition (e.g., Michel Foucault and Jean-François Lyotard), that the symbolic activities of a society — such as its religion, its ideologies, its art — cannot be explained without taking into account the technologies used by that society to record, archive, and circulate their symbolic traces (see Debray 2004, p. 67). In this sense, in his studies on next society (translated from German (*Studien zur nächsten Gesellschaft*), Dirk Baecker relates sociological developments to the advent and use of certain media technologies: the introduction of language gave rise to tribal society, the introduction of writing enabled advanced ancient society, the introduction of the printing press resulted in modern society, and the introduction of the computer will constitute the 'next society.'

As an explanation for the processes of societal change that follow innovations in media culture, which present themselves as existential crises in the sense of

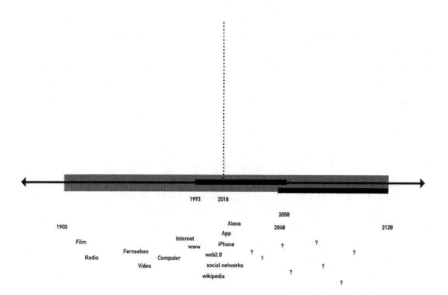

Figure 7.1 The scope of teaching teachers [see text for details]

high points and turning points of potentially catastrophic developments, Baecker offers the hypothesis that a society can only succeed in reproducing itself if it finds an answer to the problem of excess of meaning – a problem that goes hand in hand with the introduction of any new communication medium. In ancient times, for instance, the spread of writing led to an excess of symbols; modernity experienced an excess of criticism as a result of printing technology and the mass spread of books that followed; and the next society will be characterized by an excess of control stemming from the introduction of the computer (see Baecker 2007, p. 147).

Such mediological revolutions have profound effects on society and its functional systems. Initially, the search for new cultural forms that can cope with society being overwhelmed by the new communication medium throws society into fundamental crises. We are currently experiencing such a crisis. This is why it can be claimed that art after the crisis is the art of the next society. It will bring about forms that allow us 'to exploit the potential of the computer without it upstaging us' (Baecker and Hedinger, 2012; translated from German).

Just as modern society has found ways of dealing with an excess of criticism, the next society must develop forms of dealing with control that respond not only to the possibility of being controlled, but also to the possibility of controlling. An excess of control, no doubt, also means computers being able to control people, or people being able to control other people using computers. But if we only consider a society of control in terms of Orwell's 'Big Brother,' this suggests a perspective based on the experiences of modernity that is not appropriate for the complexity of the next society.

2. *Another general starting point for next art education could be: the hero of the next society, trustee of culture and an exemplary ideal for educational projects, is no longer the intellectual of the Enlightenment, who appeals to public reason, and no longer the critic, who is a master of comparing the real with the ideal. In short: the hero of the next society is no longer the sovereign subject of modernity, but is, in fact, the hacker (see Baecker and Hedinger 2008).*

Control

If the computer is the dominant medium of the next society, the significance of the figure of the hacker is evident. But this should not be taken in too concrete terms. In terms of the art of the next society, what is first and foremost meant is *cultural* hacking, and so it follows that hacking should be understood as a general, fundamental principle of working and action, only involving the computer insofar as it is reacting to the current society being overwhelmed by the computer, i.e., responding to control with control. Therefore, the hacker is simply someone who masters the cultural techniques required to understand that 'controlling' and 'being controlled' are two sides of the same coin.

Precisely in this sense, Düllo and Liebl also describe cultural hacking as the 'art of strategic action' (Düllo and Liebl 2005; translated from German). They characterize cultural hacking as critical and subversive play with cultural codes, meanings, and values. It is about exploring cultural systems with the aim of finding one's way around them and at the same time introducing new orientations into these systems. The hacker installs faults within the system. She or he is nesting in existing control projects like a parasite. In doing so, she or he responds to the excess of control by putting his or her own control projects on top of other people's control projects.

'The art of the Next Society is light and clever,' predicts Baecker. 'It evades and binds with wit. Its images, stories and sounds attack, without actually doing so' (Baecker 2011; translated from German).[2] This can be read as the work of a cultural hacker. The artist of the next society is someone who is able to crack a code, whether that code is technological, social, psychological, or cultural (see Baecker 2008, p. 80). They use coding techniques to conduct experiments that are formally rigorous, yet in their effects highly liberating – translating different image and language games into each other.

3. *A further insight for next art education would be orientation is based on the cultural techniques necessary for dealing with excess of control. The artists of the next society master (control) the cultural techniques of their time. Their art 'trembles in the network' and 'vibrates in the media' (Baecker and Hedinger, 2012 ; translated from German). They do not have to be an expert in computer science, but they do maintain a creative approach to coding techniques and control projects.*

Post-art

The crisis that marks the transition into the next society is catastrophic for art. Régis Debray already announced this in his *Une histoire du regard en Occident* (Debray 1995). In intellectual proximity to the idea of the next society, he exposes art (or rather *the* art) as a symptom of the mediosphere dominated by printing and central perspective. Here, art is 'not an unchanging component of the human condition,' neither is it a 'transhistorical substance' that runs unchanged through cultural history as an anthropological constant, but rather a concept that first emerged 'late in the modern West,' the persistence of which is 'in no way' secured. Art – according to Debray – 'the sensational, monosyllabic word, is an obstacle to every attempt at explaining the changeability of images. It presents an artefact as nature, a moment as something essential, and folklore as something universally valid' (Debray 1999, p. 149; translated from German).

The chief curator of the world's largest and most important exhibition of contemporary art also doubts now whether 'the category of art can be regarded as a given. Nothing is simply given,' says Carolyn Christov-Bakargiev and she explains that she aims during Documenta 13 to shake the certainty 'that a field called art even exists' (Christov-Bakargiev and Hohmann 2012, p. 62; translated from German). She describes the conception of art 'which examines colour using colour, form with form, history with history, space with space' as a 'bourgeois, Eurocentric idea,' and as such she is, 'to be honest,' not sure whether 'the field of art' – in terms of the great Western narrative – 'will survive through the 21st century' (Christov-Bakargiev 2011, p. 27; translated from German). Hence, she decided to gather in Kassel art by *outsiders*, i.e., by people who are not or do not wish to be (professional) artists and who only really know the 'field of art' from the outside (outsider art), and – as has been a reasonable standard in contexts of contemporary art since Okwui Enwezor's Documenta 11 – by people who live outside the Eurocentric dominance of culture (global art).

Next art leaves the 'bourgeois, Eurocentric' field and the usual mechanisms of inclusion and exclusion. 'It breaks free from its shackles of high culture and leaves the prison of its autonomy. It will,' as Dirk Baecker explains in a discussion with Johannes Hedinger, 'seek new places, new times and a new audience. It will experiment with formats in which the usual institutions become variables' (Baecker and Hedinger 2012; translated from German).

Next art is no longer art. It is beyond art. Jerry Saltz introduced the rather elusive term *post-art*: 'Post Art – things that aren't artworks so much as they are about the drive to make things that, like art, embed imagination in material [...] Things that couldn't be fitted into old categories embody powerfully creative forms, capable of carrying meaning and making change' (Saltz 2012b). He is thinking here of things 'that achieve a greater density and intensity of meaning than that word usually implies' – for example the sign next to the small, unassuming landscape paintings in Documenta 13's *Brain*, which tells visitors that, in the late 1990s and early 2000s, artist and physicist Mohammad Yusuf Asefi prevented around 80 paintings from the National Gallery in Kabul being destroyed by the Taliban. He did this by carefully and meticulously (and reversibly) painting over in those landscapes the human figures who were prohibited to be depicted under the fundamentalist regime: 'A number of things at Documenta 13 that weren't art took my breath away, in ways that turned into art' (Saltz 2012a).

4. *Next art education breaks with the history of art as a great narrative of Eurocentric high culture. It enters uncharted territory. It opens up to the unknown, to next art, and attempts to think in terms of post-art. It is recognizably connected with the field of art, but thinks beyond it. And it knows: next art does not remain unaffected by the world in which it is created. It deals with aspects of contemporary life by utilizing current methods of presentation, operating on the ground of everyday culture.*

Natives

Jimmie Durham considers himself an *American native*. His ethnically coded works, which he has been producing since the 1970s as a radical cultural criticism of America's (European) settlers, the *American immigrants*, are born out of a self-conception that the artist himself describes as follows:

'According to some official documents I was born in Arkansas in 1940, but that state is a recent invention. The 'united states' were all invented against American Indians, and as a Cherokee I was born in Cherokee territory under the aggressive political act called "Arkansas"' (cited in Cahan and Kocur 1996, p. 120).

The generation of people born into the crisis are called *digital natives*. This generation has grown up with what we sometimes still call 'new media.' But the attribute 'new' no longer means anything to them in connection with the things that surround them on a daily basis. They are natives of digital media cultures.

If we transpose Jimmie Durham's perspective to the much discussed and rather controversial metaphor of the *digital native* – and, for the sake of the argument, let us take this metaphor very seriously for a moment – then it would be possible to relate current discussions about inter-culture and post-migration to the media culture of the next society as well. But this would entail a serious disfigurement of our usual signs, and of our 'normal' understanding of causality. This is because then we should use the future perfect tense to look into the future past. On the one hand, teachers, parents, and other educators are then to be understood as 'migrants.' Children and young people, on the other hand, must then be considered as the indigenous people of digital cultures. Therefore, not unlike Jimmie Durham's description of the 'aggressive political act called "Arkansas",' they are subject to an *aggressive [cultural] act called [school]*, which is intended to impose on them the culture of the 'migrants'.

5. This is the next insight for next art education, and specifically in relation to digital immigrants: The 'dominant culture' of next art education is the culture of the digital natives. It is a culture which is emerging at this very moment. It is alien to us. Respect for the indigenous people of the next society commands our special attention.

Inside out

The metaphor of the digital native emerged from the Declaration of the Independence of Cyberspace: 'You are terrified of your own children, since they are natives in a world where you will always be immigrants' (Barlow 1996). This 'cyberspace' was one of the metaphors used in the early years of the internet in an attempt to make this new medium tangible and understandable. When William Gibson invented the word in 1984, he was to leave a lasting impression on our collective imagination; 1990s' science fiction films also played their part, and so it was that we imagined this cyberspace to be a large, dark, cold, 'virtual' space (based on ideas about outer space), a sort of 'world beyond,' a 'virtual reality.'

This 'virtual reality' was sharply separated from so-called real life. For some reason, the boundary between the two worlds was very important. The virtual reality involved the non-real, the fictional, dreamlike, imaginations, and illusions, sometimes even the imaginary, the magical, and the uncanny. On this side of the divide we had 'real life,' the real reality. If someone ventured too far into the other side, the side of virtual realities, if they were too deep *inside* cyberspace, then they might not be able to make their way back; they risked suffering a 'loss of reality,' etc.

Now, a sixth of the global population are inside this supposedly virtual world: i.e., one billion people. With web 2.0, with blogs, wikis, and social networks, mainstream has arrived on the internet. Cyberspace has become inhabitable. But it is not inhabited by the weird cyborgs of early science fiction fantasies. The natives of digital culture don't dress in cybernaut suits in order to immerse themselves in parallel worlds. Instead they have the internet in their pockets, Wikipedia and social networks on their smartphones. They have – as wonderfully put by Aram Bartholl in his investigations into the relationships between 'net data space' and 'everyday life' – brought the internet into 'real life' and thus, to a certain degree, turned cyberspace inside out. Piotr Czerki describes what this means very vividly in his Web Kids' Manifesto: 'We do not "surf" and the internet to us is not a "place" or "virtual space". The internet to us is not something external to reality but a part of it: an invisible yet constantly present layer intertwined with the physical environment' (Czerski 2012).

6. Next art education must be based on the principles of cyberspace being turned inside out into reality: the connection of everyone with everyone, the creation of virtual communities and collective intelligence (see Lévy 2008 , p. 72). Next art education must position the issues, problems, and phenomena it addresses in its teaching against the backdrop of a digitally interconnected global society. And this means that it can no longer maintain the modern educational goal of working 'critically,' and, at the same time, contemplatively, with books and images; instead, it must be based on dispersion in the networks and on the operational handling of complexity (see Baecker 2007 , p. 143).

The Global Contemporary

Contemporaries experience the world simultaneously: they are in a spatio-temporally common world the size of which – both spatially and temporally – depends on the nature of the currently dominant means of communication and information. They become socialized, and constitute an environment and system, for and with each other. Such contemporary constellations give rise to new ideas, new knowledge, new art, and other new artefacts of human imagination. Through contemporary constellations, youth subcultures, for example, develop new music and new images, new forms of culture and new forms of self-conception.

The communication processes in the exhibition 'The Global Contemporary,' which tends towards innovation, are fundamentally opposed by principally conservative communication processes in the family, school, university, academy etc., which aim at transmitting the cultural knowledge and skills, as well as the cultural self-conception of a generation into the consciousness of the next generation. Traditionally, these processes of cultural transmission tend to be related to people sharing places or spaces, rather than sharing temporality, i.e., contemporaneity.

Cultural tradition and cultural heritage are – as we know from the past – based on territory, nation states, speech communities, etc.

People communicate with one another in space and in time. The next society prefers the new means of communication for disseminating information in space, which comes with ignoring the means of disseminating information in time. In keeping with the concept of the exhibition "The Global Contemporary," this development can also be read from the recent history of art: in the 19th century, art was a matter of national relevance. As the general focus on historical origin became more established, national museums were opened, the discipline of art history was invented – primarily as *national* art history – and *inter*national shows comparing culture – such as the Venice Biennale – saw the light of day. In the 20th century, the newly formed, internationally oriented avant-garde turned against old nationalisms, and, at the same time, adopted the 'primitive art' of (former) colonies as a new source of inspiration. But behind this there was, as Belting and Buddensieg (2013) stress, 'a hegemonic modernity which declared its concept of art to be universal' (p. 61; translated from German). In contrast to and emphatically to be distinguished from modernity, art in the 21st century is trans- and hypercultural. The art that is now emerging all over the world claims 'contemporariness without limits and without history' (Ibid.).

7. *This would be a further proposal for next art education: the next society no longer regards time primarily as a line stretching from yesterday to tomorrow, which causally links origin with future. History belongs to the age of modernity, as does teleology. For the next society, time is a series of discrete 'presents' distributed around current events – 'the now' is what matters. Having been turned inside out, cyberspace is becoming the medium of a global contemporariness. This makes cultural globalization a constantly present layer of reality.*

Postproduction

The artist of the next society no longer asks 'what can we make that is new?' but rather 'how can we produce singularity and meaning from this chaotic mess of objects, names, and references that constitutes our daily life?' (Bourriaud 2002, p. 17). The artist of the next society no longer refers to a field of art as a museum of high culture, full of works that have to be 'referenced' or 'exceeded.' They refer to global contemporariness – being the world shared by all. For Nicolas Bourriaud, this is 'a territory all dimensions of which may be travelled both in time and space' (Bourriaud 2009a) – i.e., a huge hypertext experienced as a 'global space of exchange' (Bourriaud 2009b, p. 203; translated from German), in which artists wander around, browse, sample, and copy like DJs and web surfers 'in geography as well as in history.'

Somewhat aptly, Bourriaud calls this 'postproduction' – a term borrowed from the vocabulary of TV and film production, which refers to processes that are applied to previously recorded raw material: montage, editing, combination, and integration of audio and video sources, subtitles, voiceovers and special effects. Bourriaud attributes 'postproduction' to the 'tertiary sector' of the economy, so as to metaphorically underline how it is different from the production of 'raw materials' in the agricultural and industrial sectors. So, what is at stake here is not producing beautiful or new images, for example, but *dealing with* all the beautiful and new images already stored in the (inter)cultural heritage available to the global contemporary. The image is no longer the aim of art, rather it is its raw material.

Postproduction is not concerned with the image as a thing and as an object. It is about how the image is dealt with symbolically. Next art invents models for using images; it no longer composes the *forms of the visible*, but instead programs the *formats of seeing*.[3] This involves the interactive adoption of different cultural codes and forms of everyday life worlds – with the aim of *making them work* in the global contemporary. This can be understood as cultural hacking: instead of transforming raw materials (blank canvas, lumps of clay etc.) into beautiful or new forms, the artists of postproduction make 'use of data' *as* the raw materials. He or she does this by taking existing forms and cultural codes and remixing them, copying and pasting them, and translating them into each other.

8. *Next art education knows that next art no longer considers the image as the goal of art, but as its raw material. It no longer strives for one grand masterpiece, but deals primarily with the plurality of images. It produces profound knowledge about the codes that structure our reality, and develops the ability to interactively adopt culture in the form of samples, mashups, hacks and remixes. And it senses that control over our global reality of life can only be attained through forms of participatory intelligence and collective creativity.*

Next nature

The excess of control associated with the introduction of the computer not only provokes a next society, but also a next nature, from which the next society distinguishes its own culture. Cyberspace, turned inside out into real life in the global contemporary, is the *natural* environment of digital natives. The natives of the next society are confronted with the fact that the largest part of their life is out of their control and unpredictable. Their environment is dominated by the need to anticipate that – as Baecker puts it – 'not just things have other sides than people previously thought, and the individuals other interests [...] than people previously assumed of them, but that each of their interconnections generates formal complexes which fundamentally and thus irreducibly overwhelm the understanding of every observer' (Baecker 2007, p. 169; translated from German). If the complexity of the interaction of information in this sense exceeds the subject's powers of imagination, this is an indication of what Michael Seemann most appropriately refers to as *ctrl-Verlust* or *loss of control* (Seemann 2013). This 'loss of control' is the fertilizer of the next nature.

Koert van Mensvoort defines next nature as 'culturally emerged nature' (see Mensvoort 2013). He examines the changing relationships between humans, nature, and technology, and in doing so notices two things. On the one hand, (old) nature – being just a simulation, i.e., a romanticized notion of a balanced, harmonious, inherently good entity, which therefore is worthy of protection – has become an extremely well-marketed *product* of culture. On the other hand, he makes clear that technology – traditionally understood as that which protects us from the 'raw forces' of nature – is itself developing into something that is just as unpredictable and menacing, as savage and cruel, as that which it is supposed to protect us from, i.e., 'nature' (as traditionally understood).

This radically tweaks the distinction between art and nature, which dates back to the 18th century. Traditionally (and etymologically), nature is associated with concepts such as 'birth' and 'growth,' while culture is associated with concepts like 'being made,' 'creation,' 'artificiality'. In keeping with the concept of next nature, the opposition of *controllable* versus *uncontrollable* now seems to be the better dividing line. Nature can be 'cultivated' by bringing it under the control of people. We have been doing that for tens of thousands of years. And for a relatively short amount of time now, the reverse has also been true: culture can, if it becomes too complex, become 'nature like' (i.e., out of control). The products of culture, typically thought of as being under people's control, become autonomous and unmanageable. Next nature describes that which escapes control (see Meyer 2010).

9. This final point (for the time being), in particular, requires a very thorough rethinking of the basic reference points of any next art education. This is because tweaking the opposition of nature/culture implies that we say goodbye not only to the idealization of nature as a harmonious reference point for art (which, to a certain extent, steps in for nature by creating that which nature would create if it simply let images, music, sculptures, colour, forms etc. 'grow'), but also to that paradigmatic figure of the artist as an aesthetic subject 'gifted' with a corresponding, quasi-natural power of creation. However, the notion of this aesthetic subject, geared towards individuality, originality, expressivity, ingenuity, and authenticity, has, in only slightly varying forms, represented the foundation of common theories of aesthetics, fine arts, and cultural, artistic education or instruction ever since the Enlightenment and Romanticism. What Jean-Jacques Rousseau brought into play with the 'homme naturel' as a standard and benchmark for the cultural criticism of modernity (see Meyer 2014) as well as for its educational ideals, was set out in theoretically more elaborated forms in Schiller's letters 'On the Aesthetic Education of Man' and Humboldt's idea of the 'genius' as an ideal model for processes of 'Bildung' (see Hubig 1983 , p. 207). And this has endured ever since as a cultural counter-principle of an 'aesthetic utopia' closely connected to the idea of the sovereign subject and the autonomous artist (see Reckwitz 2012).

Next art education has not only left behind the opposition between art and technology dating back to the 18th and 19th centuries, but it has also moved past the related opposition between nature and culture. The homme naturel 2.0, as a contrast to and a starting point for cultural criticism and for the educational projects of the next society, is a being in the state of next nature. As a role model for next art education projects, it follows that the artist of the next society must – very carefully with respect to the depth of the rootedness in the professional argumentation – be thought of in terms of Immanuel Kant's premise – updated by Koert van Mensvoort: The 'genius [of the artist of the next society] is the innate mental aptitude (ingenium) through which [next!] nature gives the rule to art' (Kant 1790, para. 46).

Notes

1 This chapter is loosely based on the article Next Art Education: Eight theses future art educators should think about. *International Journal of Education through Art 13(3)*, 369–384.
2 'Die Kunst der nächsten Gesellschaft ist leicht und klug. Sie weicht aus und bindet mit Witz. Ihre Bilder, Geschichten und Töne greifen an und sind es nicht gewesen.'
3 Thanks to Manfred Faßler for pointing this out.

References

Baecker, D. (2007). *Studien zur nächsten Gesellschaft*. Frankfurt am Main: Suhrkamp.
Baecker, D. (2008). Intellektuelle I, in D. Baecker, *Nie wieder Vernunft. Kleinere Beiträge zur Sozialkunde*. Heidelberg: Carl-Auer Verlag, pp. 74–81.
Baecker, D. (2011). 16 Thesen zur nächsten Gesellschaft. *Revue für postheroisches Management 9*, 9–11.
Baecker, D. and Hedinger, J.M. (2012). Thesen zur nächsten Kunst. *Schweizer Monat 993*, February. Accessed July 13, 2012: http://www.schweizermonat.ch/artikel/thesen-zur-naechsten-kunst.
Barlow, J.P (1996). *A Declaration of the Independence of Cyberspace*. Accessed March 28, 2013.http://w2.eff.org/Censorship/Internet_censorship_bills/barlow_0296.declaration
Belting, H. and Buddensieg, A. (2013). Zeitgenossenschaft als Axiom von Kunst im Zeitalter der Globalisierung. *Kunstforum International 220(March–April)*, 61–69.
Bourriaud, N. (2002). *Postproduction. Culture as Screenplay: How Art Reprograms the World*. New York, NY: Lucas & Sternberg.
Bourriaud, N. (2009a). *Altermodern Explained: Manifesto, Tate Gallery London 2009*. Accessed April 22, 2013. http://www.tate.org.uk/whats-on/tate-britain/exhibition/altern odern/explain-altermodern/altermodern-explainedmanifesto.
Bourriaud, N. (2009b). *Radikant*. Berlin: Merve.
Cahan, S. and Kocur, Z. (Eds.) (1996). *Contemporary Art and Multicultural Education*. New York, NY, London: Routledge.
Christov-Bakargiev, C. (2011). *Brief an einen Freund/Letter to a friend*. Ostfildern-Ruit: Hatje Cantz (Documenta 13. 100 Notizen /100 Gedanken.
Christov-Bakargiev, C. and Hohmann, S. (2012). Vielleicht gibt es Kunst gar nicht. Interview mit der Chefkuratorin der Documenta12. *Monopol. Magazin für Kunst und Leben 6*, 60–63.
Czerski, P. (2012). *We, the Web Kids*. Accessed February 22, 2012http://boingboing. net/2012/02/22/web-kids-manifesto.
Debray, R. (1995). *Vie et mort l'image. Une histoire du regard en Occident*. Paris: Editions Gallimard.
Debray, R. (1999). *Jenseits der Bilder. Eine Geschichte der Bildbetrachtung im Abendland*, Rodenbach: Avinus.
Debray, R. (2004). Für eine Mediologie, in C. Pias, J. Vogl, and L. Engell (Eds.) *Kursbuch Medienkultur. Die maßgeblichen Theorien von Brecht bis Baudrillard*. Stuttgart: DVA, pp. 67–75.
Düllo, T. and Liebl, F. (Eds.) (2005). *Cultural Hacking. Kunst des strategischen Handelns*. Vienna, New York, NY: Springer.
Hubig, C. (1983). 'Genie' – Typus oder Original? Vom Paradigma der Kreativität zum Kult des Individuums, in E. Wischer (Ed.) *Aufklärung und Romantik. 1700–1830*. Berlin: Propyläen, pp. 187–210.

Kant, I. (1790). *Kritik der Urteilskraft*. Stuttgart: Reclam 1963.
Lévy, P. (2008). Menschliche Kollektivintelligenz bedeutet Symbolische Kollektivintelligenz. Ein Gespräch mit Klaus Neumann-Braun. *Kunstforum international Bd. 190*, 72–75.
Lucarelli, F. (2012). *Documenta 13: Czechoslovak Radio 1968*, by Tamas St. Turba. Accessed April, 22, 2013. http://socks-studio.com/2012/08/01/documenta-13-czechoslovak-radio-1968-by-tamas-st.
Mensvoort, K.V. (2013). *What is Next Nature?* Accessed April 22, 2013. http://www.nextnature.net/about.
Mensvoort, K.V. and Grievink, H.-J. (2011). *Next Nature: Nature Changes Along With Us*. Barcelona, New York, NY: Actar.
Meyer, T. (2010). Next Nature Mimesis, in D. Schuhmacher-Chilla, N. Ismail, and E. Kania (Eds.) *Image und Imagination*. Oberhausen: Athena, pp. 211–227.
Meyer, T. (2014). Cultural Hacking als Kulturkritik?, in S. Baden, C. A.Bauer, and D. Hornuff (Eds.) *Formen der Kulturkritik*. Munich: Fink, pp. 157–176.
Reckwitz, A. (2012). Der Künstlermythos zwischen Exklusivfigur und Generalisierungstendenzen, in C. Menke and J. Rebentisch (Eds.) *Kreation und Depression. Freiheit im gegenwärtigen Kapitalismus*. Berlin: Kadmos, pp. 98–117.
Saltz, J. (2012a). Eleven Things That Struck, Irked, or Awed Me at Documenta 13. *Vulture on 15.6.2012*. Accessed April 22, 2013. http://www.vulture.com/2012/06/documenta-13-review.html.
Saltz, J. (2012b). A Glimpse of Art's Future at Documenta. *Vulture on 16.6.2012*. Accessed April 22, 2013.http://www.vulture.com/2012/06/documenta-13-review.html.
Seemann, M. (2013). *ctrl-Verlust*. Accessed April 22, 2013. http://www.ctrl-verlust.net/glossar/kontrollverlust.

Section 3

Interventions

Chapter 8

Looking at ourselves looking through a screen. A case study of media education

Anna Caterina Dalmasso

Interrogating the extensions of our body

We often think about looking as if it concerns an automatic action, one that comes along with our being open to the world by means of our body. But what if we start to look at the world via screens? What if we learn, relate with others, and express ourselves by looking at the screen? The new scopic regime brought about by the diffusion of screens, and especially of mobile and augmented reality technologies, calls for a phenomenological investigation, to be developed both theoretically and practically.[1]

As a matter of fact, today, we are surrounded by screens and we live our lives through them. In our everyday life, we have become familiar with a continuous exchange and production of audiovisual documents, in which it seems there is no interruption between the human eye, the lens of a digital camera, and the gesture of sharing Snapchat shots, Instagram stories, YouTube videos, etc. In the last decade, the diffusion of digital mobile media has radically transformed – and *is* still transforming – our perceptive experience: portable and wearable screens have become permanent extensions of the user's body, they act like prosthesis expanding human possibilities of knowledge and action. Within a short time after their appearance, they have become incorporated as modalities of perception, especially by those who are commonly referred to as the 'natives' of the digital world (Prensky 2011).

Nevertheless, such a metamorphosis of our perception and intersubjective relationships, brought forth by technology, entails, as its historical possibility, the danger that we forget that perception and appearance are involved. Indeed, technologies tend to disappear in the accomplishment of our goals: every technical 'amplification' of the body entails a deformation or transformation of our experience, but, in the process of mediation, the medium seems to become transparent (Bolter and Grusin 1999). Indeed, when we experience reality through a device, our perception is mediated, and this often goes unnoticed because the world seems to appear as immediate. And yet, the specific ways to express the world that we have been acquainted with do not completely leave us, since our perception as well as our imagination, our way of thinking and feeling, has been informed by the relationship we entertain with our devices. The modalities of our sensibility are *remade* by the media experience to which we have been initiated (Sobchack 2004, p. 135; see also Grusin 2010).

It is by virtue of a process of dissimulation operated by technology, that today the 'new generations' appear to be *innately* familiar with digital devices and practices, whereas in reality their perception undergoes a progressive *training* during their contact with these media. Referring to the spectators' experience of early cinema, Walter Benjamin spoke of a 'shock' and even a sort of 'psychic immunization' (Benjamin 2008, p. 38) operated by media in the spectators' bodies, as they have the power to affect human perceptive, cognitive, and social relationship to the world, resulting in a training of the sensibility to the conditions of modern life. At the same time, the so-called *digital immigrants*, that is, people brought up before the widespread use of digital technology, and whose experience has therefore been shaped in relation to *other* optical and technological devices, and according to the complex systems of beliefs, ideologies, and forms of subjectivity that each of them conveys, or, in Foucaultian terms, according to the *dispositive* in which they are inscribed (Foucault 2012), often tend to read the habits and behaviour of the *digital natives* through the filter of concepts that have been moulded by a different media culture.

An episode from a piece of news, that recently occurred in Naples, serves as a telling illustration of how the digital divide – often simply understood as a generation gap – is underpinned by a more radical epistemic conflict concerning the inadequacy of an already established *image of thought* (Deleuze 2004), which renders us incapable of making sense of some of the phenomena that stem from contemporary mediality.[2] On February 2016, after having been missing for two weeks, an 18 year old boy was found buried in a shallow grave. This occurred around noon in the proximity of two high schools. Then, what might appear simply as a part of local crime news – unfortunately, pretty common in the Naples area – suddenly became breaking news, since a group of teenagers who had just come out from school started to take selfies in front of the grave and to share them with friends and family through instant messaging and social networks, before the police could prevent them getting close to the restricted area. In the aftermath, this behaviour seemed to have shocked public opinion (see Figure 8.1). As a result, the press published commentaries and declarations by experts in psychology and education, claiming that the teenagers' reaction – taking selfies in front of a grave where a boy of their own age had just been found dead – was a clear symptom of disrespect and, far more important, of a lack of empathy. One of the experts in particular argued that the grave *immediately* provokes in 'us' (the digital immigrants) respect and dignity, because it *immediately* represents for 'us' the death, so implying the assumption that such an immediacy derives from the fact that the digital immigrants got acquainted with the world *without mediations*. According to the expert, the digital natives, on the contrary, seem not to be touched by such an event because they are *only* able to establish relationships *in a mediated way* (Del Porto 2016).

Looking at ourselves looking 109

Figure 8.1 Teenagers taking selfies in front of Vincenzo Amendola's grave, Naples, February 2016 (c) La Repubblica: https://napoli.repubblica.it/cronaca/2016/02/20/news napoli_gara_di_selfie_ all_uscita_da_scuola_ucciso_un_ragazzo_mando_la_foto_a_casa_-133829397/

This argument puts to display the logic and conceptual framework by which behaviour related to digital devices is often explained. But, why should we infer that looking at the world without a smartphone means to see it in a *non-mediated way*? Isn't our encounter with the world and others *always mediated*, if only by the categories and experiences that enable us to understand it in the first place? And why does the fact that teenagers have a mediated experience of the world, exclude that for them this could also be an opportunity to negotiate — not without difficulties and risks — another way of making sense of what happens all around them, especially of the most traumatic aspects with which they are constantly in contact? It could be equally argued that, maybe, for the teenagers the grave does not immediately *represent* death, precisely because their relationship to reality can no longer be just described by the term 'representation' anymore, to which the experts referred to.

Furthermore, if we examine what taking a selfie implies on the level of the very positioning of the subject within the visual environment, we can observe that this specific way of taking pictures is primarily concerned with the gesture of putting oneself *on the same side* of the spectacle, which reveals a completely different relationship between the beholder and the visible, if compared to the distance and detachment that the digital immigrants seem to judge as the 'right' and 'empathic' reaction to the event of death.

As this simple example shows, screen practices bring about new forms of expression and along with them different ways for the beholder to picture and to inscribe themselves within the visible world. As it is worth noting, the screen is in the first place a *screen*, i.e., an apparatus that, according to its etymological ambiguity (Avezzù 2016; Carbone 2016b), at the same time shows and conceals the visible, configuring itself as a filter or medium for accessing reality.

Reversing the perspective

A climate of distrust regarding digital technologies, similar to the one described above, has characterized the introduction of mobile phones in the school environment since their very first appearance, long before the advent of smartphones and wearable devices. In Italy, as well as in other countries, this hostility was also triggered by several scandals related to cases of sexting and cyberbulling, addressed towards both teachers and students, and specifically associated with the use of mobile technologies. This is why in 2007 the use of mobile phones was banned from school by the Ministry of Education.[3] These preventive measures also ended up accentuating the digital gap and confining the mobile and online life[4] of teenagers to the private sphere. Hence, it became for a long time a taboo to use and interact through mobile technology in the school environment.[5]

Against the background of this social and cultural context, the pedagogical and documentary film project *Vedozero*, realized by the Italian director Andrea Caccia, offers a ground-breaking case of media education that goes against the flow and that challenges the general consensus of the period. Being the very first example of both a pedagogic and a film project about the creative use of mobile phone built-in cameras,[6] it aimed at exploring the expressive potentialities of the device that would soon become the dominant and hegemonic medium of our epoch.

The essential idea of the project stemmed from the director's experience in filmmaking literacy classes, often addressed to high school students and usually revolving around the realization of a short film. Over the years, Caccia observed how in these pedagogic experiences the creative process gave way to a hierarchical logic, which reflects the dynamics of power in the cinema industry. In the high school microcosms, this always entails the issue of the management and control over who could use the camera, and who not. The only way to overturn this mechanism consisted of giving a camera to every student in the class. But, with the appearance of mobile phone built-in cameras, this suddenly became possible and against very reasonable production costs. Moreover, the fact that this pocket device, at everyone's disposal, is ready for use in every moment of life made it an extraordinary instrument for recording reality from one's own point of view, and thereby an essential means for documentary cinema.

Launched in 2008, at the very beginning of the smartphone wave,[7] Caccia's *Vedozero* aimed at reversing the perspective, as well as the feeling connected to digital mobile technology in the world of education. Through a series of workshops, the Italian director wanted to realize a movie on the world of teenagers, entirely shot by teenagers themselves with their mobile phone cameras – the same cameras that were the reason of public scandals around the lack of respect and outright voyeurism to which adolescents are prone these days. Reversing this logic, Caccia saw in the mobile phone an opportunity for teenagers to share their own experience through the cinematic medium and 'to let the eighteen years olds tell their life from their own point of view,' by directing instead their objectives towards themselves, and using the mobile phone like a private journal (Caccia and Dalmasso 2014).

In fact, Caccia's goal was to bring into focus the change that screens and digital technologies are about to cause to our contemporary scopic regime. Discussing with teachers and stakeholders in education, the director strongly maintained the idea that only a creative work and pedagogic exchange could lead to a concrete understanding of the new technologies. This would then raise awareness of the role they were about to play in our lives.

Indeed, *Vedozero* offers a unique case study, since the project was repeated twice over a decade, with some significant differences in its implementation, but with the same essential core elements: the first edition took place in the school year 2008–2009, at the dawn of the spread of smartphones, whereas the second one was realized in 2014–2015, when the proliferation of digital devices had dramatically increased. Hence, the latter version allows us to come to understand significant shifts that have occurred over just six years. Through this case study, which offers an outstanding example of creative media education practices, we will then be able to highlight different aspects that emerged from the implementation of the two projects, as well as to shed light on the perceptual and epistemic transition engendered by digital screens in our contemporary techno-culture.

Moreover, Caccia's project interrupts the transparency and automatism of the familiar and basically unconscious act of producing pictures. As such it interrogates the very act of looking. In fact, if the cinematic genre of *Vedozero* can be defined as a documentary, its subject is not so much the daily problems of teenagers, as it is the digital gaze and the necessity of questioning it. In fact, by launching this project, the director was not in search of making another portrait – more or less truthful – of adolescence: his aim was to concentrate on vision, on that odd, postmodern, and sometimes blamed, kind of mediated vision, that began to emerge with the diffusion of mobile cameras. *Vedozero* is not so much a window through which to contemplate or to spy on the mysterious habits of the web generation (actually, teenagers of different epochs seem to resemble one another a lot). Rather, the project is conceived of as *a dispositive for questioning the gaze*: a gaze that perceives the world through a digital camera, having become familiar with screens and pixels, and with new forms of digital storytelling. To put it in a nutshell, the whole project was born as an *invitation to vision*, an 'invitation to take possession once again of a gesture, the act of looking, and to do it without prejudice,' as Caccia writes (Caccia and Dalmasso 2014).

A mobilized virtual gaze. *Vedozero* (2009)

The project of *Vedozero* had first been developed in collaboration with three high schools in Milan's Hinterland, thanks to the financial support of an open call for creative pedagogic projects promoted by the City Administration. For six months, 70 boys and girls aged between 17 and 18 attended a series of after-school workshops, meeting the director Andrea Caccia and other cinema professionals in order to acquire the fundamentals of videomaking (cinematography, screenplay writing, editing). Without specific assignments or constraints, except the assignment to tell their own experience by means of the mobile phone camera, they shot 4000 minutes of footage that was collected daily on a website over a school year.

Caccia's method sets out a workflow, which allows students to put into practice a composition and screenwriting process *in real time*. The materials shot by the young authors and actors were discussed in class, during a collective exchange. This puts into question the complex notion of authorship within the cinematic apparatus. Thus, the final editing of the film carried out by the director has to be considered as a part of this trajectory. But, what interests me most in this project comes to the fore when we examine from a phenomenological point of view some of its technical and formal elements, related to both the spectator's perception and the teenagers' directing experience. In fact, when it comes to a device as familiar as the mobile phone, the challenge is to be able to overcome the apparent acquaintance with such medium, in order to be able to apprehend its expressive possibilities.

The most evident feature of this film is that it shows a *point of view in motion*. As such, it reveals how the mobile phone has been modifying the way we live and inhabit public spaces, and especially the urban and suburban environment. It also shows the way one perceives and pictures oneself within this environment. The camera objective is constantly moving, at the same time roving and physically dislocating, be it on the bike, the bus, or the rollercoaster. This testifies to a new sense of place entailed by mobile technology. Developing further what Anne Friedberg has called the 'mobilized virtual gaze' of postmodernity and cinema, this is a gaze, the history of which is rooted in pre-cinematic performances as well as in the cultural activities that involve walking and traveling, and that took shape when 'the mobilized gaze of shopping and tourism was combined with the virtual gaze of photography to produce a new form: the mobilized and virtual gaze of the cinema' (Friedberg 1994, p. 184; see also Verhoeff 2012). The montage of *Vedozero* restores to the viewer the feeling of a *flanerie*, often muddled with *routine*. The film makes perceivable the coming and going, from the bedroom to the urban space, where the mobile gaze wanders around the landscape of the suburbs. Indeed, *Vedozero* presents the world through a mobile gaze, in a way that is sometimes too mobile, so that the viewer can actually become seasick. Besides, to those who have criticized the film for causing motion sickness, as a side effect due to the handheld camera, the director readily answers that 'it is not the camera, but the teenage itself [sic] that makes you seasick' (Caccia and Dalmasso 2014).

Another specific feature that strikes the spectator is the apparent *unity of place and action* of a film that has been shot by 70 people living in different places and in at least as many locations. The characters follow one another, but, from one clip to the other, places, experiences, gestures, and thoughts appear on the screen in an extraordinary continuity. The editing style of *Vedozero* plays with editing actions and links together clips without any concern for continuity or lighting consistency. And yet, this celebrates nothing but the fundamental nature of cinema itself, that is, its capacity to create a virtual space.[8] By the simple act of putting together shots that have been taken in different places at different moments, the editing creates a perceptible virtual world, as it has been shown by the very first editing experiments of Soviet filmmakers.[9] That is why *Vedozero* can be rightfully called a cinematic work and not just a blog movie: it shows the construction of such a virtual space, which has to be rediscovered continually.

In the interaction with digital mobile media, the mobilized virtual gaze of cinema is extended and spread out, because the film as a medium is no longer spatially confined to the institutional sites of cinema, but definitely ubiquitous (Bolter and Grusin 1999; Casetti 2012). In so doing, *Vedozero* could be identified as a dispersed and 'expanded cinema' (Youngblood 1970; Biserna et al. 2010; Gaudreault and Marion 2015; Jaudon et al. 2015). At the same time, thanks to the use of mobile technology, the creative process of the film has caused teenagers involved in the project to get a progressive understanding and awareness of the cinematic apparatus of vision as such. This turns the moving image into an instrument to reflect on the act of looking itself.

At the very beginning, the camera, in the hands of the teenagers, worked as a digital eye, recording what was happening. It was just as if a hidden camera was installed on their head, so that the vector of the shooting angle often departs from the body and wanders around in the horizon, describing a circle or sections of circles. But the spectator can observe that progressively the angles of shooting varied and multiplied; sometimes, we even witness a sort of shooting plan and little by little the composition becomes more interesting and original, as some personal shooting styles come to stand out. Indeed, we witness a transformation of the gaze. Viewers does not embrace a single point of view anymore, but realize they are at the same time both the viewer *and* part of the visible environment. The relationship with the camera allows the young directors to recognize and understand the world as populated by gazes and themselves as embodied subjects that are both viewing and being viewed.[10]

Besides the technical skills that could have been developed through practice, what is progressively explored and sometimes consciously enabled is the reflexive potential of the camera. Leaving behind a passive and voyeuristic attitude (the one that inhabited, at the time, vlogs and YouTube videos), the cinematic gaze allows the teenagers involved in the project to develop a personal and intimate reflection. The very act of filming becomes a chance to get engaged in or surprised by a situation, a relationship with a friend or a parent, a cityscape, etc. The mobile phone camera transforms itself into an embodied gaze, as much as teenagers become aware that no framing can be neutral, that every picture incorporates a memory, a dream, a thought, which is acting and moving. The medium is not anymore perceived as a transparent glass through which one can record reality, but rather becomes a prism or a screen whose mediation makes it possible to project and to look at one's own thoughts, fears and desires.

A smartphone native film. *Vedozero*[2] (2016)

Whereas the first *Vedozero* film and project stands out for its dialectical relationship to the cinematic apparatus and authorship, the second realization is deeply concerned with post-digital remediations and witnesses to the radical transformation brought forth by contemporary mediality. The second *Vedozero* project was carried out in Palermo, during the school year 2014–2015, with the support of the Film Commission of Sicily. While in 2008 the production had to provide the students with the smartphones, because at the time none of their mobile phones was equipped with a camera, in 2014 all the participants to the workshops already owned a smartphone, even though the boys and girls involved in the project were considerably younger, being aged between 14 and 15, that is, born after 2000. The choice to involve younger participants was motivated by the will to grasp the feeling of those who are fully 'digital natives' – a term by which mass media often refer to a much larger generational range spanning from the *millennials* or *generation Y* (born between the early 1980s and the early 1990s) to the so-called *generation Z* (born between mid-1990s to mid-2000s). The boys and girls involved in the second project were also experiencing a particular period in life, that is, the transition from pre-adolescence to adolescence, in which they are confronted with the beginning of high school and the impact of adult life.

Another significant difference with the first *Vedozero* film concerned the school environment: just a few years after the first project, most teachers and school representatives were unprepared to face the challenges of a changing digital horizon, but they were much more aware of the underexploited potentialities of the smartphone, and thus eager to find a way to turn it in a creative instrument that serves education. Therefore, they were more willing to let the pedagogic environment become part of the film project. This meant a significant difference vis-à-vis the context in which the first experiment took place. Hence, the school – which occupies such an important role in the life of a teenager – became the protagonist or at least the main focus of the documentary (see Figure 8.2).

As a result, the setting and workflow of the project needed to be adapted to the new conditions and technical context,[11] which had radically transformed in just six years. The structure of the project needed to suit the particular attitude of digital natives with regard to digital practices: despite the fact that boys and girls were already familiar with smartphones and acquainted – to a greater or

Figure 8.2 Still from *Vedozero²* (2016)

lesser degree – with digital photography and video, their nonchalant use of those devices testified to a lack of awareness and reflexivity.

Hence, the second project cannot be seen as just a sequel or a second edition of the first one. That is the reason why it is called *Vedozero²* – Vedozero 'squared.' The film, released in 2016, takes on the essential features of the previous project and raises them to the second power, since it incorporates and is doubled by a further virtual dimension. The workshop experience developed in Palermo was inseparable from the hyperconnected life that spontaneously came about together with the project – especially a Facebook and a WhatsApp group, by which the teenagers involved in the project were able to find follow- ups of the meetings and to exchange thoughts and writings. From this, originated the texts used in the film.

Moreover, a specific application had been designed so that the participants could automatically upload or download videos on a server, and to share them using their computers. It should be noted that this was something many struggled to manage, since, opposed to what may people hold true today, the digital natives' familiarity with the use of information technology conceals a significant lack of command of the most basic procedures and computer literacy – which is in line with what has been recently shown by different surveys and studies.[12]

Now, if we compare both films, a most interesting change in creative output can be found. In *Vedozero* (2009), a project that was deeply engaged with the proliferation of the cinematic dispositive, teenagers came to progressively master the filmic construction of a virtual space by means of a multiplication of perspectives and points of view. *Vedozero^2*, however, brings along the emergence of a post-cinematic dispositive. The audiovisual materials show that cinema is no longer the visual reference for the young directors and actors. Here, the cinematic apparatus is no longer at work (even not in a fragmented and disrupted way as it was the case in the first project). Caccia's second project shows that youngsters specifically use digital and post-digital aesthetics, which can no longer be associated with classic cinema constructs.[13]

Indeed, the shooting style implemented by the young directors is strongly influenced by a variety of audiovisual practices. Their digital gaze *remediates* the post-cinematic first-person perspective (Eugeni 2012) of video games, and especially the *survival mode* gameplay,[14] one can find in popular games such as *Left 4 Dead* or *Call of Duty*. In fact, through ironic or parodic dramatizations, the teenager-directors referred to the school in terms of a struggle for existence, and even modelled their shooting style on the aesthetic techniques of the survival gameplay, implicitly or explicitly comparing their experience to the attitude and challenges that are typical to the survival gameplay. Thus, in a sequence of the film, a boy stages his own return home after school, acting as a surviving hero in a war or zombie video game. Another boy has even rebuilt a model of his own classroom setting within the extremely popular game *Minecraft* (see Figure 8.3), and set his avatar inside the room before being attacked by creepers – enemy creatures within the *Minecraft* universe. Such an overlapping of reality and avatar experience shows how for the teenager-directors there is no sharp gap between their virtual/digital life and the environment that surrounds them. Furthermore, the survival style implemented in their videos, giving the impression that someone is chasing or hunting them down, reveals that one significant trait of their experience as viewing and mediated subjects is intimately connected with their being constantly framed and put under surveillance. Through this apparently simple and playful aspect, *Vedozero^2* touches one of the major concerns raised by contemporary techno-culture, given the increasingly pervasive biometric systems that affect our embodied existences and determine our social and political visibility or invisibility, as well as our circulation in the geopolitical space.

Figure 8.3 Still from *Vedozero*[2] (2016)

Two other distinctive features of *Vedozero*[2] are particularly noteworthy: the generalized use of direct address, descending from vlogs and YouTube videos, going hand in hand with the figure of the *selfie*. Let us examine this prominent visual construct, which emerged in the last few years, as symbolic form typical for our time. The selfie has been variously classified as a symptom of a turn in human relationships towards compulsive attachment to visibility and recognition (Fox and Rooney 2015; Weiser 2015; McCain et al. 2016; Sorokowska et al. 2016). Selfies are often indicted as vain and indulgent self-celebrations, and understood as evidence of a narcissistic, voyeuristic, and exhibitionist tendency of the millennial and Z generations. As Giovanna Borradori points out in her insightful analysis of contemporary selfie culture, such a *pathological reading* of the selfie is ultimately underpinned by a representationalist theoretical framework that 'takes the self as a given and accomplished fact, which is supposedly transferred to a photograph' (Borradori 2018, p. 227; see also Bollmer and Guinness 2017; Eckel et al. 2018). This dominant interpretation misses out on the complexity of both image and selfhood entailed by the figure of the selfie, and it also risks ending up by reinforcing the very objectification of the self that it charges selfies to have.

Selfies cannot simply *represent* the self, at least for two reasons: ontologically, because the self they are supposed to convey, at least according to a pathological reading, is not already constituted but always *in formation*, and *performed* through the practice of the selfie itself,[15] and aesthetically, since the selfies we are familiar with respond to multifarious tropes and codes to which any selfie producer needs to conform, such as *duck-face, halfie, smize, smooch, peace, mug, tongue, surprise face, dab*, etc. Hence, if the practice of the selfie urges us to expose the most intimate details of our experience, thought, and emotion, at the same time, these poses and visual strategies function as *masks* – like in the distorted masks of the ancient Greek tragedy and comedy, i.e., like filters, modulating, and standardizing the appearance of the subjects. These codified features contribute to canalize and to discipline what Borradori calls the *narratable subject*, 'the docile political subject produced and maintained by the reversible camera' (Borradori 2018, p. 223) who continuously projects itself through the lens of imagined others.

In this context, the pedagogic strategy implemented by Caccia aims precisely at deconstructing the clichés that occupy the horizon of expectation of audiovisual production in the digital iconoscape, to liberate the gaze from the multiple codes and conducts they are supposed to perform. In contrast to the common approach to media education and classes in audiovisual creation, that usually rely on series of assignments and constraints aimed at stimulating production and making the training process easier, Caccia avoids giving the students specific assignments and indications, as this would inevitably influence the videos they make. In fact, the mechanism of expectations often brings the pupils to comply to the image they believe authority figures expect from them, even if they are not required to, involuntarily endorsing a relational and generational lack of communicability. Therefore, in the workshops developed by Caccia, instead of following hints or indications, the teenage directors are confronted with the freedom of creation and thereby with the responsibility connected with the gesture of filming.

The results of Caccia's pedagogic work emerges first in the opacity and hypermediation (Bolter and Grusin 1999) that characterize many videos, that is in the fact that the very operation of mediation is not hidden, in order to achieve a smooth and transparent audiovisual output. On the contrary, the digital interface becomes part of the aesthetic and expressive strategies, through constant and explicit reference to the recording tools. Such visual strategy involves selfie videos. Moreover, in $Vedozero^2$, the screen often becomes not just metaphorically but literally a reflection tool, as boys and girls look at themselves as if they were looking in a mirror (see Figure 8.4). They do this by adjusting their hair or commenting on their make-up and their appearance onscreen – which was impossible in 2008, when in the *Vedozero* project only phones with built-in cameras were used: they did not yet feature a reversible camera or selfie camera. This can be often observed in vlogs and YouTube videos, that let appear the material presence of the medium, with the effect of thematising the audiovisual dispositive as part of the process of expression. Thus, the practice of selfie is put into play beyond already standardized codes, reaching a complex dimension that overcomes the repetition of already beaten tracks for exploring forms of personal expression.

This allows for bringing into focus that when we look at a selfie we are not simply *looking at someone posing for us*, but *looking at the eyes of someone who is looking at themselves, while they pose for us* (Borradori 2018), or rather looking at the eyes of someone who is looking at themselves *through a screen* while they pose for us. For the practice of shooting a selfie video, far from being a vain self-celebration, for the teenagers involved in the project it becomes a fundamental tool for *learning to look* and *for learning to look at themselves* through a screen.

In fact, in $Vedozero^2$, the selfies are not dominant, but they alternate with first-person shots mentioned above, revealing the world the teenagers are looking at. Surprisingly, most of the time nothing spectacular or exceptional is captured, and sometimes nothing at all appears within the frame. In fact, while *Vedozero* makes extensive use of recorded *voiceover*, the participants of $Vedozero^2$ deliberately use live *off-screen voice* and do not hesitate to shoot in complete darkness or under bad visibility conditions. This might lead to completely black frames associated with words. The way they address the camera reveals that showing one's own image on screen, as it happens in selfies, is not perceived as being more intimate than exposing one's own perception of reality through the camera and the voice. Conversely, the most personal and most confidential shots, in which boys and girls share their dreams, fears and desires, are those in which they choose to *expose to the spectator their own gaze looking at the world* while they give free rein to their imagination and hopes.

Figure 8.4 Still from *Vedozero²* (2016)

The future of school and cinema

The overarching transformation brought about by contemporary mediality is expressed by another aspect of *Vedozero²*, viz. the *vertical format* of the film, which literally accomplishes a *revolution* of the cinematic dispositive that is turned upside down, to a ratio of 9:16. Indeed, the choice of this format directly results from the creative and pedagogic exchange that occurred during the workshop, after the teenagers showed a clear inclination for filming in a vertical format. Far from obliging them to adhere to the classic horizontal cinematic format, Caccia decided to go along with this new direction imposed by the digital practices and to seize the opportunity for interrogating further the changes imposed by the device in the creative process.

The vertical format of the film required an unprecedented form of projection and diffusion – just only because no movie theatre is provided with a 9:16 screen. Thus, this film was intimately concerned not only with intermedial overlapping of different media codes, but with the process of what Francesco Casetti has called 'cinema relocation' (Casetti 2012). When the film was premiered, a double projection was designed: in Palermo, where the workshop was conducted and the film shot, the film was projected onto a six-meter tall digital screen inside a church, whereas in Milan, where it was post-produced, *Vedozero*[2] was presented at the Filmmaker Festival in a movie theatre: however, not on the cinema screen, but on as many tablets as the spectators in the theatre had. Thus, such an intermedial premiere accomplished the vision informing the whole project: it created asynchronies and led to a collective sense of space that allowed the spectator to share a common and intimate practice, like watching a film on tablets and digital screens, usually done at home, sometimes in bed or on the couch. Hence, the concept of public space was challenged and the movie theatre was transformed in a post-cinematic dispositive (see Figures 8.5 and 8.6).

In the two *Vedozero* projects, cinema is called to interrogate its fundamental premises and to radically question its dispositive: the issue was raised whether is cinema to be conceived as the experience of watching a film in a movie theatre into a dark room and with a collective audience (see Aumont 2012; Belloun 2012), or should it include the diverse experience of the moving image that has invaded public and private spaces?

By virtue of its vertical format, *Vedozero*[2] is incompatible with classic – horizontal – cinema, but it cannot be simply inscribed in the *expanded cinema* that inhabits museums and exhibiting places, for it claims to be a cinema work in its own right. Indeed, Caccia's film claims to reinvent from the inside the cinematic dispositive, to show that 'cinema' – understood in a broader framework – is not a medium of the past, but is still able to express the metamorphoses of our experience of the world, brought forth by our relationship to contemporary screens.

Besides the potential it has for audiovisual and media education, the peculiar interest of *Vedozero* also resides in its capacity to connect cinema with the universe of school. The environment of school has been variously explored in the history of film, from *Zéro de conduite* (Jean Vigo, 1933) to *Elephant* (Gus Van Sant, 2003), passing by *Picnic at Hanging Rock* (Peter Weir, 1975). Today, school and cinema seem to face a similar challenge. In fact, they both need to question their structure and operational system, without taking for granted that the dispositive they instituted is valid under all social, cultural, and even perceptive conditions. But, this doesn't mean that they have to accept to become obsolete dispositives. As much as it is the case for cinema, the school is a *laboratory of future*, in which technological transformations are continually put to the test, and anthropological shifts emerge in a prominent way, in the contact with new generations and their vision.

Figure 8.5 and 8.6 Premiere of *Vedozero*² (2016) at the Filmmaker Festival in Milan (c) Massimo Schiavon [same caption for 8.5 and 8.5]

Thus, *Vedozero* offers a powerful insight, in that it shows that the school can only reinvent itself if it radically puts into question its operational horizon. It should do this not just by updating already existing methodologies or a body of knowledge: it also needs to include a permanent interrogation of the future of the emerging dominant technological dispositive, now that it is constantly brought to our attention due to the experience of looking at the world through a screen and of looking at ourselves by looking through a screen.

Notes

1 For an analysis of the contemporary screenscape and the theoretical implications of screens in contemporary techno-culture, see Casetti 2015; Mitchell 2015; Chateau & Moure 2016; Bodini & Carbone 2016; Bodini et al. 2016; Carbone. 2016a; Bodini et al. 2018; Monteiro 2018.
2 For a further exploration of the philosophical implications of this event see the Introduction to Bodini et al. 2016: 5–13.
3 See 'Circolare n. 14. Linee di indirizzo ed indicazioni in materia di utilizzo di "telefoni cellulari" e di altri dispositivi elettronici durante l'attività didattica', March 15, 2007.
4 Luciano Floridi suggests to speak of *onlife*, in order to characterize 'the new experience of a hyperconnected reality within which it is no longer sensible to ask whether one may be online or offline,' so avoiding to a narrow separation between our real or immediate experience and our virtual life within the media environment: Introduction to Floridi 2014.
5 See also: Meirieu et al. 2012; Tisseron et al. 2013; Tisseron 2017.
6 See also ground-breaking Pippo Delbono's *La paura* (Italy-France, 2009). A crowdsourcing project like *Life in a Day* has been released in 2011.
7 The first iPhone was released on June 29, 2007, whereas the first phones with built-in cameras became publicly available in 2002, including the Nokia 7650 featuring 'a large 176x208 pixel colour display.'
8 On this dynamic, see the fundamental classic essays: Bazin 2005: 41–52 and Francastel 1983.
9 Such as the Kouleshov's or Pudovkine's experiments. See Pinel 2001.
10 For a phenomenological account of film experience, see Sobchack 1991 and 2016.
11 After having acquainted myself with Andrea Caccia's work because of my research interests in transmedial documentary cinema, I started a professional collaboration as a consultant with the executive production of the project *Roadmovie production*. Thereafter I had the chance to be involved with the production of *Vedozero²* as first assistant director. Therefore, the analysis I will develop will be partially biased by my internal and experience-based perspective on the project.
12 The problematic notion of digital *innateness* is discussed in detail in Bennett et al. 2008; see also Small 2008; Battro and Denham 2010; Ferri 2011; Rivoltella 2011.
13 For more on post-digital aesthetics, I refer to Berry and Dieter 2015.
14 The survival mode or horde mode is a type of gameplay that can be either selected or in-built in the game interface, in which the player must continue playing without losing their 'life' in an uninterrupted session, while the game presents them with increasingly difficult and often unexpected challenges.
15 About the use of the notion of performativity, I refer to Butler 1990 and 1993.

References

Aumont, J. (2012). *Que reste-t-il du cinéma?* Paris: Vrin.
Avezzù, G. (2016). Intersections between Showing and Concealment in the History of the Concept of Screen, in D. Chateau and J. Moure (Eds.) *Screens*. Amsterdam: Amsterdam University Press.
Battro, A.M. and Denham, P.J. (2010). *Verso un'intelligenza digitale*. Milano: Ledizioni.
Bazin, A. (2005). *What is Cinema?* Berkeley, CA, Los Angeles, CA, London: University of California Press.
Bellour, R. (2012). *La querelle des dispositifs: Cinéma, installations, expositions*. Paris: POL.
Benjamin, W. (2008). The Work of Art in the Age of Its Technological Reproducibility. in M.W. Jennings, B. Doherty, and T.Y. Levin (Eds.) *The Work of Art in the Age of Its Technological Reproducibility, and Other Writings on Media*. Cambridge, MA: Harvard University Press.
Bennett, S., Maton, K., and Kervin, L. (2008). The 'Digital Natives' Debate: A critical review of the evidence. *British Journal of Educational Technology* 39(5), 775–786.
Berry, D. and Dieter, M. (Eds.) (2015). *Postdigital Aesthetics. Art, Computation and Design*. Basingstoke: Palgrave Macmillan.
Biserna, E., Dubois, P., and Monvoisin, F. (Eds.) (2010). *Extended cinema. Le cinéma gagne du terrain*. Pasian di Prato: Campanotto.
Bodini, J. and Carbone M. (Eds.) (2016). *Voir selon les écrans, penser selon les écrans*. Paris: Mimesis.
Bodini, J., Carbone M., and Dalmasso A.C. (Eds.) (2016). *Vivre par(mi) les écrans*. Dijon: Les presses du reel.
Bodini, J., Carbone M., and Dalmasso A.C. (Eds.) (2018). *Des pouvoirs des écrans*. Paris: Mimesis.
Bollmer, G. and Guinness K. (2017). Phenomenology for the Selfie. *Cultural Politics* 13(2), 156–176.
Bolter, J.D. and Grusin, R.A. (1999). *Remediation: Understanding New Media*. Cambridge, MA: MIT Press.
Borradori, G. (2018). De selfie en selfie. L'espace confessionnel du soi narrable. In J. Bodini, M. Carbone, and A.C. Dalmasso (Eds.). (2018). *Des pouvoirs des écrans*. Paris: Mimesis, pp. 221–237.
Butler, J. (1990). *Gender Trouble*. New York, NY: Routledge.
Butler, J. (1993). *Bodies that matter*. New York, NY: Routledge.
Caccia, A. and Dalmasso, A.C. (2014). Intervista a Andrea Caccia. *Vedozero* in condotta. Interrogare la scuola e il futuro del cinema. *Materiali di Estetica* 1, 'Pensare nella caverna. Incontri tra cinema e filosofia,' 193–204.
Carbone, M. (2016a). *Philosophie-écrans*. Paris: Vrin.
Carbone, M. (2016b). Thematizing the 'Arche-Screen' through Its Variation,. In D. Chateau and J. Moure (Eds.) *Screens*. Amsterdam: Amsterdam University Press.
Casetti, F. (2012). The Relocation of Cinema. *NECSUS*. Autumn2012 'Tangibility'.
Casetti, F. (2015). *The Lumière Galaxy: Seven Key Words for the Cinema to Come*. New York, NY: Columbia University Press.
Chateau, D. and Moure J. (Eds.) (2016). *Screens*. Amsterdam: Amsterdam University Press.
Del Porto, D. (2016). Napoli, gara di selfie all'uscita da scuola. Ucciso un ragazzo mando la foto a casa. *La Repubblica*. http://napoli.repubblica.it/cronaca/2016/02/

20/news/napoli_gara_di_selfie_all_uscita_da_scuola_ucciso_un_ragazzo_mando_la_foto_a_casa_-133829397/.
Deleuze, G. (2004). *Difference and Repetition*. London: Bloomsbury.
Eckel, J., Ruchatz, J., and Wirth, S. (Eds.) (2018). *Exploring the Selfie. Historical, Theoretical, and Analytical Approaches to Digital Self-Photography*. Basingstoke: Palgrave Macmillan.
Eugeni, R. (2012). First Person Shot. New forms of subjectivity between cinema and intermedia networks. *Anàlisi, Quaderns de Comunicaciò i Cultura. Audiovisual 2.0*, 19–31.
Ferri, P. (2011). *Nativi digitali*. Milano: Mondadori.
Floridi L. (Ed.) (2014). *The Onlife Manifesto: Being Human in a Hyperconnected Era*. New York, NY: Springer.
Foucault, M. (2012). *Discipline and Punish: The Birth of the Prison*. New York, NY: Knopf Doubleday Publishing Group.
Fox, J. and Rooney, M.C. (2015). The Dark Triad and Trait of Self-Objectification as Predictors of Men's Use and Self-Presentation Behaviors on Social Networking Sites. *Personality and Individual Differences* 76, 161–165.
Francastel, P. (1983). *L'image, la vision et l'imagination, L'objet filmique et l'objet plastique*. Paris: Denoël-Gonthier.
Friedberg, A. (1994). *Window Shopping. Cinema and the Postmodern*. Berkeley, CA, Los Angeles, CA, London: University of California Press.
Gaudreault, A. and Marion, P. (2015). *The End of Cinema? A Medium in Crisis in the Digital Age*. New York, NY: Columbia University Press.
Grusin, R. (2010). *Premediation: Affect and Mediality After 9/11*. London: Palgrave Macmillan.
Jaudon, R., Marchiori, D., and Vancheri, L. (Eds.) (2015). *Revue Écrans* 3, 'Expanded Cinéma'. Paris: Classiques Garnier.
McCain, J., Borg, Z.G., Rothenberg, A.H., Churillo, K.M., Weiler, P., and Campbell, W.K. (2016). Personality and Selfies: Narcissism and the dark triad. *Computers in Human Behavior* 64, 126–133.
Meirieu, P., Kambouchner, D., and Stiegler, B. (2012). *L'école, le numérique et la société qui vient*. Paris: Fayard.
Mitchell, W.J.T. (2015). Screening Nature (and the Nature of the Screen). *New Review of Film and Television Studies* 13(3), 231–246.
Monteiro, S. (2018) *The Screen Media Reader: Culture, Theory, Practice*. London: Bloomsbury.
Pinel, V. (2001). *Le montage: l'espace et le temps du film*. Paris: Cahiers du cinéma.
Prensky, M. (2011). Digital Natives, Digital Immigrants. *On the Horizon* 5.
Rivoltella, P.C. (2011). *Neurodidattica. Insegnare al cervello che apprende*. Milano: Raffaello Cortina.
Small, G. (2008). *iBrain: Surviving the Technological Alteration of the Modern Mind*. New York, NY: HarperCollins.
Sobchack, V. (1991). *The Address of the Eye. A Phenomenology of Film Experience*. Princeton, NJ: Princeton University Press.
Sobchack, V. (2004). *Carnal Thoughts. Embodiment and Moving Image Culture*. Berkeley, CA, Los Angeles, CA, London: University of California Press.
Sobchack, V. (2016). The Active Eye (Revisited): Toward a phenomenology of cinematic movement. *Studia Phaenomenologica* 16, 63–90.

Sorokowska, A., Oleszkiewicz, A., Frackowiak, T., Pisanski, K., Chmiel, A., and Sorokowski, P. (Eds.) (2016). Selfies and Personality: Who posts self-portrait photographs? *Personality and Individual Differences* 90, 119–123.
Tisseron, S. (2017). *3–6-9–12. Apprivoiser les écrans et grandir.* Paris: Erès.
Tisseron, S., Virole, B., Givre, P., Tordo, F., and Triclot, M. (Eds.) (2013). *Subjectivation et empathie dans les mondes numériques.* Paris: Dunod.
Verhoeff, N. (2012). *Mobile Screens. The Visual Regime of Navigation.* Amsterdam: Amsterdam University Press.
Weiser, E.B. (2015). #Me: Narcissism and its facets as predictors of selfie-posing frequency. *Personality and Individual Differences* 86, 477–481.
Youngblood, G. (1970). *Expanded Cinema.* New York, NY: Dutton.

Chapter 9

Digital literacy in the age of the screen? Re-imagining the social pedagogy of the archive

D.-M. Withers and Maria Fannin

How do learners acquire digital literacy, and what kinds of digital literacies are required to effectively participate in a digital society? This question has underscored political, cultural, and social anxieties about widespread computerization since at least the early 1980s (Lean 2016). From the vantage point of contemporary digitized culture, the pressing task is to consider digital literacy beyond the limitations of what has been 'dictated by [the] tech companies and self-interested venture capitalists' of Silicon Valley (Emejulu 2014). Can digital literacy ever be thought of as the everyday acquisition of operational grammars that provide individuals and communities with the skills and techniques to read, write, and build a digitized world that exists *under and around the screen*? What competencies and pedagogical activities need to be invented to support such ambitions? Furthermore, what institutional locations and imaginaries can be leveraged and repurposed to support the forging of what Akwugo Emejulu (2014) calls a 'radical digital citizenship': practices that support 'individuals and groups [to] critically analyse the social, political and economic consequences of technologies in everyday life and collectively deliberate and take action to build alternative and emancipatory technologies and technological practices'?

During the 21st century, digitization has radically reconfigured the relationship between knowledge, archives and society (Berry 2016). We are embedded in society *through* the digital archive. This makes 'the archive' into something far more than a repository in which artefacts are preserved; it is also a tool for population surveillance, control, and governance (Day 2014). In this chapter, we start from the position that what the digital archive *means*, and *how* it is used within society, should remain an open question. This enables us to *imagine* the digital archive as an important site through which the power and knowledge stored within digital infrastructures might be broken down and demystified. We re-imagine the digital archive as a *social pedagogic location,* one that is embodied, sensory, materialized, and animated in the everyday. As an infrastructural form deeply embedded in the everyday life of a digitized society, the archive is an educational institution – comparable, perhaps, to the school in the 19th century – in which new conceptions of digital literacy and citizenship could be acquired.

This pedagogical orientation to the digital archive, which aims to re-imagine the social role of the digital and archives, opens up compelling possibilities. Yet there are many barriers to realizing such potential, including the changing conditions of reading and writing within digitized societies. A range of thinkers, such as Bernard Stiegler, Vilém Flusser, Giorgio Agamben, and Dennis Tenen, have theorized the generalized condition of illiteracy that has been created through digital 'disruption.' We use these perspectives on illiteracy as an incitement to invent new pedagogical practices that take place within an expanded conception of the digital archive. We argue that the digital archive has an important pedagogical role in re-imagining digital literacy. To do this, however, the *social contexts* of the digital archive need to be reconsidered. Pedagogical activities must extend beyond the content of archives – sources, texts, images, and information – to include the infrastructures – and Meta-Data[1] – that organize such materials. Digital infrastructures – the 'meta' space *about and around* the archival content – are social contexts, in other words, within which new forms of collaborative knowledge can be practiced, shared, and developed, and new social encounters with digital il/literacy can become possible.

In this article, we place these theoretical, yet pragmatic, provocations in dialogue with the archival legacies of the Women's Liberation Movement. Like many other 'community archives' (Flinn 2010) established in the wake of social movements of 1960s and 1970s, the Feminist Archive is the outcome of grassroots activists who took initiative to collect, organize, and preserve heritages that challenged the society they lived in. The archive, in the hands of Women's Liberation activists, became the location where communities learnt how, in practical terms, to take care of their history, culture, and knowledge. This meant collecting content, but also re-imagining *how* building archives might be a social and emancipatory project. We begin this chapter by outlining how the Feminist Archive provides tangible theoretical inspiration through which we re-imagine the social pedagogical role of the digital archive. We then analyze how tropes of illiteracy and dispossession feature in theorizations of the digital, before discussing the pedagogical activities we created to generate dialogue across these different contexts.

Feminist Archival legacies – inspiring social pedagogical action

Activists involved in the UK Women's Liberation Movement established the Feminist Archive in 1978. Originally a modest collection stored in an attic in Shepton Mallet, a town in the southwest of England, the collection grew throughout the 1980s to its current size of over 325 meters of archive material covering transnational women-centred social movements of the 1960s–2000s. It is stored across two locations: Feminist Archive South (Bristol) and Feminist Archive North (Leeds). From its improvised, grassroots, and precarious beginning, the Feminist Archive is now housed in Special Collections at the Universities of Bristol and Leeds respectively.

The institutionalization of archival collections generated within revolutionary, women-centred social movements is symptomatic of significant shifts in the construction of knowledge in the late 20th and early 21st centuries. The increased normalization of gendered perspectives across varied disciplines is notable, and feminist perspectives are increasingly viewed as 'proper knowledge' (do Mar Pereira 2017) within universities (see also Scott 2008). The Feminist Archive was, however, not established with the sole aim of influencing academic debate. The founders of the Feminist Archive were amateur, non-archivists who did not ask permission to archive, but did so anyway. They understood that in collecting the documents produced by a 'woman-centred' or 'wmyn-centred' social movement they were making an epistemic intervention that sought to 'restructure' knowledge in a feminist way (Freer 1986). Indeed, the archive was established as *a community resource*. It aimed to empower women with information that would help them transform their consciousness and become politically active.[2] It is easy to forget the activist social contexts and cultural practices that shaped the genesis of the Archive when readers encounter the collections in a Special Collections department at an elite, British university. How then do we:

> access and engage [the] archive, from our own time, in a manner which avoids unwittingly lapsing back into and reproducing the underlying rules of discursive and disciplinary foundations? [...] How can we resist the 'containing' of these histories and archives of struggle in and through the *methods* and *practices* of academic expertise? (Grufydd Jones 2017, p.71; emphasis added)

Our response to this question has been to develop social pedagogic exercises that enable participants to learn about the radical social, political, and cultural practices (and the hours of activist labour) that built the archive, and shaped its social purpose. The organizational structure of the Feminist Archive – its building blocks, as it were – was a 'wmyn-centred' classification system invented to ensure women's lives were not only legible but *prioritized* within the catalog. This system was the idea of Archive founder Jean Freer who viewed archival classification as an important tool for transforming the political consciousness of those who used it. Her scheme was admittedly eccentric by today's standards – it was based on numerological principles and separatist feminist spirituality, designed to remove 'man's' influence from the construction of knowledge. Such intentions are clear in the following categories: A Cosmology, B Communication, C Healing and Divination, D *Humun* Society, E *Hystory* and Politics, F Ecology, and G Technology.

Freer's creative approach to feminist information science was not practiced in isolation. Librarians and archivists at the International Archives for the

Women's Movement (now known as Atria) and the University of Utrecht, Netherlands, developed the European Women's Thesaurus, a separate women-centred classification system. In the world of archiving, a thesaurus is a 'controlled and dynamic vocabulary or list of terms, aimed at describing (or indexing) and locating (retrieving) information in the collections of libraries and documentation centres' (Vriend 2009, p. 3). As Tilly Vriend states, major classification systems such as the Dewey Decimal and Library of Congress systems are not neutral tools for organizing and classifying information and materials, but reflect the particular presumptions of their creators and are the products of social and political forces. The Universal Decimal System has the more well-known examples of how sexism shapes the practices of indexing: in this system, for example, 'the term Women could be found under the category Morals and Customs, Menstruation under Medicine, and Lesbian women under categories such as Psychopaths and Hysterics' (Vriend 2009, p. 3). The European Women's Thesaurus and its precursor, the Dutch Women's Thesaurus, sought to explicitly reject these tendencies and generate new categories. The Feminist Archive adopted the Thesaurus to index its catalogs, and uses it to this day.

The Feminist Archive catalog – the 'Meta' space surrounding the collection – has always, therefore, been a *political* location. It is a site where activists and feminist information scientists have interrogated, and generated new understandings of, the material and *social* implications embedded in the description and organization of information. Such activities highlight the power wielded by those who categorize, and how information architectures can reproduce cultural marginalization unless there are deliberate attempts to disrupt their arrangements (see also Brown et al. 2016). Understanding these histories encouraged us to focus our pedagogical activities on the archive catalog. We wanted to explore how digital infrastructures could be opened up through pedagogical practice, enabling practical insights into the constructions of power and knowledge that work through the context of the digital archive.

Our focus on the archive catalog as a social location in the digital era is also pragmatic. Quite simply, the archive lacks the kind of detailed description required to make it a truly effective resource in a digital information environment. This is wholly due to the technological conditions in which the archive was initially created. Built with the then contemporary technologies at hand – pens, paper, typewriters, photocopiers, and, only later, desktop computers – its catalog was largely untouched by the rapid technological and infrastructural change of the 1980s and 90s, as global economies became deeply penetrated by 'computerization,' and culture and society underwent a 'process of total digitalization' (Ross 2013, p. 248). The archive was also maintained for many years through dedicated voluntary, part-time labour. This means both the extent and digitality of the catalog is limited: basic records are searchable on the University of Bristol's archival collection management system (CALM), yet consulting a paper list remains the most detailed way to learn about parts of the collection. Second, the descriptions that do exist are limited. Catalog items might refer to the theme of a particular topic box, for example 'Health/Medicine 6: Reproductive technology,' 'Media 2: Archives, libraries, information services, Fawcett Society, IIAV Amsterdam,' or 'Education/Training 2: Sexism in schools, research, equal opportunities, EOC colleges, FE, HE,' but these box files in themselves might have 100 or more individuals' items in them. In this sense, all the feminist information science in the world will not help us to 'discover' the full breadth of these collections because there simply isn't an adequate description for the items.

Collective annotation/archival discovery

Between June and July 2017, we held two, three-hour workshop sessions called 'Collective annotation/archival discovery.' An audience of non-archivists that included academics, artists, and those with an interest in the topic were invited to learn about, and participate in, feminist archive catalog making. These workshops built on Withers's research and teaching that explore how Meta-Data can become a discursive and collaborative context within which new modes of historical experience, conditioned by digital technology, can be practiced (Withers 2016, 2018). This work is informed by Bernard Stiegler's claim that 'the epistemic, political and economic stakes of the "digitalisation to come" rest on the conception, development and mass socialisation of such production models of the épistémè founded on polemical annotation systems' (Stiegler 2011, p. 32–33). Meta-Data, in its capacity to enable readers to link and navigate information, he argues, 'will affect more and more both the elaboration of knowledge as well as the conditions for its socialization and transmission' (Ibid.). These workshops, then, attempted to create a context where such polemical annotation systems might be realized. They were spaces to explore how the digital might support the invention of annotation systems that enable participation, collaboration, and enrichment of a text or dataset.

From the outset we understood that such systems are very much 'to come,' that is, they are not yet here, and also require *new modes of socialization*. The concept of Meta-Data itself was not intuitive for many participants, despite increased vernacularization after the Edward Snowden affair (Dencik et al. 2016). In a previous session at the Centre for Contemporary Arts in Glasgow (2016), and in informal conversations with colleagues prior to our sessions, Withers found that framing the activity in ways that foregrounded technical knowledge (i.e., we will learn how to write Meta-Data *correctly*) generated subtle anxieties about 'getting it right.' We therefore wanted to mitigate this kind of psychic resistance in the early part of the session. Instead our aim was to create an environment in which participants could feel comfortable in their state of a generalized and shared 'illiteracy,' transforming these feelings into a tool for self-reflection and empowerment. Our sessions then, were an opportunity for to 'go back to kindergarten [...] to get back to the level of those who have not yet learned to read and write' (Flusser 2011, p. 157). This is not to say that psychic resistance and discomposure did not circulate within our sessions. They did, certainly, and especially in moments when we invited participants to incorporate digital grammars from the Meta-Data schema Dublin Core in their annotation activities, as shall be described below. Overall, our intention was to introduce learning practices extracted from and inspired by the technical potential of Meta-Data – systematically categorizing artefacts, writing descriptions, tagging items with keywords – using them to animate pedagogical conversations and activities.

Our first activity focused simply on generating new descriptions for archival material. We wanted to see how different people responded to the same artefact. In doing so, this facilitated conversations about the role of subjectivity when writing archival descriptions. The archive profession is traditionally guided by the principle of the archivist's neutrality; in reality, such neutrality is harder to achieve. As we have already made clear, the Feminist Archive is not a *neutral* archive. It was established as an epistemic intervention; its contents have been directly extracted from the embodied experiences of a diverse social group who have been silenced, rendered invisible, and caricatured throughout most of history. There are also multiple voices in the archive: it documents everyday, vernacular experiences rather than polished, detached, *rational* knowledge. The materials in the feminist archive are excessive – they are archives of feelings, created in the vicinity of trauma (Cvetkovich 2003). How can the neglect and violence suffered at the hands of a sexist medical establishment be described without acknowledging the sense of such enduring injustice encountered through the archival record? Is it possible to remain detached when describing the border violence of the immigration system, and its impact on women and children? If we bring our personal feelings and responses into the catalog, is this how the digital archive becomes social, that is, relational?

To begin to explore these questions, we invited participants to describe the same item we had preselected for the workshop. This was an anonymous girl's account of her first experience of menstruation, written in the late 1970s. Already the document of an excessive, leaky body, we prompted descriptions with the following instructions and questions:

- Describe the item to someone as if they cannot see it.
- How will its 'materiality' be included in the description?
- What keywords or 'tags' can you use? (Generate as many as you want.)
- What should /shouldn't be included?
- Be as detailed as you can.

As might be expected, the descriptions of the artefact varied greatly among participants. Some skillfully and succinctly constructed a summary of the item, offering detailed keywords and detaching themselves from the emotional struggles the account depicted. Others laboured in the mundane details, mentioning names of particular sanitary products, experiences of acute bodily pain and emotional shame, and additional translations of the author's subjective reflections. Material details about the artefact – that it is typed, two pages long, and includes manual corrections – were included on some of the descriptions. On a pedagogical level, inviting participants to describe the artefacts, and discuss their descriptions with the group, generated confidence and immediate engagement with the activities. This provided a solid ground on which to introduce more challenging exercises later in the session that explicitly connected description practices with learning about Meta-Data.

Digital deskilling and developing interior pedagogies

The opening exercise opened up the 'Meta' space of the digital archive through familiarizing participants with how archival practices are used to organize information in digital infrastructures. Initially, non-technical language was deployed to establish confidence and facilitate participation. Yet we wanted to go further: in line with the intellectual and practical legacy of the Feminist Archive, our aim was to explore how we might use the archive as a social context in which non-experts could acquire digital literacies—how non-experts could build (on) the Archive. Within a digitized society, digital grammars are the operational sociotechnical knowledge that structure existence and everyday environments – even if such structuring is not always transparent – suppressed under flatly designed screens that foreground 'simplicity, minimalism, and lightweight approaches to complexity' (Berry 2016, p. 113). Such grammars are often framed as resolutely Other to human existence (Evens 2015), written for the digital's 'grammar machines' (Flusser 2011, p. 6), opaque and difficult to assimilate. Indeed, according to Flusser, numeric code cannibalizes alphabetic literacy and its legitimacy.

Is it fanciful to suggest that humans could ever acquire digital grammars, especially at the cognitive level? Perhaps the mass alphabetic *literacy* projects of modernity were equally as ambitious? And *'just as, in print culture, the school was created to develop this kind of knowledge [i.e., alphabetic literacy], we can imagine that a kind of knowledge of the image [the digital] might be constituted'* (Derrida and Stiegler 2002, p. 58; emphasis in original). Anxiety of inscription characterizes much theoretical work about the impact of the digital on writing, knowledge, and its transmission. This suggests that the acquisition of digital grammar is in no way as intuitive or automatic. Agamben, for example, writes how, within the digital, 'the page as material support of writing has been separated from the page as text' and the reading 'gaze', as an operational technical apparatus, can no longer '"stroll" and move around to gather the characters of writing like the hand gathers a bunch of grapes' (2017, pp. 106–107). In this context the eye, as well as the hand, becomes dislocated: 'digital devices are not immaterial but founded on the obliteration of their own materiality' (Ibid., p. 107).

The obliteration of materiality is one aspect of the wider interruption of the circuit of interiorization and exteriorization caused by digitization. Dennis Tenen describes the double process of interiorization/exteriorization as 'the passage of inscription into understanding' (2017, p. 80), and argues that it 'echoes through the canon of Western philosophical tradition' (Ibid., p. 68). Interiorization/exteriorization is how knowledge is encountered, processed, imprinted, retained, and transformed in a circuit that conjoins psyche, technics, body, and the social. The digital interrupts this process, particularly when information is encountered primarily, and seductively, through the image that screens over its grammatical operations – requiring no exterior mark to convey meaning. How deep, then, should the grammatical 'scratch' be, to effectively inscribe digitized knowledge (Flusser 2011, p. 11)? To enable the reader/writer to execute it and evolve toward a condition of maturity that, Stiegler argues, was central to the institutionalization of alphabetic literacy within the context of the Enlightenment? (Stiegler 2010, p. 28) If we accept the claims of Flusser, Stiegler, Tenen, and Agamben – that learning, as a process that intertwines inscription and understanding, has been dislocated by the digital – what pedagogical practices can be developed to re-inscribe the integrity of the circuit?

These questions informed the second half of our learning session that enabled participants to encounter and interiorize digital grammars. We drew on Withers's practice of using archival descriptions to write collaborative, Meta-Data 'diaries' or 'letters' to a future reader in the archive. Reframing Meta-Data as an epistolary, always already relational form (Hui 2016) helps us appreciate how the way archive catalogs operate is hidden from view (behind the screen), private, and interior. Nevertheless, such writing is often *for* a public audience, even if that public does not 'read it' in a straightforward manner: it is often executed through search activities, even if it is never clearly revealed to the person looking for information. Meta-Data, therefore, simultaneously traverses the broken envelope of public/private. The imaginary of 'interior' forms of writing – diaries as a space of learning and reflection, and the relational quality of letters – were also used to encourage experimentation within an informal environment in which participants might feel safe and grow. We wanted to ensure people felt like it was perfectly ok to make mistakes, and not 'get it right.' The main point of the pedagogical exercise was precisely not to pass on a set of instructions that participants could *adapt* to. Rather, it was to enable those present to encounter digital grammars – and institute that encounter within an embodied, psychosocial circuit. For all participants, this was the first time the textuality of the digital was revealed to them.

With pencil and paper, handwritten archival descriptions were generated, using the categories from the Meta-Data schema, Dublin Core. Dublin Core was chosen over a number of other schemas for several reasons. It is relatively simple to learn, and participants would have encountered it in their everyday navigations of the internet, albeit without realizing it, since it operates 'behind' the screen. Dublin Core is also widely adopted in archives internationally. As with the prior exercise, participants were asked to be as detailed as possible (to explore the 'Meta' as a space of excess), and pay attention to the materiality of the artefact (corrections, paper tears, staples, if the document is handwritten or typed, etc.). Hand writing the schema categories took additional time, which initially generated frustration for some participants. Yet others commented that the format made them 'pay attention in a more detailed way' (Participant a 2017) to what they were describing, and *how* they were describing it. Another participant reflected on the temporal richness of the activity – it enabled her to spend time thinking about what she was reading and writing (Participant b 2017). In this sense, these descriptive activities socialized time and spaces of reflection – delay or *différance* – increasingly compressed by the speed of the digital (Stiegler 2008).

Figure 9.1 Images of handwritten description using Dublin Core

Figure 9.2 Images of handwritten description using Dublin Core

Many participants reflected on how learning about Meta-Data schemes increased their overall operational knowledge of 'the world in' (Participant c 2017) the Feminist Archive. Others talked about the value of 'thinking about descriptions – purpose and intent and use of tags and keywords' (Participant d 2017). One person spoke of how she 'enjoyed thinking about how knowledge and information is categorised, particularly in relation to archives and feminist perspectives' (Participant e 2017). Others commented on the scale of the challenge, that the 'amount of information to discover and investigate is huge' (Participant a 2017), and that there is 'so much to learn' (Participant f 2017). This feedback indicates how the exercise extended the social location of the archive, enabling it to become a site to be explored and contribute to.

One participant wrote a detailed reflection on the activity, and drew an analogy between collaborative feminist archival practices and the sewing of a patchwork quilt:

> Each piece of archive material is quite different in content, size, shape and form, and must be carefully analysed, in order to hand sew it into place within the archive, through giving it; a title, creator, subject, description, publisher, contributor, date, type, format, identifier, source, language, relation, coverage and rights. Each piece needs to be carefully positioned in relation to other pieces. Eventually this information will be threaded together on the world wide web, to create a large, open ended quilt of meta data. The experience of describing the archival material was

mesmeric, repetitive, labour intensive and relational. It is women's work. *The act of archiving, became for me, a handmade act, an act from the body and an act of making herstories visible* (Bossom 2017).

Reintroducing the writing hand as a technical instrument and 'giver' of embodied grammar was a vital part of our activity. As Bossom's description makes clear, the pedagogical context we created was active and embodied, a site to examine how 'ideas have become external and to copy them out is repossession', and the ways 'the physical act of writing is aligned to the act of thinking' (Leslie 2017, p. 48). Theorizations of digital illiteracy often present the digital as an unforgiving and absolute rupture, yet the reality is we exist in a hybrid state, pressed into and against diverse modes of technical inscription and transmission. As Flusser notes: '[W]e are just about to leave notation ([linear] writing as such) to apparatuses [...] we are about to emigrate into the "universe of technical images" so that we can look down from there at history being written by apparatuses. But this colonisation is an extremely complex process. "*Writing cannot just be overcome*", because "the images we contemplate feed on history" and the process "stumbles on literal thinking, on letters" (Flusser 2011, p. 21; emphasis added).

Our aim, then, was to reclaim the stumbling hand in order to reactivate an inscriptive circuit between 'inside' and 'outside,' the passage from inscription to understanding that, several theorists claim, has been interrupted by the digital. We created a collaborative social context within which the textualities of the Meta-Data schema – the ingestion of peculiar, alien, machine readable forms like – might enfold archival description and 'pass through your mind, your body, your hand, completing a full circuit, from body into language, from language back through the body again' (Leslie 2017, 48). We reiterate here that within the pedagogical activity the need to learn the schema of classification *perfectly* was secondary to the psychic and embodied interiorization of grammatical forms. In reality, one learns with the whole body, not just the mind. Yet if we accept that the digital interrupts the learning circuit in some fundamental way (our minds cannot imprint the grammar, and the paper does not hold the mark), such sensory and embodied encounters with grammars of the digital aim to create initial contact points where such circuits might be recalibrated. Such activities may seem infantile but, as noted earlier, we remain in the kindergarten of digital literacy. Such moments of familiarity, we speculate, need to precede movement under and around the screen/image that always already obstructs the very possibility of such an infantile encounter.

Digital archives as social pedagogic spaces of speculative possibility

The Feminist Archive presents itself as a gift. Composed by layers of feminist knowledge, accrued through deliberate acts of acquisition in the recent past, it remains a social location on which we might project our imaginations of what a socially engaged digital archive might be. Such mobilizations of imagination and action are vital if the digital archive is to be reconfigured as a cultural, institutional, and *social* location in which, and through which, digital literacies can be acquired *in the long term* – those literacies that exist above, alongside and under the screen, in the 'Meta' space, in and around a digitized society.

We have argued the digitized era opens up the potential to realize the archive as an animate location where (lifelong) learning occurs. If the deskilled society is to be reskilled, why not turn to the archive, an institutional site where knowledge is preserved and transmitted across generations? Viewing the digital archive in this manner requires a modification in how we approach it, certainly. But such a modification is supported by the practical action we inherit from the Feminist Archive – a lived context in which operational technical and social knowledge can be seized and redistributed to empower the marginalized and deskilled.

Notes

1 We use the term Meta-Data (always hyphenated and capitalized) rather than the more common version 'metadata' to underscore the existence of 'Meta' as a distinct social location.
2 The founding documents of the Feminist Archive can be consulted in the Feminist Archive (South), Bristol: DM2123/1/Archive boxes 68.

References

Agamben, G. (2017). *The Fire and the Tale*. Stanford, CA: Stanford University Press.
Berry,, D.M. (2016). The Post-Archival Constellation: The archive under the technical conditions of computational media, in Blom, I., Røssaak, E., and Bossom, F. (Eds) Archive. Accessed January 9, 2018. https://www.francesbossom.com/single-post/2017/07/01/Archive.
Bossom, F. (Ed.) (2017). *Archive*. Accessed January 9, 2018.https://www.francesbossom.com/single-post/2017/07/01/Archive.
Brown, N.M., Mendenhall, R., Black, M.L., Van Moer, M., Zerai, A., and Flynn, K. (2016). Mechanized Margin to Digitized Center: Black feminism's contributions to combatting erasure within the digital humanities. *International Journal of Humanities and Arts Computing* 10(1): 110–125.
Cvetkovich, A. (2003). *An Archive of Feelings: Trauma, Sexuality, and Lesbian Public Cultures*. Durham, NC: Duke University Press.
Day, R.E. (2014). *Indexing It All: The Subject in the Age of Documentation, Information, and Data*. Cambridge, MA: MIT Press.
Dencik, L., Hintz, A., and Cable, J. (2016). Towards Data Justice? The ambiguity of anti-surveillance resistance in political activism. *Big Data & Society* 3(2). 1–12.
Derrida, J. and Stiegler, B. (2002). *Echographies of Television*, translated by Jennifer Bajorek. Cambridge: Polity.
do Mar Pereira, M. (2017). *Power, Knowledge and Feminist Scholarship: An Ethnography of Academia*. Abingdon: Routledge.
Emejulu, A. (2014). Towards a Radical Digital Citizenship. Accessed January 9, 2018. http://online.education.ed.ac.uk/showcase/towards-radical-digital-citizenship/.

Evens, A. (2015). *Logic of the Digital*. London: Bloomsbury.
Flinn, A. (2010). An Attack on Professionalism and Scholarship? Democratising archives and the production of knowledge. *Ariadne* 62. Accessed May 11, 2017. http://www.ariadne.ac.uk/issue62/flinn.
Flusser, V. (2011). *Does Writing Have a Future?* Minneapolis, MN: University of Minnesota Press.
Freer, J. (1986). Feminist Archive: Explanatory notes by the founder, Feminist Archive South DM2123/1/Archive boxes 68.
Grufydd Jones, B. (2017). Comrade, Committed, and Conscious: The anticolonial archive speaks to our times, in El-Malik, S. and Kamola, I.A. (Eds.) *Politics of African Anticolonial Archive*. London: Rowman Littlefield International, pp. 57–83.
Hui, Y. (2016). *On the Existence of Digital Objects*. Minneapolis, MN: Minnesota University Press.
Lean, T. (2016). *Electronic Dreams: How 1980s Britain Learned to Love the Computer Hardcover*. London: Bloomsbury.
Leslie, E. (2017). Acts of Handwriting, in Hiller H. and Treister S., (Eds.) *Monica Ross: Ethical Actions A Critical Fine Art Practice*. Berlin: Sternberg Press, pp. 42–52.
Ross, D. (2013). Pharmacology and Critique after Deconstruction, in Howells, C. and Moore, G. (Eds.) *Stiegler and Technics*. Edinburgh: Edinburgh University Press, pp. 243–259.
Scott, J.W. (Ed.) (2008). *Women's Studies on the Edge*. Durham, NC: Duke University Press.
Stiegler, B. (2008). *Technics and Time, 2: Disorientation*, translated by Stephen Barker. Stanford, CA: Stanford University Press.
Stiegler, B. (2010). *Taking Care of Youth and the Generations*, translated by Stephen Barker. Stanford, CA: Stanford University Press.
Stiegler, B. (2011). Distrust and the Pharmacology of Transformational Technologies, translated by Daniel Ross. In Zülsdorf, T., Coenen, C., Ferrari, A., Fiedeler, U., Milburn, C., and Wienroth, M. (Eds.) *Quantum Engagements*. Heidelberg: AKA Verlag, pp. 27–30.
Tenen, D. (2017). *Plain Text: The Poetics of Computation*. Stanford, CA: Stanford University Press.
Vriend, T. (2009). It's a Women's World in the Women's Thesaurus: On the history, development and use of the (European) Women's Thesaurus, in Fatma Türe D. and Talay Keşoğlu, B. (Eds.) *Women's Memory: The Problem of Sources: 20th Anniversary Symposium of the Women's Library and Information Centre Foundation*. Istanbul: Kadir Has University, pp. 1–12.
Withers, D. (2015). *Feminism, Digital Culture and the Politics of Transmission: Theory, Practice and Cultural Heritage*. London: Rowman Littlefield International.
Withers, D. (2016). Meta-Data Diaries: Collective annotation. Workshop given at the Centre for Contemporary Arts, Glasgow. http://www.cca-glasgow.com/programme/invisible-knowledge-metadata-diaries.
Withers, D. (2018). Meta-Data Diaries 1: The Feminist Archive, in Johansson K.M., (Ed.) *Inscription*. Gothenburg: Regional State Archives, pp. 177–204.

Chapter 10

Scholastic practices in digital education: on grammatization and poetization in bMOOC[1]

Nancy Vansieleghem

Introduction

There is currently a strong tendency within educational practice and policy to virtualize and digitize higher education. This trend is exemplified most clearly by the current interest in Massive Open Online Courses (MOOCs). MOOCs are new forms of open education that have a profound influence on the daily functioning of higher education. The main objective of MOOCs is to offer unlimited access and free admittance to educational resources to thousands of students, and to offer them the opportunity to learn everything, everywhere, and when they desire, in spite of institutional, economical, or geographical barriers. As such, MOOCs not only make it possible to learn outside institutions, they also make education more in line with current trends for flexible learning trajectories. The European Commission, for instance, claims in regard with MOOCs:

> The potential benefits of the digital revolution in education are multiple: individuals can easily seek and acquire knowledge from sources other than their teachers and institutions often for free; new groups of learners can be reached because learning is no longer confined to specific classroom timetables or methods and can be personalised, new education providers emerge; teachers may easily share and create content with colleagues and learners from different countries; and a much wider range of educational resources can be accessed. Open technologies allow All individuals to learn, Anywhere, Anytime, through Any device, with support of Anyone. (European Commission 2013, p. 3)

Therefore, thanks to advanced digital education, we no longer need to go to school. Everyone can complete individualised learning trajectories at one's own pace and driven by one's own interests.

This transition towards personalized education is more often than not regarded as being at the vanguard of progress and innovation. In this regard, authors have mentioned that today a 'revolution' and massive 'disruption' is taking place within higher education (see Shirky 2012; Barber et al. 2013; Haggard 2013). It goes without saying that this (r)evolution is appealing. However, based on the work of Jan Masschelein and Maarten Simons, I discuss in this chapter the meaning and importance of 'scholastic' practices as different from learning practices. Not because I am opposed to digital technologies in education, and advocate to go back to a time and age before digital media. On the contrary, I argue for the possibility of reconsidering digital education in terms of its scholastic potential, meaning a time space in which learning is not an issue of acquiring credits, and of maximal investing potential resources, but an issue of free time and of indeterminate potentiality (cf. Lewis 2012; Masschelein, Simons 2013). To explore this, I discuss in this chapter a concrete online course for the arts (bMOOC). The main question for bMOOC is: *How to think a MOOC through the 'eyes' of the arts?* Art education implies, so Boris Groys says, exercises and study that make it possible to go beyond what is known in order to see – not in time, but in the moment (Groys 1997). Taking this advice to heart, one might suggest that what is at stake in digital art education is not the efficient and effective production of personalized learning outcomes, but a bringing together of people around a subject matter in a way that it becomes an issue, and hence a disclosure of (certain aspects) of the world (cf. Rogoff 2006). In their book *In Defense of the School: A Public Issue*, Masschelein Simons (2013) refer to this attempt with the notion of *scholè* and relate it to free time (cf. Infra).

Therefore, in this chapter I want to present another view on digital education: one that shows how a particular way of thinking and of problematizing education is constituted and transformed through a perspective on MOOCs that seems most opposed to the idea of indeterminate potentiality. More exactly I want to argue that certain operations might be required for digital education that go beyond aiming at clear and comparable outcomes. Hence, I want to defend a view on digital education that calls for study practices, to be conceived of in terms of digital grammatization and poetization. More specifically, the question at stake in this chapter is not how to design a MOOC that responds to the need of creating an effective learning environment and of preparing students for the next society, but to look for digital education that generates scholastic practices. These are practices that enable us to see and think 'relationally,' in the sense that they allow the user to turn 'dispositives'[2] into an issue, and potentially open a way for maintaining unforeseen relationships to them. Before describing the bMOOC project, I briefly discuss the currently dominant discourse on MOOC platforms. I do so not in order to engage in an argument in favour for or against MOOCs, but rather to understand what mode of thinking and acting this discourse assumes and to see whether it is possible to think and design digital education in a slightly different way.

What kind of learning and education traditional MOOCs allow for?

Within the dominant discourse on MOOCs, learning in general is no longer situated within a fixed time and space. This is different from traditional (institutional) ways of learning that always took place within the school. Over and against this, learning within a MOOC environment is a continuous process that takes place everywhere and all the time. Moreover, it needs to be facilitated and stimulated. From a MOOC perspective, the school is to be criticized for obstructing rather than stimulating learning processes, since it is subject of all kinds of institutional regulations and barriers. Learning in a MOOC environment, on the contrary, is presented as a personal and self-directed process that responds to learners' needs and aspirations. A learner should not only choose the courses he or she likes, but should get optimal technological support in the composition of his or her personal learning trajectory. The aim of MOOC platforms is not to lead students towards obtaining a final degree within a regular amount of time (i.e., a goal-oriented curriculum). Rather, they want learners to obtain employable competences and qualifications at their own pace. This way, MOOC platforms offer a wide range of courses students can subscribe to, according to their personal or professional desires and needs. There are no requirements in terms of having a particular age or holding specific degrees: the learner only needs to find out what kind of courses fit with his or her learning needs. Hence, monitoring systems that are based on individual profiles direct the learner towards a list of potentially interesting courses. Take the following introduction by the platform Coursera as an illustration:

> Welcome to Coursera,
> On Coursera, you can take hundreds of courses from the world's best universities and instructors. Courses are open to anyone, and are available anytime, anywhere. Follow these 4 simple steps to start accomplishing your learning goals, and discover what you're capable of today. (blogpost by Coursera 2018)

Moreover, MOOCs do not only offer a service that fits individual needs and aims, a tracking system also identifies new learning needs and adjusts the list on the basis of new data. Besides a permanent updated list of courses, the platform details the learner also about the course: about the required time investment in relation to the expected return and the precise outcome students can expect, but also about which top universities organize the courses. Therefore, MOOCs provide personalized information and trajectories to be picked up by the learner. Together with monitoring systems and automatized feedback loops, MOOCs serve as 'educational positioning systems' that navigate students through their curriculum along individual 'pathways and routes to maximize (their) success' (Bear and Campbell 2012, cited in Mazoue 2013, p. 63). This is also clear, again, from the European Commission reports:

> Technology makes it possible to develop new solutions for better personalised learning, by allowing teachers to have a more accurate and up-to-date follow up of each learner. Through learning analytics, new and more learner-centred teaching methods can emerge since the evolution of learners who use ICT regularly can be closely monitored: teachers may know the exact learning outcomes of each individual and

identify needs for additional support depending on each individual's learning style. (European Commission 2013, p. 5)

Differently put, in a MOOC environment, tracking and monitoring systems function as a GPS that redirect and recalculate the learners' position time and again.

Furthermore, individual and permanent support and advice is constantly given, and the promise of MOOCS leading up to direct employability, based on an accumulation of competences, is emphasized. As such, knowledge acquisition is no longer the guiding principle of learning in a MOOC environment. Rather it is the accumulation of competences and in particular competences regarding learning how to learn. According to the discourse on MOOCs, learners no longer 'study' courses, but acquire competences in an efficient way. Courses and learning materials are configured in such a way that an optimal learning output for each individual person is generated. By a sequence of (weekly) well-organized units, the learner directs him or herself towards the preferred learning outcomes in a straightforward way. Contents and instructions that do not serve immediate progress and that do not respond to the users' specific needs are removed. This means that:

> Learning materials are offered in small units that are easy to understand and process, usually 12–20 minutes long. Instead of reading, the main medium to transfer content and information is video. Other means are online tests, exercises and games. Short video and exercises follow each other, so that students have to practice what they have learnt. In addition, forums and wiki pages are used to give participants a social learning experience. (EDATU 2016, p. 12)

In this sense, MOOCs also respond to personal aspects of experience, wellbeing and participation. Against this background, new multimedia forms are put at use. Professionally produced clips, equipped with features such as playback and speed control, allow for sections of the lecture to be skipped, speeded up or slowed down according to the needs of the learner. Moreover, techniques are integrated, such as fast and slow motion, or aerial views and microscopic views, so as to give the students the comfort of their own homes and to grant them the opportunity to come in touch with things that were non-accessible before (Koumi 2006). See, for instance, KU Leuven MOOC: *Existential Well-Being Counseling: A Person-Centered Experiential Approach* by Professor Mia Leyssen.

Hence, in a MOOC environment the learner is not addressed as a passive receiver of information, but he or she feels always personally addressed (Tseng et al. 2016). Insofar as the lecturer in a MOOC environment still has a function, his or her role is defined based on such a logic of personalization. The learner, so it is argued, benefits most from the online 'presence' of the teacher, and hence eye contact between the viewer and the lecturer is highly recommended. While the teacher in real-life classroom situations is only able to have eye contact with one student at a time, in a MOOC environment, the teacher is always there for every individual. 'The viewers,' so it is argued, 'feel like they are the only person in a room' (Warrington Newsroom 2018).

MOOCs are thus effective to the extent that learning is conceived of as a personalized and smooth process geared at the acquisition of predefined learning outcomes. Personalized feedback and monitoring systems are the beginning and endpoint of the production of learning output. With this, I mean that these systems function as apparatuses that encourage the student to think about him or herself in terms of the acquisition of deployable competences, a process that time and again needs to be recalculated and that never finishes.

Hence, it could be said that in comparison with other learning environments, the MOOC learner appears as someone who experiences full autonomy over his or her educational trajectory. And that, thanks to digital technology, the learner can finally escape the hierarchical power that is traditionally associated with the figure of the teacher and the school. In fact, from a MOOC perspective, the student no longer needs the school to learn something. He or she learns solely by using his or her 'smartphone.' This might look like the perfect actualization of self-regulated learning. The learner can acquire, produce, and pass on information as the result of monitoring and tracking systems that are made precisely for that. At the same time, however, these self-regulating environments come with a mode of thinking and acting that makes that students no longer can touch on something 'out there.' They are caught in an apparatus that closes them in onto themselves (cf. Decoster 2016). In this sense, it can be argued that MOOC platforms codify the world by digits so that it becomes manageable and accountable, but also out of the reach of the learner's touch (Knox 2018). MOOCs operate on the basis of automated processes in which the student's voice is recognized as a calculation of employable competences and learning outcomes to invest in. This is to say, the participant has to adopt to the logic of personalization and as a result all interactions are 'secured against any possibility of interruption on the pole of the addressee' (cf. Readings 2011, p. 157). In other words, in a MOOC environment the student first of all experiences learning needs and aims, but not something unforeseen. The operations on the basis of which MOOC platforms are constituted could be described as actions that follow a route that is determined in advance, in the form of learning environments that guide learners toward determined destinations.

Returning to the main concern of this chapter, I will reflect in the following sections on the question whether there is a possibility to design digital education in another way. This question could be formulated as follows: can we conceive of digital operations and actions in a way that they do not predetermine the future, but open it for the new generation.

About grammatization and poetization: actions and operations digital education might allow for

In view of these considerations it could be argued that MOOC practices differ considerably from scholastic practices. The term *scholastic* is derived from the Greek word *scholè*, which refers to the time during which political, religious, or economic obligations are suspended. As Masschelein and Simons suggest, scholastic practices do not enact productive time, but free time. Whereas it is often assumed that education should address societal needs and ensure employability, *scholè* has meaning in and of itself. *Scholè*, as Masschelein and Simons (2011 and 2013) argue, is a pedagogic form, invented in Greek Antiquity. It is first of all a form of separation of time and space that respects a logic that is opposed to a logic of production. It has no external finality, and hence no predetermined outcome. More exactly: 'In a pedagogic form something is for common use: something is de-appropriated or disconnected from particular interests (…), usages (…) and words (…)' (2011, p. 81). In the Middle Ages, this pedagogical form reappeared as the *universitas magistrorum et scholarium*. Here it referred to 'a unique assembly of scholars and students where something (a text, a thing, …) is made public; a carefully constructed time and space where people gather around something, where a public is made able to think in the presence of something and where something is able to call a public into being' (Ibid., p. 81). As Bill Readings writes in relation to the university, this 'implies that students are not simply intellectuals or managerial professionals in waiting. Rather the University implies the time of pedagogy: a thought or study in excess of the subject which rejects the metanarrative of redemption' (Readings 2011, p. 145). According to these authors, the minimal condition of pedagogy is that it opens a series of incalculable differences. In this respect, Reading argues that 'education, as e-ducere, (…) is not a maieutic revelation of the student to him-or herself, a process of clearly remembering what the student in fact already knew. Rather, education is this drawing out of the otherness of thought that undoes the pretention to self-presence that always demands further study' (p. 162). The acquisition of knowledge and skills, then, are not directed towards an external finality or personal ideal, but is a way of becoming attentive for the possible and hence a way for students to constitute themselves as a new generation.

In assembling this pedagogical form, reading and writing technologies, and, in particular, the textbook and the blackboard, appear as crucial elements (Illich 1996; Marin etal. 2018). This is to say, it is the technology of reading and writing, and the corresponding gestures and exercises, that turns someone into a student: someone who relates to the world as text (Ibid.). In this sense, it is important to mention that there is no school without the textbook. The text creates a space between the student and the world. Or as Marin et al. write, 'the text provide(s) a means to take distance from the world while also making possible its study' (2018, p. 6). The text transforms a continuous flow of speech or thought into something discontinuous (in the form of clearly distinguished letters, words, sentences, etc. written or printed on the book page). It lays down what we think and say in material inscriptions according to a set of rules and conventions (the grammar). To refer to this materialization of the temporal flow, Stiegler (2013) uses the term grammatization. The materialization and spatialization of the temporal flux is, according to Stiegler, the condition for not being absorbed by the flow, so that one can take a distance to the world and the world is turned into an object of study. The invention of the school can be described as the creation of the time and space in which students and professors gather around a text in order to speak, think, and discuss about something external. It allows them to become involved with what they are reading and writing. They can also take distance towards it in order to analyze, memorize, and criticize it. The school, as such, is a time and place that makes study possible. However, to study a book, it must be read in a certain way, and the reader must develop and employ certain practices and technologies. The most well-known and probably the most efficient school technology is the blackboard. On the blackboard one can put down schemes, sentences, and words. When a teacher writes something on it, he or she may direct students' attention towards it. In this sense, it could be said that there are always technologies involved that demand attention and that put personal needs and aims between brackets. It could be said that within a school arrangement text (e.g., in a book or on the blackboard) externalizes and materializes (aspects of) the world: it puts into question what is there.

Therefore, the grammatization of the temporal flux is not aimed at the reproduction of the world. Instead it is in the first place about disclosing the world: making the world available for new and other uses, so to say. This, perhaps, explains why grammatization is close to poetization. Reading and writing texts demands interpretation and improvisation. This means that students always read and write what affects, infects, addresses, or even pushes them. Reading and writing is always a form of returning to what is known, which allows for a certain distance towards it, and as such for thinking. It is in the act of reading and writing that a thought gets form. A text in this sense never coincides with one thought or one meaning, but always enacts or even provokes thought. Put differently, it is in such a moment of disconnection or distance that students may have the experience of being (not un)able to speak, to begin with the world and to say something that is not claimed by someone or something. What is at stake here is the experience of being able to play with the letters, words, sentences, or their syntaxes, so that we may set them free for use; but also to alter them and try out different ways of using the rules or the syntaxes. As a result, the text is never taken for granted as an authority: a text needs voices to make or let it speak. In the act of gathering around a text, in copying, memorizing, analyzing, or writing text, fragments or words are brought to someone's attention, and therefore they can get alternative voices. What happens here is situated at an individual level, but it can also become collective. Hence, these practices lead to questioning, but also to being questioned. As such, school practices are self-forming practices, or in the words of Stiegler (2013) they individuate or even transindividuate. At least, my argument is that this precisely happens when technology is used in a scholastic way, i.e., not aiming at any kind of predefined outcome.

How to design a MOOC that integrates practices of grammatization and poetization?

What seems to happen in most digital environments today is that education is no longer able to mediate grammatization and poetization in a direct way. With this I mean that grammatization and poetization (i.e., the conditions for taking distance, suspension, and improvisation) are captured by ICT tools. In this regard, Stiegler argues that when we use digital devices as the sole or prevailing means to read and create text, we enter a different space of experience: we no longer relate to language as text and 'become alienated to our own productive capabilities' (Vlieghe 2015, p. 220). Or at least, in a digital environment there is no longer a direct and intimate relationship with the production of text as text. The grammar is inside digital devices and remains hidden there – numerically codified (based on 1s and 0s) and hence unreadable for the human eye. This is to say that the structure of the digital device does not represent the world, but computes it and visualizes it (on a screen) according to a program or algorithm that makes sense out of it. Hence, where the grammar that facilitates traditional reading and writing is firmly and intimately embodied in the literate person, the code in a digital environment remains invisible and hidden. As Lev Manovich writes, digital technology in its perfect form works because it is invisible or transparent (Manovich 2001).

This, however, is no reason to be opposed to the use of digital media as such. One of the challenges within digital education is how to relate to the digital in a way that the possibility of grammatization and poetization isn't ruled out (cf. Vlieghe 2015). That is to say, how to create conditions in which the grammar of the code may show itself, so that we can find a certain distance towards it in a way that makes us think – and not only consume?

In view of this, we could ask the question whether we can give shape to a virtual space as a scholastic technology? This is, as an interface by which the programs and algorithms (the backed, or b-side of the digital course) become matter(ial). Or differently put, an interface by which the algorithm is exteriorized and brought under our attention.

I explore these challenges on the basis of a description of a concrete project called bMOOC, set up in 2014 by students, lecturers, artists and graphic designers of LUCA school of Arts and KU Leuven[3]. I will use this project as a case study to articulate the grammatizing and poetizing potentiality of the digital, and to reimagine digital education in a less apparatus mode of thinking and acting than the dominant form of MOOCs we know today. A vital characteristic of bMOOC is that it is a technology that tries to grasp how the digital works and to see how these operations could be used scholastically, i.e., as digital objects, discarding in this way instrumental and essentialist notions of technology (Storme et al. 2016). The central issue for students working with bMOOC, therefore, is: how to design a digital platform in which the user becomes engaged in the life of the digital, viewed as a heteronomous assemblage in which discourse and technology are bound up with one another.

In order to investigate this issue, bMOOC is first of all designed in such a way that it is open and accessible for everyone. It is open in the sense that particular qualifications, age or enrollment at the host institution are not required. Everybody can register to bMOOC and from then on participate. This means contributing with techno-images. I borrow this term from Vilèm Flusser (2011) in order to refer to the coded structure of the images, and to indicate that pictures, texts, videos, films, audio, and all sorts of hybrid media form can be included. Even PDF files are displayed as techno-images. What is furthermore unique to bMOOC is that no learning outcomes are defined. This means that in bMOOC there is no optimal route or personal trajectory to take. BMOOC is an online arrangement between students and lecturers who gather around different issues or topics that include particular exercises and instructions (see Figure 10.1). Hence, the term openness refers not only to availability to each and all despite existing geographical and institutional barriers. It first and foremost means that the content is not fixed, and that it is produced collectively. Not the lecturer or the learner but the *collective* makes the course. There is thus always a communal dimension to bMOOC.

Of course, communality is an ambiguous term that most often refers to how some contents are produced and how educational openness is organized. The way I use it, the term also refers to a public dimension – meaning 'resources' that are available for everyone, but not owned by anyone. In contradistinction to traditional MOOCs, the content matter in bMOOC is not something already given, neither is it centered around the individual learner's needs. Instead, lines and routes are collectively produced by students who relate to them in terms of knots (see Figure 10.2). Knots differ from building blocks. While building blocks are assembled into structures according to an external order that makes them fit perfectly together, knots, so Tim Ingold argues, 'are not articulated and do not connect. They have no links. Nevertheless they retain within their constitution a memory of the processes of their formation' (2015, p. 15). Knots, therefore, 'are always in the midst of things, while their ends are on the loose, rooting for other lines to tangle with' (Ibid., p. 22). This way, instead of providing a smooth connection from one point to the other towards points of achievement, for instance learning outcomes, the lines in bMOOC flow without

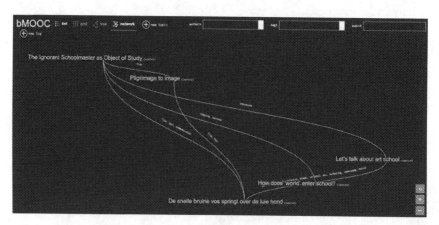

Figure 10.1 Screenshot of the opening page of bMOOC

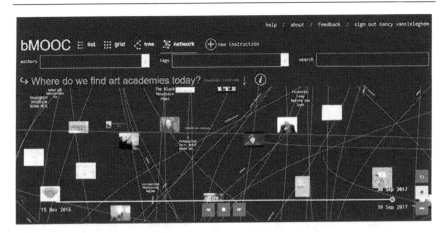

Figure 10.2 Screenshot of contributions within one particular topic on bMOOC

leading to a particular end. A student uploads a contribution always next to an already existing one in the topic, wherever he or she wants to. Every contribution is thus connected to others and forms together a network of techno-images.

Therefore, the order of the steps users of bMOOC take is not given by intention but by attention. The posts which students find meaningful to contribute, is not determined in advance, it just makes sense at the moment of paying attention. While navigating, the participant sees which images come next and he or she can become attentive to them. Clicking on an image within the network makes pop up two images alongside each other, with the possibility to navigate to other images (see Figures 10.3 and 10.4).

The content is thus constantly changing. Every post engenders an immediate effect and demands the user to relate to the previous contribution. The bMOOC

Figure 10.3 Screenshot of two images alongside each other on bMOOC

Figure 10.4 Screenshot of the instruction page that pops up when the user wants to add a new contribution to bMOOC

student has to respond to what is there to see, to what he or she thinks of it, and how he or she can contribute? Hence the actions of the users are not at random. The student must be attentive to the path that invites him or her to see and read what is written, and to search for a possible response. Even though a topic or issue may have specific instructions, there is no fixed connection, as each contribution waits for a next contribution. This process has no predefined direction. It is only thanks to the connection with another post that a new contribution receives meaning. As such, no contribution is like any other. Each contribution confronts the student with a sense of his or her own movement through the MOOC, leaving a trace in the process of forming a path. On this path, then, the digital world is present for the student. With each step, he or she has a bodily experience that provides him or her with a clear sense of the path that he or she is 'shaping.' Contributing images, then, is not primordially about producing, but is rather a relating to what constitutes the digital as digital: a relationship in terms of a becoming part or in the midst of it. Stated differently, the digital world in bMOOC is brought into existence and hence, emerges not as a fixed apparatus of power, but as something in the making. This means that in bMOOC the digital world is transformed into an object of study, which involves the crucial experience of digital grammatization and poetization.

Let me give an example of one topic that was a part of the bMOOC project, viz., the one on 'the ignorant schoolmaster as object of study' to make this clearer (see Figure 10.5). Left without instructions other than to annotate the text of Jacques Rancière and to relate to other students' uploads, the course of this topic performed a series of translations and transcodings. Beginning with the posting of a pdf of the first chapter of Jacques Rancière's book in English, the lecturer contributes a video-clip in which she recorded herself while reading the first chapter.

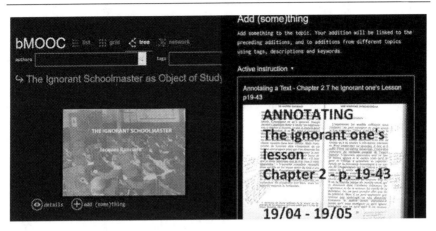

Figure 10.5 Screenshot of the topic of the ignorant schoolmaster – an example of educational commonality

One student reacted on this by writing down a translation of the reading of Rancière in French. Another student contributes with a drawing of the reading, and yet someone else records the Dutch texts while reading and highlighting important fragments in yellow (see Figure 10.6). Hence, without being instructed to do so, the students resort to translating the digital objects they have in front of their eyes, without being ever told to do so. Translation as an issue was never planned by the instructor: there is no item in the course that explicitly demands this to be the issue. Translation is what the text of Rancière itself is about, and it emerges as something the students not only paid attention to, but had started to put into practice. While the text of Rancière touched on translation as a means to show

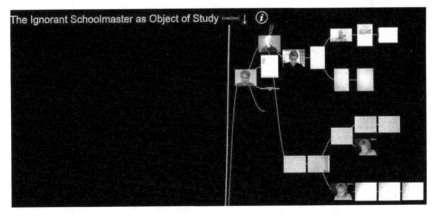

Figure 10.6 Screenshot of the topic of the ignorant schoolmaster – an example of educational commonality

something about the equality of intelligences, students made translation the central issue of their thinking. In this sense, it could be argued, that in the online exercise on Rancières text, a collective response emerges, evoked by the students who responded to contributions within the course. In this exercise, then, the students were not only thinking about translation, they were performing it through their contributions. Hence, bMOOC allowed for something new to emerge that functions collectively.

Returning to Flusser, it could furthermore be argued that what the exercise on the ignorant schoolmaster finally showed is the possibility of the formation of a collective techno-image. As Flusser (2011) says, techno-images are not representational, but aggregative. They are computed according to models and algorithms that give meaning to them. The final techno-image which emerges from the aggregation of all the techno-images uploaded by the students, however, is not computed by an apparatus according to a programmed model. The techno-image is 'computed' by the students contributions of which nobody knows the direction in advance. The direction of the topic emerged only at the end. This way, the course enables students not only to gather around and to perform the issue of translation, but also revealed the digital structure of media objects and media visualizations. In other words, what bMOOC made them think about, is that what media visualizations do: making relationships between data operative and active, and presenting these in such a way that they create something new. Therefore, the potentiality of media visualization consists in the fact that students become able to enact a space in which it becomes possible to navigate and traces out the thinking space of the course to a great degree.

This brings us to a deeper understanding of the relationality of educational practices and of how media visualizations might play a crucial role in sustaining relationality. In this respect, bMOOC shows how media visualizations might show the relationality of the educational practice, rather than the personal trajectory of the student in terms of achieving predefined outcomes. That is, what media visualizations might do is not only directed to 'who' contributes, and 'what' is contributed, but also to 'how' the relations between contributions look like, and to 'where' particular contributions are positioned. In that sense, media visualizations allow for asking questions such as: what is specific about particular relations, where are they to be found, which contributions trigger many reactions, which contributions are almost never responding with new contributions, and what sort of thinking is enacted.

Hence, in posing these questions, bMOOC discards a way of thinking about teaching practice in terms of a structure that is pre-given, and replaces it by a specific enactment of particular constellations of relations between actors. This means that constellations that make that something comes into being as stable and ordered appear not as a structure that is pre-given, but as something that is in the making (cf. Latour 2005). Hence, the potentiality of digital education is made manifest by bMOOC. And this happens mostly by rendering the relations between the users visible. In this respect, relationality rather than linearity is the prime analytic lens of bMOOC. Media visualizations display relations between actors in such a way that they do not function in order to represent an existing world, but they bring forth a new kind of reality. Hence, the advantage of media visualization is that it, in contradistinction to pictures and texts that are often conceived of as representations of something 'out there,' play a much more non-representative role, because they are expressive objects in their own right. In other words, the relations that emerge through media visualizations are not to be conceived of in terms of a passive correspondence with the world, but rather in terms of active presentations, for which what is presented create something new. It forms a space where thinking may unfold.

Hence, media visualizations as thinking spaces can be understood diagrammatically. Referring to Foucault and Deleuze, a diagram, 'although unidentifiable in itself, is that which brings forth the system of statements upon which articulation depends as well as the machine upon which consonant visibilities depend' (Lilley 2001, p. 68). A diagram is, more precisely, a seeing-saying machine, a form in which the (non)relations between the discursive and the non-discursive forces that constitute power are displayed. Insofar as a visualization is a mapping between data and visual representations, the concept of the diagram is indicative for its formative potential. In a similar way to a diagram, a visualization can be understood both as a paradigm of the forces that constitute present power, and as constituting 'a space of imagination and opportunity' (Hetherington 2011). Media visualizations, in other words, determine that characteristics and relations of the data are shown and trace out the thinking space of the platform to a great degree. Depending on the visualization different possible relations between the images as such can be displayed. The strength of media visualizations, then, is that they allow students to experience exactly this lively aspect of the diagram, namely that it is a movement that constantly redraws itself. This means, among other things, that media visualizations may express the movements of thought and imagination that are involved in digital activities (such as navigating and posting, deleting and reposting, arranging, and rearranging media). They allow us to see our thought processes, rather than our thoughts.

Furthermore, since the structure of the digital allows not only for visualizing relations, but also for altering visualizations, this opens up the possibility of starting to interact with the diagram. The variability of media visualizations makes a form of *remapping* possible: we can *rearrange* the elements of an already existing map and intervene with it (Manovich 2010). By designing the interface in such a way that its media visualizations become part of its navigational structure, bMOOC turned the variation of media visualization into an activity users can control themselves. The chosen form of visualization (e.g., in terms of structuring the contents as a tree, a network, a grid, or a list) determines which characteristics and relations of the data will be shown to the users. By default, in bMOOC all images in the 'list' are sorted chronologically. Pressing the button 'tree' makes appear the order of posts within one topic according to its genealogy, and the 'network' reveals relations between contributions or posts according to the tags that are added with each post (see Figures 10.7a, b and c). This enables users to set the diagram free for use and to operationalize it, i.e., to turn it into an activity, into a verb: the scholastic practice of diagramming. Hence, diagramming can be understood as an excessive form of grammatization in which we visualize power relations.

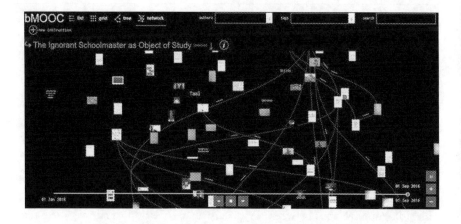

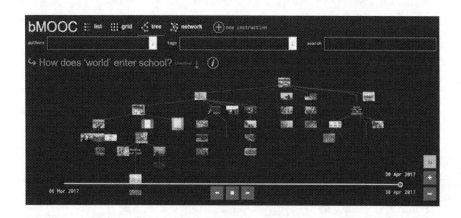

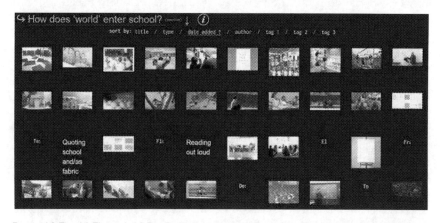

Figure 10.7a, 10.7b and 10.7c. Different forms of media visualizations: a network, a tree, and a grid

Whereas a classical MOOCs allow for drawing schemes in order to refer to something else (i.e., the distance towards the expected learning outcome), bMOOC specifically allows to show different schemes with the same dataset, and disclose, expose different characteristics, and relations of a single dataset. Hence, bMOOC allows to see the b-side or the backend of the digital course.

By way of conclusion we can say that in order to design digital education and technology that generates scholastic practices, the designers of bMOOC started from the features the digital itself has. This is opposed to the logic of traditional MOOCs, where the potentiality of the digital remains black boxed. In contrast, bMOOC tries to exteriorize the possibilities of the digital in order to use it as a scholastic technology, and as such to turn digital operations and actions into objects of study. BMOOC, thus, allows for computational operations to become educational objects. To put it differently: in bMOOC digital operations are grammatized. Due to grammatization students may experience being in the middle of the digital world *and* thus experience what it means to speak and to think through digital constellations. Therefore bMOOC is not a MOOC *for* the arts, but a research on what the digital makes us do, as such to open it for imaginative worlds to come.

Notes

1 This chapter is part of the OOF research project: 'The imaginative side of online learning: A MOOC to think with eyes and hands' funded by the Association KU Leuven (2014-16). Hence it is the result of a process in which all the project members were involved. Special thanks goes to Jan Masschelein, the co-supervisor of the project, and Thomas Storme, researcher on the project. Their collaboration and input was of crucial importance for the development of this chapter.
2 I borrow the term dispositive from Michel Foucault, in order to refer to the presence of power apparatuses that are constituted through an assemblage of discourses and governing technologies, and that constitute a horizon against which people understand and govern themselves and others (see Bussolini, 2010)
3 See www.bMOOC.be . BMOOC is part of and one of the realisations of the OOF project mentioned in footnote 1. Researchers involved in the project are: K. Cardinaels (co-supervisor) M. De Blieck, T. De Greve, D. Deschrijver, S. Devleminck, R. Kerkhofs, J. Masschelein (co-supervisor), M. Simons, T. Storme and N. Vansieleghem (supervisor)

References

Barber, M., Donnelly, K., and Rizvi, S. (2013). *An Avalanche Is Coming: Higher Education and the Revolution Ahead*. London: Institute for Public Policy Research.
Bussolini, J. (2010). What Is a Dispositive? *Foucault Studies 10*, 85–107.
Coursera. (2018). Get started at Coursera (blog post) accessed online, October 5, 2018. https://groups.google.com/forum/#!topic/me-heat-power-2014-15/wsyc4LwFLA8
Decoster, P.-J. (2016). *From Cinema Education to the Omnipresence of Digital Screens. Challenging the Assumptions in View of Educational Experiences*. Unpublished dissertation, Gent University.

EDATU, Erasmus+. (2016). Output5 Score 2020. Instructional design models for different types and settings of MOOCs. Accessed October 5, 2018. https://oerknowl edgecloud.org/sites/oerknowledgecloud.org/files/O5-Instructional_design_models_ for_different_types_and_settings_of_MOOCs.pdf.
European Commission. (2013). Opening up Education. Innovative teaching and learning for all through new technologies and open educational resources. Communication from the Commissions (COM 2013, 654, final), Brussels: European Commission.
Flusser, V. (2011). *Into the Universe of Technical Images*. Minneapolis, MN,London: University of Minnesota Press.
Groys, B. (1997). *Logik der Sammlung, Am Ende des musealen Zeitalters*. Munichen, Vienna: Carl Hanser Verlag.
Haggard, S. (2013). *The Maturing of the MOOC: Literature Review of Massive Open Online Courses and Other Forms of Online Distance Learning* (BIS Research Paper No. 130). London: Department for Business, Innovation and Skills. Accessed May 5, 2018. http s://www.gov.uk/government/uploads/system/uploads/attachment_data/file/ 240193/13-1173-maturing-of-themooc.pdf.
Hetherington, K. (2011). Foucault, the Museum and the SDiagram. Accessed May 5, 2018. http://oro.open.ac.uk/29709/1/Foucault_the_Museum_and_the_Diagram_v611.pdf
Illich, I. (1996). *Text and University. On the Idea and History of a Unique Institution*. Accessed May 5, 2018: http://www.davidtinapple.com/illich/1991_text_and_uni versity.PDF.
Ingold, T. (2015). *The Life of Lines*. London, New York, NY: Routledge.
Koumi, J. (2006). *Designing Video and Multimedia for Open and Flexible Learning*. Oxford: Routledge.
Knox, J. (2018). Beyond the 'C' and the 'X': Learning with algorithms in massive open online courses (MOOCs). *International Review of Education 6*(2), 161–178.
Latour, B. (2005). *Reassembling the Social. An Introduction in Actor Network Theory*. Oxford: Oxford University Press.
Lewis, T. (2012). Rousseau and the Fable. Rethinking the fabulous nature of educational philosophy. *Educational Theory 12*(3), 323–341.
Lilley, S. (2001). The Language of Strategy, in Westwood, R. and Linstead, S. (Eds.) *The Language of Organization*. London: Sage.
Manovich, L. (2001). *The Language of New Media*. Cambridge, MA: MIT Press.
Manovich, L. (2010). *What Is Visualisation?* Accessed April 10, 2017. http://manovich. net/content/04-projects/064-what-is-visualization/61_article_2010.pdf.
Marin, L., Masschelein, J. and Simons, M. (2018). Page, Text and Screen in the University: Revisiting the Illich hypothesis. *Educational Philosophy and Theory 50*(1), 49–60.
Masschelein, J. and Simons, M. (2011). Universitas Magistrorum et scholarium: A short history of profanation, in Decuypere, M., VliegheJ., Simons M., and Masschelein J. (Eds.) *Curating the European University*. Leuven: University Press, pp. 81–89.
Masschelein, J. and Simons, M. (2013). *In Defence of the School. A Public Issue*, translated by J. McMartin. Leuven: E-ducation, Culture & Society Publishers.
Mazoue, J.G. (2013). *The MOOC Model. Challenging Traditional Education*. Accessed May 5, 2018. https://er.educause.edu/articles/2013/1/the-mooc-model-challenging-traditiona l-education.
Readings, B. (2011). *The University in Ruins*. Cambridge, MA: Harvard University Press.
Rogoff, I. (2006). Academy as Potentiality, in Nollert, A. and Rogoff, I. (Eds.) *A.C.A. D.E.M.Y.*. Frankfurt am Main: Revolver, pp. 13–20.

Shirky, C. (2012). *Napster, Udacity, and the Academy.* Accessed May 5 2018. http://www.shirky.com/weblog/2012/11/napster-udacity-and-the-academy.

Stiegler, B. (2013). The Aufklärung in the Age of Philosophical Engineering, in Hildebrandt, M., O'Hara, K., and Waidner, M. (Eds.) *Digital Enlightenment Yearbook 2013*, translated by Daniel Ross. Amsterdam: IOS Press.

Storme, T., Vansieleghem, N., Devleminck, S., Masschelein, J., and Simons, M. (2016). The Emerging Pedagogy of MOOCs: The educational design of technology and practices of study. *Journal of Computers in Education.* Advanced publication. http//doi.org/10.1007/s40692-016-0070-5.

Tseng, S.F., Tsao, Y.-W., Yu, L.-C., Chan, C.-L., and Lai, R. (2016). Who Will Pass? Analyzing learner behaviors in MOOCs. Research and practice in technology enhanced learning. *Research and Practice in Technology Enhanced Learning*, 2–11. Accessed July 5, 2018. https://telrp.springeropen.com/track/pdf/10.1186/s41039-016-0033-5.

Vlieghe, J. (2015). Traditional and Digital Literacy. The literacy hypothesis, technologies of reading and writing, and the 'grammatized' body. *Ethics and Education 10*(2), 209–226.

Warrington Newsroom. (2018). *Making Learning More Personal.* Accessed October 25, 2018. https://news.warrington.ufl.edu/faculty-and-research/making-learning-more-personal/.

Chapter 11

Reframing the making of school in digital times
How art can(not) change digitization

Frank Maet

Introduction: the contemporary context of education

If we look at the contemporary institutional context of education, we are confronted with the presence of digital technology. Many schools are changing into so-called smart schools and among educators there is an ongoing debate whether iPads, laptops, and smart phones belong in class or not.[1] At present, every educational institution is concerned with its digital future.[2]

What happens in educational settings is symptomatic for what is going on in society at large. More and more practices that were formerly not explicitly related to technology have become digitally mediated. Consider, for example, the 'Internet of Things,' which enables physical devices – from coffee machines over cars to the heating systems – to communicate with one another and to make decisions based on that 'communication.' Consequently, in relation to educational settings some of the same problems occur as they do elsewhere in society, such as the security of applications, the lack of rules and regulations, the protection of privacy, and the loss of human autonomy.

However, we need to take into account that educational settings, and especially schools, come with a specific way of thinking and practicing. Put differently, schools are a kind of tool, which are designed according to very specific ideas and practices. For example, the Western tradition of schooling is related to the Ancient Greek concept *scholê*, which is generally translated as 'free time.' During this free time men were free from work, business and occupations, which were defined as *ascholê*, i.e., the privation of free time. Being free was considered as the means to be able to learn. It was not the end of *scholê* (Kalimtzis 2018).

Among many philosophers (of education) there is an enduring concern to protect this original meaning of *scholê*. We can refer to the philosopher and political theorist Hannah Arendt (1961, pp. 17–40, 197–226), but also to present-day scholars (such as Jan Masschelein and Maarten Simons (2013) and Marc Fabian Buck (2017)). Nevertheless, there is a continuous need to review the interpretation of the concept *scholê*, since 'free time' comes to mean something different depending on time and place. As for the present, we need to examine the possibility of *scholê* in relation to the current digital condition. This digital condition not only includes databases, software, and information of all kinds, it is also the expression of ideas and cultural practices. Moreover, digitization is often associated with late capitalism and business culture (Hesmondhalgh, Meier 2018). And, as doing business was originally categorised as being *ascholê*, it is no longer evident to define *scholê* and 'free time' in relation to our current condition.

In order to illustrate how the concept of *scholê* changes over time, I would like to make a detour along the deconstructive reading of Kantian aesthetics by the French philosopher Jacques Derrida (Derrida 1987, pp. 15–147). In Kant's *Critique of Judgment*, in which he investigates and defines the preconditions of aesthetic judgement, it is suggested that the essence of a work (Greek: *ergon*) can be defined intrinsically, i.e., without taking into account anything that is external to it, such as the context in which it was created or the economic value the work might have. Also, according to Kant, the frame of a painting remains external to it, and thus it functions only as a decorative and ornamental addition, a *parergon*, to the work itself. Contrary to this point of view, Derrida argues that the frame differs from what is inside (i.e., the work of art), as well as from the outside (i.e. its surroundings). Hence the frame presents something that is missing or not shown in the work itself. Within the logic of Derrida, the frame 'comes from outside to constitute the inside as an inside' (Krauss 2004, p. 45). However, Derrida also remarks that it is very difficult to discern where a framing begins and where it ends. Derrida follows this line of thought to further deconstruct Kant's aesthetics. More exactly, he goes on arguing that the content of the third critique is already co-constituted by its own frame. In this case, the framing is the critical method[3] that Kant used to make an analysis of aesthetic judgement. So, according to Derrida, the inside cannot be defined in its purity but it is also the result of the method used to discern the content.

Although Derrida developed his reasoning about the frame in relation to artworks and aesthetics, I argue that we can also use it to gain an understanding of educational settings. As mentioned before, education is nowadays characterized, among other things, by a shift from analogue to digital devices (e.g., from blackboard to smart board). We can understand this as a transition from one kind of framing to another: a change from an analogue framing into a digital one. As a result, we are confronted with a different framing of the idea underlying the concept of school, and hence we need to reflect carefully on this reframing. Considering the concept of *scholê* today, we find ourselves confronted with an entire history of interpretations. These interpretations have evolved in accordance with specific circumstances and this gave rise to different meanings, practices, and attributes of education. More specifically, the history of this concept started with the Socratic question: 'What type of life is worth living?' (Kalimtzis 2018, p. 2) Hence, it is necessary to relate Plato's and Aristotle's interpretation of *scholê* to this question. Then we can understand that free time, associated with the concept of *scholê* has never been free in an absolute sense. Plato and Aristotle reflected on this concept in relation to their theories of the good life, and, in order to achieve a good life, it was believed that 'free time' was necessary. If we want to consider present-day education in the wake of the Ancient Greek concept, we need to reframe the Socratic question in relation to present-day circumstances and opinions about the good life. Eventually, we will have to pose the question whether contemporary capitalism and *scholê* can belong together.

In this chapter, I attempt to reframe *scholê* by considering the domain of art. I will look at art (and aesthetic reflection) to get to a better understanding of the present-day condition and to reflect further on the construction of our (digital) access to the world and to education in particular. In Ancient Greek, the word for art was the same as the word used for technology, namely *technê*. But art in its modern sense is very much affiliated to 'free time,' since it is considered to be free from functionality. Therefore, art is related both to the development of technology in a more calculative sense, *and* to practices involving being free from occupation. But, above all, from a philosophical point of view, art has always been reflected on in close relation with ethics. As art encompasses all these features, I am convinced that turning to the artistic can help us to find an appropriate and contemporary answer to the Socratic question: 'What type of life is worth living?'

On the relationship between art and technology

In this section, I will elaborate on the intrinsic relation between art and technology, starting from a seminal text by Martin Heidegger (1977). Next, I introduce the reflections of the philosophers Jean-Luc Nancy (1997) and Peter-Paul Verbeek (2005, 2006, 2012), that have been developed in the wake of Heidegger. This will help me to show that a reflection on art can be used to broaden our understanding of contemporary technology.

In his essay 'The Question Concerning Technology,' Heidegger (1977, pp. 3–35) defines what he sees as the essence of technology. According to Heidegger, the modern understanding of technology is mainly focused on efficiency, which he considers to be a reduced understanding of technology. In Heidegger's view, technology is, in essence, a sort of making and bringing forth of reality (Greek: *poiêsis*). Furthermore, Heidegger refers to Aristotle and his theory of the four causes that are present in every creation process: all things that involve making or becoming, be it a tree, a human being, or a statue, has a material cause, a formal cause, an efficient cause, and a final cause. Every making or becoming presupposes material (i.e., the material cause), a presentation of the thing's form (i.e., the formal cause), someone and/or something to transform the material into something according to this form (i.e., the efficient cause), and, finally, the purpose of the thing (i.e., the final cause). This means that originally 'efficiency' is only one of the features that deserve attention in the act of producing something. By referring to Aristotle's analysis, Heidegger broadens the vision on technology. He presents technology as a process of making, which should not solely be based on efficiency, but which should encompass all four dimensions that characterize becoming.

If we forget to take into account this broader perspective on technology, there is the risk of ending up with a reality solely based on efficiency. Still according to Heidegger, this can lead to a situation in which all reality is used and thought of instrumentally. Then, reality becomes a source, a standing reserve, i.e., reality is there for the sake of the functioning of technology itself. Nowadays this happens, I argue, for instance when the development of digital devices is only directed to maintain the efficient functioning of the digital network by making it faster and directed towards more economical profit.

As a correction to the modern reductive view on technology, Heidegger looks in the direction of the arts. He stresses that originally *technê* is the common noun for instrumental tools as well as for artistic practices. Consequently, he suggests that we should look at the domain of art to find out the truth about the functioning of technology. Nevertheless, in Heidegger's opinion, art is related to technology but at the same time different from it. Although Heidegger stresses the familiarity between art and technology, he also states that the essence of technology is not technological. So, Heidegger suggests in the end that we need to focus on art to escape from technology in its modern sense.

Next, I want to discuss the philosophical perspectives of Nancy (1997, 2015) and Verbeek (2005, 2006, 2012), who both extend Heidegger's analysis to the present-day context. Heidegger still contrasted the modern condition of his time with a previous situation, in which a more physical, direct and humanlike contact was possible, and in which reality was not yet totally a matter of technological functioning. A renewal of Heidegger's approach is needed to get closer to the current thoroughly technological time, wherein differences between art, media, technology, and nature are disappearing.

Nancy and Verbeek have in common that they give up the divide between *physis* and *technê*. *Physis* is often translated as 'nature,' and means that which produces itself by itself, whereas *technê*, technology, alludes to the knowledge necessary to produce something that is not made by itself. But our contemporary condition is one wherein what produces itself by itself is also manipulated or influenced by technology. Climate change illustrates this intermingling very well: natural effects are linked to technological effects, and it is hard to distinguish where nature begins and technology ends. Nancy uses the neologism 'ecotechnic' to describe our present condition. Since our ecosystem has become thoroughly technological, our 'house' (Greek: *oikos*), meaning our environment, has become technological through and through. Verbeek states that our relation to the world is always already technologically mediated. Put differently, we cannot take distance from technology or search for a purely non-technological access to reality. Human beings evolve and relate to reality based on existing technologies, because they are already co-constructed by them.

Furthermore, Nancy acknowledges that art is a 'productive technique' (1997), a method for bringing something to the fore and into existence. By showing objects in an exhibition, the public is forced to consider these objects in a way that is different from their usual functioning. Therefore, within the philosophy of Nancy, art is defined as a technology to make something present. According to Nancy, art makes us aware of the sense of the thing that is made present, because art shows us how something exists and how we are related to that existence. Given the fact that this is happening within a thoroughly technological environment, Nancy refers to art as a 'technology in the second degree' (Nancy 2015, pp. 70–71). Thus, art is not opposed to technology, neither is it considered to be in opposition with a world that has become thoroughly technological. On the contrary, art is thought of as a technology itself, which moreover takes part in and expresses an 'ecotechnic' condition. In Nancy's view, art is metaphysically enlightening: it demonstrates and exhibits our technological condition.

Verbeek, in turn, stresses in a more pragmatic sense, the value-ladenness of technology. Verbeek claims that since everything is technologically mediated, the work of engineer-designers is inherently moral (Verbeek 2006). Since technological media co-construct our point of view and instruct our behaviour, the design of technological media is at the same time the design of our social and political being.[4] According to Verbeek, different scripts can be developed in relation to the construction of artefacts. Every artefact is an object that is made and can be interpreted as a material script, which turns us into actors, whose way of acting is conditioned by the design of the object. Take, for example, a juicer. This device incorporates a script for extracting liquids from fruits and vegetables. By its mere existence, it supports a certain type of nurturing and of treating food. The script of an object can be very simple or it can be multilayered. The juicer can be designed aerodynamically and suggest that speediness and smoothness are important in life. Or, it can be made from recycled material and testify to a care about nature. No matter what the outlook or the substance is of the artefact, the object invites its user to play a role in a very specific sense. We can easily apply Verbeek's reasoning in relation to artworks. As every product offers us a material script for dealing with reality, products functioning as artworks help to reflect further on the social and political dimension of the artefact by explicitly trying out alternative scripts for social and political behaviour.

Although they are sharing a common ground and both thinkers show a similar affiliation to the thinking of Heidegger, Nancy's, and Verbeek's approach differ from each other. Nancy stresses that art shows us how we are attached to reality and how sense manifests itself in the world. This entails that art can offer us a metaphysical view on reality. Verbeek demonstrates how engineer-designers actively give sense to social and political reality. I think we need to combine both perspectives: we constantly need to move from a more reflective (and metaphysical understanding) to a more concretely, effective and productive stance (and subject-oriented point of view), in order to analyze and to design (our) presence in an ever-changing technological environment. The way we understand our relation to technology leads us to the position we take in relation to technology, and vice versa. Our understanding of technology is inherently political, because it defines the way we relate to, and act with or against technology. For example, one can become an outsider of society, by becoming an outsider to digitization. That the understanding of technology is so closely intertwined with the functioning of technology and its sociopolitical effects makes it also very dangerous. When technology changes, philosophy, society, and humankind also change.

The dark side of technology and the possible failure of art to change things

Neither Nancy nor Verbeek advocates a pessimistic view regarding the technological functioning of our present-day reality. Nevertheless, Heidegger expressed in his text already the fear that art would no longer be capable of expressing what is truly valuable. Also, many authors present a pessimistic and even apocalyptic view in relation to the contemporary technological condition. Therefore, we also need to draw attention to the dark side of technology and the possible failure of art to offer a different perspective than the one based on calculated functionality. The French postmodernist Jean Baudrillard (1995) and the French philosopher Bernard Stiegler (1998) are exemplary for taking a more negative view.

Baudrillard (1995) asserts that we live in a simulacrum, because every sign points endlessly to other signs, without any clear ground left for truth. Everything becomes illusory. Stiegler (1998) maintains that we got out of joint with technology. He gives the following explanation for this phenomenon. In the past people had a static worldview: they believed that the future would look just like the past. From the Industrial Revolution onwards, societies are no longer static. They change at an ever accelerating pace, and hence it has become impossible to take care for our societies and to be in control. With Baudrillard and Stiegler, we end up in the closed circuit of technology: it appears as a system that functions for its own sake, and wherein everything is turned into a sort of reserve for the system, just like Heidegger announced it. Both Baudrillard and Stiegler point to capitalism to identify this system. This focus on the overwhelming power of capitalism also puts the relevance of contemporary art into question. If art is but a part of the reductive, purely economical technological functioning, it turns into an accomplice of the reductive business-minded logic. Baudrillard and Stiegler share the fear that art has turned into a commodity, just like everything else.

However, in spite of their pessimistic views, Baudrillard and Stiegler also propose or practice strategies to escape from the danger of ending up in a closed circuit. Baudrillard has written so-called 'fiction theory' and has experimented with irony in his writings (Kellner 2015). Stiegler supports the rethinking of our longing in order to free it from a dominantly capitalist position.[5] In fact, both authors try to get beyond an instrumentalist worldview based on calculation in order to get in touch with something supposedly more real and valuable. In the end, they do not differ so much from Nancy and Verbeek, since they also search for a positive way to deal with the current effects of technology.

In conclusion, according to me, a pessimistic interpretation increases the opposition between humanity and the development of technology. Baudrillard and Stiegler are stressing the excessive and negative consequences of technological development. Modern technology is blamed for being the expression of a narrowed, efficiency-based, ahuman and amoral system (Baudrillard 2002). Humanity and industrial technological development are considered to be 'out of joint' (Stiegler in Barison, Ross 2009). If one side of the opposition is lost and art becomes part and parcel of capitalist development, then art fails to make a difference. But the fact that both Baudrillard and Stiegler still develop alternative strategies in spite of the dominance of capitalism seems to suggest that we have not yet ended up in a totally closed circuit.

How to deal with technological immediacy?

In order to continue a more constructive approach to new technologies and to clarify how a pessimistic view on technology can be transformed into a more optimistic one, I will discuss some present-day art and social theorists, respectively art historian Terry Smith (Smith et al. 2008) and sociologist Walter Weyns.[6] Next, I turn to the design of an artistic smart phone application, as created by the interaction artist Scott Snibbe.[7] As such I show that consciously designed technological mediation can establish new fruitful ways to engage with reality. This turn to art and social theories and my discussion of an existing art project, will add a more concrete and practical dimension to the philosophical analysis I developed so far.

The focus of Smith's analysis (in Smith et al. 2008) is an explanation of contemporary art. He opposes 'modern art' and present-day 'contemporary art.' To understand this opposition it is helpful to turn to Smith's discussion of Baudelaire as an art theorist. After doing that I contrast this analysis with his characterization of contemporary art.

In the 19th century Baudelaire wrote 'Painter of Modern Life,' an essay in which Modernity was associated with the transient, the passing, the immediate. Baudelaire suggested that art should distil timelessness from what is transitory: '*Modernité*, that is, the transitory, the fugitive, the contingent, the half of art, the other half of which is the eternal and the immutable' (Smith et al. 2008, p. 3). Smith sees in Baudelaire's proposition an affinity between ideologies of the past and an interest for the present. Whereas the past was directed to eternity, the present is characterized by the passing of daily life. A combination of both time regimes can be identified in much of the art of the 20th century, Smith explains. This is, for instance, the case when artists experiment with bringing together high and low culture, or when they develop art that is consciously antagonistic to the museum. So, values of the past and the institutions that express those values are combined with a modern, independent, and transient attitude. Following Baudelaire, Smith considers this to be characteristic for Modernity and modern art in particular.

However, in the aftermath of Modernity, we can no longer continue Baudelaire's so-called program, Smith argues. In fact, due to digitization and globalization, everything seems to have become present everywhere, and happening instantly. Moreover, institutions or disciplines that are oriented towards eternity become digital and hence start to operate in a transitory digital network. We are, Smith goes on arguing, left with the first part of Baudelaire's description: the transitory, the fugitive, and the contingent. The representations that are linked to the other half of Baudelaire's program, for example, eternity-oriented institutions, are now regarded as historically situated, too. These institutions appear as time-specific, contingent constructions, rather than as representative of an absolute truth.[8]

In view of this analysis, I would argue that today it is up to art to open up space and freedom within the transitory, but no longer with an orientation towards eternity. The freedom today, as granted by contemporary artworks, points, in my interpretation to the freedom of position one can take in relation to the present fugitive. If art can show us that there is not one possible way to deal with the passing of our time, then art sets us free from the condition we experience, and this without leaving its transiency behind. Instead, we become more aware of this transient condition, because we witness that there are different possibilities to deal with the situation, and we need to find out and discuss which hierarchy or juxtaposition is the most preferable for this situation. Artists no longer look for universal truth, but take a political point of view that depends on a human experience of reality.

Smith thinks that contemporary art can offer a fruitful answer to the current condition and its conflicting positions in relation to globalization, digitization, and the current economic divide. However, a more pessimistic view regarding the transient condition that characterizes our time is possible, too. The sociologist Weyns,[9] for example, holds that the fugitive and transient condition comes with a destruction of time experience. He explains this as follows. Whereas in former times people were looking backwards to the past in order to find out how to take care of things, Modern time is characterized by looking forwards towards the future, turning one's back to the past. Present-day time disappears in immediacy. Weyns goes on suggesting that today we are so attached to our digital screens, that there is no more possibility for distance or reflection. Hence, we have destroyed the experience of time.

The analysis and warning by Weyns demonstrates how a pessimistic and destructive view can be linked to contemporaneity. Weyns argues that human culture is threatened by immediacy. But, as I have already argued, we do not have direct access to the world or its sense. The so-called immediacy is illusory, because it is technologically mediated, and thus itself the result of technological production. Therefore, raising an alarming voice as Weyns does, can be misleading. Taking the ideas of Nancy and Verbeek seriously, we do not need to fulminate against present-day technologies and even not against the transience of our time. Instead, we need to research the transformations of meaning that take place as a result of digitization. Moreover, we need to reflect further, very concretely and practically, on how we should deal with the present technological mediation and its effects.

Let us turn to a concrete application designed for smart phones to illustrate how an active engagement with technological mediation does not only alter our experiences, but can also open up new ways of understanding and exploring our access to the world. The artist Snibbe[10] recently developed an application for a smart phone, whereby the user can manipulate music idioms composed by Philip Glass, and recreate the music of the famous composer.[11] When the app was shown to Philip Glass, he commented: 'The listener becomes the artist.' Following Glass's understanding of this possibility for renewal, I suggest we reflect further on the kind of artists we want to become, as listeners. Within my understanding, this app confronts us with an antinomy between a process of destruction and a process of construction. On the one hand, the listener no longer takes the time to devote herself entirely to music listening. On the other hand, the listener might become more involved in a composition by recreating it. Digital technologies enable us to adapt information of all kinds to personal preferences, but it also gives us the ability to become more actively present in domains other than the ones we are already mastering.

If we have arrived at a world which is experienced mainly as transient, fugitive, and contingent, then we need to reconsider how we can deal with it. Worrisome sociological analyses can help us to draw the attention to the negative effects of the modern and current technological development, but, in the end, this is also a path that might drift us away from a more constructive engagement with the world we inhabit.

Back to *scholê*

In this section, I want to reflect further on the (im)possibility of defending the idea of *scholê* at present times. As mentioned before, the digitization and the overwhelming presence of technology today make it difficult to maintain a distinction between *scholê* (free time) and *ascholê* (privation of free time). Thanks to digital technology, pupils and students can easily and effectively interact with what is happening outside the classroom. Also, educational institutions and didactical tools and materials need to adapt to the requirements of the digital age. Moreover, many new platforms for education are created in which audiovisual entertainment and study material get mixed. Consider for example the TED lectures, which began 'as a conference where Technology, Entertainment and Design converged.'[12]

Obviously, schooling has always been co-constructed by the media that were dominant during a given time. But, different media are the expression of different ideas and practices. Technological and digital media are supposed to destroy human experiences and values, as suggested by Baudrillard, Stiegler, and Weyns (as previously discussed). In the worst possible scenario, digitization can lead to the extinction of *scholê*, because it represents a system that is solely focused on efficiency and making profit. The new learning platforms might promote stardom instead of deep learning. According to TED, its aim is to spread the best ideas all over the world, but it could be argued that the platform is using ideas and knowledge as products to be styled in order to promote and sell the combination of technology, entertainment, and design. As a result, the digital evolution changes pupils and students in marketing targets and eventually education ends up being only a simulation.

Although this analysis may sound exaggerated and one-sided, the worry that *scholê* is no longer compatible with the present-day condition is shared by many scholars. Kalimtzis (2018) for example argues:

> Scholê, as a way of life, never was, nor does it seem that it ever will be, determined by economics or technological progress but from political and moral choices. Presently, it is indeed difficult, if not impossible, to imagine how the ideal of leisure might ever be transformed into scholê (…) Given our present course, it is possible that we, with our powerful technologies and ever powerful states, may yet fall victim to Aristotle's warning that republics unable to live a life of scholê are destined to collapse from the busyness of their misdirected pastimes (p. 180).

In this quote, Kalimtzis affirms the fear that nowadays 'free time' is devoted to a sort of hedonism, which is strongly related to the capitalist consumption industry. If this were to be the case, the unique strength of education is lost. However, throughout this chapter, I have been searching for a positive and constructive attitude towards present-day times and technologies. Hereby I referred to an artistic approach as a possibility of opening up the technological view in the direction of a more reflective and morally inspired view. Now I want to return to the app designed by Scott Snibbe (see above), and use its functioning as a guide to reflect on the reframing of *scholê* today.

The idea of being free from any occupation in order to study can also be decomposed and recomposed at a more individual level, just like what happened to the music of Philipp Glass by using Snibbe's app. Here the users become the co-constructors of their personal commitment to *scholê*. Maybe the pupil or student who in former times used to be a receiver of *scholê* enters now a condition under which she becomes partly self-responsible for the creation and integration of *scholê* in her own life. This does not make schooling necessarily better or easier than it was before. But if *scholê* and *aschole* get mixed up more and more, we need to take this fact into account when we look for a good life, and hence we should search for examples of good mixtures.

The *scholê* or 'free time' needed today is different than the one required in the Ancient Greek or Modern period. The means that enable education today might not be 'free time,' but the free choice concerning digital self-creation (as an individual and a community). Only if we realize that the digital technologies we rely on can be altered, we can effectively control the relation between digital culture and ourselves. Then, the awareness will arise that the content one gives to freedom involves a political choice, since the mediation of freedom co-constructs our sociopolitical identity. By realizing this, the discussion can start, and the search can start for finding out what the best possible mediation is – and with this, what the best society is. Art itself cannot and will not direct us to the right path to respond to our digital condition, but by allowing some free experimentation with technological mediation, art can help to realize and to stimulate a freedom of choice concerning further technological development.

Contemporary technologies direct us in finding possible answers to the question 'What makes life worth living?,' but the answer to it is not yet fixed. Therefore, the awareness of and the design of technology, as well as the artistic experimentation with technology should necessarily belong to *scholê* today.

By way of conclusion

In this chapter, I have sketched a contemporary version of *scholê*, which takes into account the digital technologies of our time. Referring to Derrida's analysis of the frame, I started by arguing that something like a pure, autonomous reality, of which the meaning can be defined independently from its context, does not exist. Therefore, I suggested we study the present digital framing of reality and education. In order to do this, I looked at art, because of its intrinsic relationship with technology.

Taking further Heidegger, I argued that having recourse on art, we can come to a broader and better understanding of what technology is, can and should be. From this artistic point of view, technology is no longer linked to calculation, profit, or a business-minded logic. Nevertheless, I also showed that art might also have become part and parcel of a culture based on calculation and commercialization. Furthermore, I expressed the fear that art fails to lead us to a better understanding and development of technology.

Next, based on art works and social theories, I further analyzed the transiency, fugitiveness and contingency that characterize the present-day world. I drew attention to the possible destruction of durable perspectives as a result of this volatility. At the same time, I insisted that it is still possible to explore the given impermanence in a fruitful way and pointed to an artistic application for a smart phone by way of example. In my view, the app shows how a continuing variability can stimulate the user to engage more actively with reality and get more touched and interested by it.

After this exploration of the possible interaction between technology and art, in a positive as well as a negative sense, I returned with these insights to the concept of *scholê*. By reflecting on the relationship between art and technology, I have showed that technology is not necessarily totally determined by a business-minded logic. It does not have to exist as a thoroughly calculated operation, solely directed to economical gain. Since the technological realm is not yet totally destined or known, there is the opportunity to study and to change the technological development from within. This brought me to a reconsideration of *scholê*. Again, the analysis of the interaction between art and technology served as an example. Eventually, I proposed to focus on the freedom of digital self-realization (of a person and a community). The awareness of the existence of this creative freedom is perhaps the necessary precondition to enable education today.

Notes

1 A quick search on the internet, shows there are a lot of entries, listing the pros and contras of the use of tablets in school, e.g., https://mastersed.uc.edu/news-resources/the-ipad-debate-are-ipads-truly-helping-with-education/.
2 In relation to the digital future of educational institutions it is interesting to refer to France, where school students were banned to use mobile phones on school grounds from September 2018 onwards. See https://www.theguardian.com/world/2018/jun/07/french-school-students-to-be-banned-from-using-mobile-phones.
3 The critical method used by Kant is characterized as transcendental idealism: a search for the laws of the cognitive powers that structure the way people can have knowledge of the world. In 'the Critique of the Aesthetic Judgement' Kant (1987) defines the principles that occasion and prestructure the aesthetic judgement before we have a concrete experience of the beautiful.
4 We can think here of McLuhan's (2003) famous phrasing 'the medium is the message.' As McLuhan claims, the media influence our psychosocial behaviour. Verbeek, on his part, stresses the making of the media and refers among others to Langdon, Achterhuis, and Latour to defend that artefacts define our (social) behaviour (Verbeek 2012).
5 See, e.g., the manifesto of *Ars Industrialis*, an organization initiated by Bernard Stiegler: http://www.arsindustrialis.org/node/1472.
6 Weyns presented an analysis of the present human experience of time at the *University of Flanders*, which is an initiative that broadcasts (on the internet, radio and TV) short lectures of top scientists, aimed at a big audience. Weyns posed the question whether it is possible to destroy time. See https://www.universiteitvanvlaanderen.be/college/kan-tijd-kapot/ or https://www.youtube.com/watch?v=MFxLGbqEKfc.
7 See https://www.snibbe.com/.
8 We can link this to postmodernism and the end of grand narratives, as described by Lyotard (1984). According to Lyotard, postmodernity is characterized by the loss of grand narratives, such as Catholicism, Marxism, modern utopianism, etc. that structure people's life from the beginning to the end. What is lost is the social givenness of a shared sense. Instead, we are confronted with a collection of many different small stories, existing opposed and next to each other.
9 See https://www.universiteitvanvlaanderen.be/college/kan-tijd-kapot/ or https://www.youtube.com/watch?v=MFxLGbqEKfc.
10 See https://www.snibbe.com/.
11 See https://www.snibbe.com/apps#/rework/.
12 See https://www.ted.com/about/our-organization. The *University of Flanders* is a similar organization.

References

Arendt, H. (1961). *Between Past and Future. Six Exercises in Political Thought*. New York, NY: Viking Press.
Baudrillard, J. (1995). *Simulacra and Simulation*, translated by Sheila Faria Glaser. Michigan, MN: University of Michigan Press.
Baudrillard, J. (2002). The Spirit of Terrorism, in Berberich, F. (Ed.) *Der Schock des 11. September und das Geheimnis des Anderen – Eine Dokumentation*. Berlin: Haus am Lützowplatz/Lettre International, pp. 323–335.
Buck, M.F. (2017). Gamification of Learning and Teaching in Schools – A Critical Stance. *Seminar.Net, 13*(1). Accessed https://journals.hioa.no/index.php/seminar/article/view/2325.

Derrida, J. (1987). *The Truth in Painting*, translated by Geoff Bennington and Ian McLeod. Chicago, IL, London: University of Chicago Press.

Drucker, J. (2014). *Graphesis. Visual Forms of Knowledge Production*. Cambridge, MA, London: Harvard University Press.

Heidegger, M. (1966). *Discourse on Thinking*. (Translation of *Gelassenheit* by M. Anderson and E. Hans Freund.) New York, NY: Harper & Row.

Heidegger, M. (1977). *The Question Concerning Technology and Other Essays*, translated and with an Introduction by William Lovitt. New York, London: Garland Publishing, Inc.

Hesmondhalgh, D. and Meier, L.M. (2018). What the Digitalisation of Music Tells us about Capitalism, Culture and the Power of the Information Technology Sector. *Information, Communication & Society 21(11)*, 1555–1570.

Kalimtzis, K. (2018). *An Inquiry into the Philosophical Concept of Scholê. Leisure as a Political End*. London, New York, NY: Bloomsbury Academic.

Kant, I. (1987) (1790). *Critique of Judgment*, translated by Werner S. Pluhar. Indianapolis, IN, Cambridge: Hackett Publishing Company.

Kellner, D. (2015). Jean Baudrillard, in Zalta, E.N. (Ed.) *The Stanford Encyclopedia of Philosophy*. https://plato.stanford.edu/archives/win2015/entries/baudrillard/>.

Krauss, R. (2004). Poststructuralism and Deconstruction, in Foster, H., Krauss, R., Bois, Y.-A., and Buchloh, B.H.D. (Eds.) *Art Since 1900*. London: Thames & Hudson, pp. 40–48.

Lyotard, J.-F. (1984) (1979). *The Postmodern Condition: A Report on Knowledge*, translated by Bennington and Massumi. Manchester: Manchester University Press.

Masschelein, J. and Simons, M. (2013). *In Defence of the School. A Public Issue*, translated by Jack Mc Martin. Leuven: E-ducation, Culture & Society Publishers.

McLuhan, M. (2003). *Understanding Media. The Extensions of Man*. (Critical edition, edited by W. Terrence Gordon.) Corte Madera: Gingko Press.

Nancy, J.-L. (1997). *Technique du présent: essai sur On Kawara*. Villeurbanne: Nouveau Musée/Institut d'Art Contemporain.

Nancy, J.-L. and Barrau, A. (2015). *What's These Worlds Coming To?*, translated by Travis Holloway and Flor Méchain. New York, NY: Fordham University Press.

Shiner, L. (2001). *The Invention of Art. A Cultural History*. Chicago, IL, London: University of Chicago Press.

Smith, T., Enwezor, O., and Condee, N. (Eds.) (2008). *Antinomies of Art and Culture. Modernity, Postmodernity, Contemporaneity*. Durham, NC, London: Duke University Press.

Stiegler, B. (1998) (1994). *Technics and Time, 1*, translated by Beardsworth and Collins. Stanford, CA: Stanford University Press.

Verbeek, P.-P. (2005). *What Things Do: Philosophical Reflections on Technology, Agency and Design*, translated by Robert P. Crease. Philadelphia, PA: Pennsylvania State University Press.

Verbeek, P.-P. (2006). Materializing Morality: Design Ethics and Technological Mediation. *Science, Technology & Human Values 31(3)*, 361–380.

Verbeek, P.-P. (2012). Politiek in het geding. Over kunst en de democratisering van de dingen. *Open 24*, 18–29.

Other media (film – DVD)

Barison, D. and Ross, D. 2009. *The Ister. Based on Martin Heidegger's 1942 Hölderlin lectures*. Black Box, Sound and Image.

Chapter 12

Epilogue

Nancy Vansieleghem, Joris Vlieghe and Manuel Zahn

The purpose of this book project is to give an account of the impact digital technologies have on ways of thinking about education, and how it is and can be organized today. It concerns an attempt to develop a theoretical language that enables us to observe more closely the current media culture and the effects it has, so that we can ask the 'right' questions. In this respect, the first contributions of the book analyze the changed conditions in which education (can) take(s) place today. The digital has confronted us with total new and unforeseen circumstances, for which each of the contributions try to find a new 'grammatization,' to use the words of Bernard Stiegler (2009). Other contributions set a first step in coming to terms with the consequences of the digital in the domain of education, by zooming in on detailed examples of practices that map our digital educational presence. Besides these more anthropological approaches, there are other contributions in this book that try to provide some concrete answers as well. These answers, however, do not function as a kind of solution – as if our current digital condition is a problem that needs to be solved. Instead, they are interventions that make us attentive for the here and now: they make us face the present and provoke thinking, more exactly about education in the age of the screen.

It is against this background that we want to conclude this book. We do not see this book as an endpoint, but rather as a beginning, so that we can start to think and speak differently. By way of epilogue, we finish the book with three concrete exercises that are based on the films the contributors to the book watched together during the seminars that preceded the writing of this book. The aim of these exercises is to draw the reader into our digital present, but also to bring about an aesthetic experience of our digital future. These three exercises render us capable of thinking not only about practices of looking and listening, but also about 'ecologies' that allow such practices to be developed and exercised. With this, we refer to the material conditions of social and cultural life. As such, we try to open up and further the exploration towards new digital ecologies and practices.

Father and Sons

The film *Father and Sons* (2014) by the Beijing-based director Wang Bing records the life of a Chinese migrant worker, Cai, and his two teenage sons in the outskirts of Fuming. The film consists almost entirely of a handful of fixed long shots filmed in a four square meter room where the three men live together. Within this tiny space, which looks like a barrack more than a room, there is an oven and a bed. The filmed images are mainly confined to this room, and they contain nothing but the sons, their father, and the stuff in the room. We see clothes and plastic bags hanging on a coat rack on the wall, a red blanket, a tea kettle, flip flops on the floor, and two puppies seeming to look for shelter in the already crowed hut. Hence, *Father and Sons* is restricted to one kind of image, and one kind of shot: a fixed framework in which the boys apparently do nothing. This is contrary to the 'usual' Wang Bing documentary films, which are driven by an unceasing desire to film and explore new places and situations. In order to come into contact with the world Wang Bing moves through the world with a cheap camera, tirelessly following the everyday lives of people who find themselves in the margins of a society amidst the transitions taking place in 21st-century China (Claes, Debuysere 2018). He tries to capture the world with his camera, experiencing constantly the restrictions inherent to it. For Wang Bing, these restrictions are no limitations, but move the filmmaker to navigate with his camera and to come closer to the people he is following.

The energy and movement that is felt in most of his films, however, seem to come to a standstill in *Father and Sons*. The camera is put on a tripod and there are only long static shots in which nothing really happens. The contextual information, which Wang Bing usually manages to provide through real-life dialogues and situations are squeezed in *Father and Sons* into a title screen page before the final credits. In this regard, for some looking at *Father and Sons* is nothing but a long, demanding and boring experience, e.g.: 'In spite of the sense of closure achieved through a well-executed "24 hours in the life of ..." montage, the feeling is that we are watching some rushes for a film-to-be' (Guarneri 2015). This way, it is argued that *Father and Sons* 'is far from matching the dissection of human emotions Wang Bing achieved in his previous features.' Furthermore: 'There wasn't enough filmed material to work on in the editing phase in order to provide the spectators with a comprehensive reconstruction of the real life of all three family members' (Ibid.). Indeed, there was not enough time for *Fathers and Sons* to grow and to come into being. In fact, Wang Bing had set out his usual tactic of spending time with the three persons in his film and recording their lives without interfering, with the aim of collecting hours and hours of footage to be condensed and shaped during the editing phase. However, in this case, after a few days shooting, the father's boss and the owner of the room started to send threats to Wang Bing and forced him to stop filming. Hence, it could be said that *Father and Sons* is indeed more of an exercise in looking than a fully finished film. However, whereas in his other films the act of moving with the camera makes the viewer experience the restrictions of what there is to be seen, we can only see what is in front of the camera, it could be said that here these restrictions are made more tangible and that in this sense the tension between presence and distance is even nowhere so radically present as it is in *Father and Sons*.

Wang Bing usually moves through the world in order to make it present to his audience, but in *Father and Sons*, the filmed space itself prevents any movement. It is as if we entered a situation (a world) in which we are no longer able to move (Wyns, Driesen 2018).

We see two boys in a small room, who, in turn, are just looking at their mobile phones. The TV is switched on and one can hear the sound from the broadcast, but the boys don't seem to be watching it. They are engrossed in their mobile phones – intermittently shifting their gaze to the TV. The sound of the television set as well as the glow coming out of a mobile phone screen captivate the eyes and fingers of the two boys. The shots show them moving from one screen to the other, only barely engaging with the 'real' world that surrounds them. Besides this, the film shows a room that is filled with shadows and spots of light that the sun throws through the door on the walls. We see that the day descends into night, but although it is night and dark, we still see the glow of the mobile phone. It is as if the day goes sleeping, but life on social media never ends. This image, we think touches on the heart of the film.

Father and Sons seems to draw our attention to what is happening in our digitized world more generally speaking, viz., that it becomes increasingly difficult to be in touch with 'reality,' in the sense that something can arrest our attention and move us. There is, of course, the attention for the screen, but there is also the impossibility of not looking. The gaze is captured by the screen. Everything that happens beyond the screen remains unnoticed, while all what appears on the screen is promoted to be the only thing that is important and significant. The film seems to suggest that the condition of the ubiquity of digital and social media in our lives is related to the disappearance of the experience a world 'outside.' For the boys in the film, the world only happens on the screen, which is functioning independently of a time and a place. On the screen, the world is always accessible – it is always there. The difference between inside and outside, private and public, day and night does no longer make sense when one finds oneself in front of the screen. Of course, there is still an indication of day and a night. We see the father's shadows on the wall and we hear a voice requesting to turn off television because it is time to sleep. But both, the darkness and the voice, seem to refer to a time before the advent of the digital screen: they are like a kind of ghost figures that only remind the young generation of the existence of another world.

Hence, the viewer is confronted with these questions: What does it mean to be a father in a society that is based on consumption? What does it mean to have a night time and a day time? What does it mean to have time as such? Rather than giving and opening a world that provides the possibility of a new beginning, the condition of the screen seems to heavily obstruct or even prevent this experience. In a world filled with digital technologies and social media there seems to be no beginning and no end. Consider in this regard the way in which the boy responds to his father: 'I can always turn it on again.' The messages that appear on the screen of the mobile phone cannot exhaust the energy of the user, or move her. Instead, there is the permanent feeling of an inexhaustibility, i.e., of not having enough of it. The film seems to be all about a gaze that clings itself to the will to be connected and to be in contact with others. Hence, relationships do not seem to be anything more than an urge for instant connectivity. As such, it seems that connectivity has replaced conversations. In *Father and Sons*, there are no conversations and we hear no voices speaking. We only hear the noise of the television and signals appearing on mobile phone screens.

By way of contrast, what the film also seems to suggest is that the experience of time and of paying attention for what happens here and now relies on a certain practice and discipline. As mentioned above, *Father and Sons* is not a documentary, neither is it a fiction film. It is an exercise. This means that looking at *Father and Sons* requires making an effort and the willingness to simply sit and watch through a window that gives access to what is present here and now. So maybe we can say that *Father and Sons* is, both in its content and its form, a real school film. Rather than teaching us something about another culture, poverty or youth, the film brings about free time or *scholê*. That is time that has no function. It enables nothing but looking at and speaking about what there is to see on the screen.

Lo and Behold

In his 2016 documentary film *Lo and Behold: Reveries of the Connected World*, Werner Herzog paints a fascinating and at times grim picture of a world in which digital technologies have become ubiquitous. We refer here to this film not solely because it has an obvious connection with this book, but also because we were struck by the particular *form(at)* in which Herzog has chosen to tell us his views on our digital present.

It could be argued that this documentary performs a double operation in the sense that it details our present conditions (the growing importance of screen-based technologies in our lives) by using and intensifying these conditions – exactly by *screening* the impact of these technologies. This might explain for some of the odd and puzzling aspects of the film, which seems to bounce back and forth between the traditional genre of the classical documentary that passes on information (e.g., about the possible disruption of our communication networks as the result of solar prominences or about the original idea behind the internet as a citation machine, which allowed users always to go back to the original sources, but which never materialized) and an intentionally staged and at times most ironic comedy show, especially because of the contrast between the farcical content and Herzog's well-known eloquent and stern voiceover (e.g., the overdramatized staging of a grief-struck family that has lost a daughter and that is now confronted with cyberbullying, or the over-enthusiastic reactions of developers of new technologies).

The question that might arise here is one of veracity and trust: it is a matter of doubt whether or not Herzog's particular way of screening his subject succeeds in painting a true picture of our present digital conditions. However, as Jeff Frank remarks in an article on documentary making from a Cavellian perspective:

> Documentary is interesting in that it acknowledges its limited perspective, and nonetheless aims at creating a public from that perspective. It creates a public not through direct argument, but through the creation of a space where its position is made manifest, and where a viewer can engage in a process of letting herself learn from the film if she finds that the film is (somehow) representative of (some part) of her experience of the world. (Frank 2013, p. 1025)

Frank's point is that the documentary is a genre of its own (and that it is markedly different from genres such as the news or pornography that are also after a particular reality effect). The question at stake here is whether or not the filmmaker is successful in giving images the quality of 'representativeness.' This term doesn't refer to correctly representing the world as it is, but to the challenge to put one's own subjectivity and situatedness at stake, in order to show to the audience that there is something new and interesting to be experienced – and hence to be learned. This is, to make a world (and not-yet experienced aspects of it) *present*. The fact that the film is made from a particular and biased perspective (e.g., by choosing not to present average situations – and hence to respect reality as it is – but to focus on the extraordinary) is a requirement for the documentary to work and to educate.

Following Stanley Cavell, Frank claims that we need to trust our own experience and become 'authorities in our own experience' (Cavell 1981, p. 12 as quoted in Frank *op. cit.*, p. 1023). Only then the audience might experience the subject of the film *as* something relevant and *as* something that demands further thought and a public debate. And in a sense, this is exactly what happens in *Lo and Behold*. The possibilities that screen technology offer are used – and played with – in order to make something about the screen present. It is in this sense that the aforementioned exaggerations that are so typical for this documentary and the contrast between the visual content and Herzog's own voiceover play an important role.

As a result, digital technologies appear simultaneously as objects of suspicion and fear *and* as things that cause fascination and demand awe ('Lo and behold'). The relation we are supposed to take to them is never clear, but it is clear that we need to take a relation: that we have to start *caring* about them. We can take a distance and connect back to our screen-based technologies. Doing this in a 'care-full' way then means that we must take a critical stance, but also that we go on with the present conditions – refusing to take an indifferent attitude, but also refusing to accept that we are the slaves of a system that is utterly beyond our control. In order to do so, we need to be affected and start to imagine our world in ways that are not-yet given. In that sense, Herzog's documentary presents us indeed with 'reveries.'

The Human Surge

The experimental film *The Human Surge* (*El auge del humano*, 2016), directed by the Argentine director Eduardo Williams, is structured around three separate geographical segments: Buenos Aires (Argentina), Maputo (Mozambique), and Bohol (Philippines). In every segment, Williams (literally) follows one protagonist while he/she is performing (more or less) his/her all day routines like getting ready in the morning, going to work, meeting friends and peers, and hanging around at home with family. In between, there are long sequences in which the characters move between spaces, such as workplace and home. The characters depicted in the three segments are invariably poor, restless, and on the search for connection with other human beings. The segments are linked with unexpected transitions.

Williams distances himself from using a continuous dramatic narrative and from casting figures endowed with a story the way we are used to it from watching fiction films. Rather, he presents a more open structure, a mapping of fragments of biographies, micro-plots, situations of people in constant motion in search for connection and communication. The film therefore is a way of thinking that unfolds in the course of its performance; a way of thinking through moving images that invite us as spectators to *re*think, to reflect. *The Human Surge* thinks about the impact of digital media technologies on all dimensions of our world. Digital media and communication technologies of all sizes and types (from smartphones to desktop computers) are ubiquitous in Williams' film. They can be seen in almost every shot: in private, public, and work spaces. But also in places deep in the jungle (like in the last of the three segments), digital devices are present. And they play an important role in structuring the relations between the figures depicted, or they become thematized in their dialogues – especially when they don't work. Communication in *The Human Surge* fails as often as it is successful: the technological devices we make to improve our communication (as shown in the last long sequence in Bohol) seem to make it equally difficult to communicate. Either the smart devices are defective (e.g., they have fallen into the water), their batteries are not charged, or they receive no signals.

The Human Surge shows not only the omnipresence of digital screen media, but reflects this ubiquity also through the aesthetics of the film. As with *Father and Sons* and *Lo and Behold* we are interested in the specific form of *The Human*

Surge through which it mediates its 'thinking.' Its form shows clearly traces of the so-called 'postdigital aesthetics' (cf. Berry, Dieter 2015) of current media culture. The prefix 'post' in this expression emphasizes the omnipresence of digital media and at the same time focuses on a new quality of digitality: the transformations of the digital into new social, economic, cultural, and also aesthetic structures (Cramer 2015). Just to name a few observations: the use of the camera is strongly influenced both by the aesthetics of online videos and by new digital camera technology, and as a result we get long, uncut shots with a blurred hand camera following the characters. The camera always remains at a distance from the figures depicted. There are no close-ups of people in Williams' film. The few close-ups are of computer screens, cell phone displays, and of ants. Furthermore, the film material of the three segments is the product of distinctly hybrid moving-image technologies: for the first section, Super 16mm; the second, shot using a Black Magic camera, then filmed off a monitor in Super 16mm; and the third, simply RED digital video. Also, the handling of the light and the alignment of the image, subvert a visual regime as we know it from feature films. Again and again, there are long phases of low-key shots in which we hardly see anything, in which we see the figures only schematically and in which are forced to listen to their conversations or to sounds caused by their actions.

Williams also invites us as viewers to think 'beyond' the digital devices, their screens, and the new visual regimes and aesthetics they bring about, so as to see the network character of digital media. This happens when the film connects two teen bedrooms via the close-up onto a computer screen, and more exactly through an open Chaturbate webpage, which functions as a 'passage.' It becomes clear then that the film investigates the temporal and spatial dimensions of a globally networked, digital infosphere. One can say that Williams tries to make connectivity conceivable in the global contemporary: between people, between people and nature, between people and their time, between times, and between continents, regions and things. This is metaphorically represented in the film by the flooded streets in Buenos Aires or by the small lake in the jungle in Bohol. In and through the water, bodies are connected to one another in a non-directional way. These images can be thought of as an analogy for the embeddedness of people in the medium of networked digital media. In this perspective, one can add that *The Human Surge* discovers an abundance of media and networks. Streets, water, roots, and underground passageways all connect spaces and people in ways similar to fibre optics, mobile screens and digital networks. This title-giving 'surge' might be less singularly human and more general, and hence more difficult to properly categorize. In Williams' film, this pulse of energy is everywhere, running through and between all of the (in)dividuals: human, animal, material, and mechinic.

The Human Surge reflects on how networked media technologies have infiltrated our everyday lives, how they have changed them, and thus how they influence our everyday practices. In addition, in the specific manner of his staging, the film demonstrates how artists can intervene in the screen-based, post-digital practices.

References

Berry, D.M. and Dieter, M. (Eds.) (2015). *Postdigital Aesthetics. Art, Computation and Design*. Basingstoke: Palgrave Macmillan.

Cavell, S. (1981). *Pursuits of Happiness; The Hollywood Comedy of Remarriage*. Cambridge, MA: Harvard University Press.

Claes, G.J. and Debuysere, S. (2018) *Wang Bing. Filming a Land in Flux*. Amsterdam: Graficon, NV.

Cramer, F. (2015). What Is Post-Digital'? *APRJA*. Accessed February 19, 2019. http://www.aprja.net/what-is-post-digital.

Frank, J. (2013). The Claims of Documentary: Expanding the educational significance of documentary film. *Educational Philosophy and Theory 45(10)*, 1018–1027.

Guarneri, M. (2015) *Shadows of the Opus Magnum: Wang Bing's 'Father and sons'*. Accessed February 19, 2019. https://mubi.com/nl/notebook/posts/shadows-of-the-opus-magnum-wang-bings-father-and-sons.

Stiegler, B. (2009). The Carnival of the New Screen: From hegemony to isonomy, in Pelle, S. and Vondereau, P. (Eds.) *The YouTube Reader*. Vilnius: Logitopas, pp. 40–59.

Wyns, Q. and Driesen, M. (2018). Vier camerabewegingen. De arme mise en scène van Wang Bing. *Sabzian*. Accessed February 19, 2019. https://www.sabzian.be/article/vier-camerabewegingen.

Index

Page numbers in **bold** refer to figures.

academic freedom 12
actors 17, 53, 54
Adams, C. 62–63
aesthetic education 85–90
aesthetic experience 44
aesthetic judgement 159
Agamben, G. 4, 42, 81, 82, 83, 84, 85, 128, 133, 134
Agarwal, A. 17
agency 75, 84; schools 36
Alberti, L. B. 47n5
algorithmic thought 41–42
apparatus 81
archives: annotation systems 131–133; classification 129–130; community 128; as community resource 129; contents 132; digital 127–138; digitization 127; feminist legacies 128–131; institutionalization 129; keywords 132–133, 136; Meta space 131–133, 133; as social pedagogic location 127; as social pedagogic spaces of speculative possibility 137–138
area mapping 37
Arendt, H. 158
Aristotle 159–160, 160
Arnheim, R. 9, 20
art 160; failure of 163, 164; freedom 165; productive technique 161–162; and technology 160–163, 168; turn to 164–166, 167–168
art education 141–155: and becoming 94; communication processes 99–100; cultural codes 101; cultural hacking 95–96; digital natives 97–98; dominant culture 98; and Eurocentric dominance 96–97; and the excess of control 96; hero of 95; and the image 101; and nature 101–102; orientation 96; post-art 96–97; postproduction 100–101; time and temporality 99–100; virtual reality 98–99
art teachers 92
Asefi, M. Y. 97
Asselberghs, H. 5
attention, direction of 62; formation 5; levels 2
authority 65
authorship 112
automatism 111
autonomy 144

Baecker, D. 69, 92, 94–95, 96, 97, 101
Barthes, R. 28–29
Bartholl, A. 99
Baudelaire, C. 164–165
Baudrillard, J. 163–164, 166
becoming 94
behaviour, mediated 108–109, **109**
Belting, H. 100
Benjamin, W. 108
Bing, W. 5, 172–174
blackboards 54, 60, 145–146
Blumenberg, H. 37, 38
body, screens as extensions of the 107–110, **109**
Bolter, J. D. 46
book culture 24, 32, 38; transition from 36
books 23–24, 38; disappearance 39
Borradori, G. 118
Bossom, F. 137

Bourdieu, P. 18, 21n3
Bourriaud, N. 73, 100–101
Bring Your Own Device (BYOD) model 52, 53; classrooms 55–65, **56, 58, 60**
broadcasting 13–14
Broadcasting Corporation 14
Buck, M. F. 158
Buddensieg, A. 100

Caccia, A., *Vedozero* (film) 110–123, **115, 117, 120, 122**
cameras 17, 28–29, 29, 33n5, 33n6, 81, 107, 110–112, 113–114, 114, 118, 119, 123n7, 172–173, 177
capitalism 163, 164
Carbone, M. 30–32, 47n5
Castells, M. 92
Cavell, S. 175
celebrity lecturers 17
choice 2
Christov-Bakargiev, C. 96–97
cinema 26, 28, 81, 120–123
cinema relocation 121
cinematic gaze 113–114
classic screens 81
classic, the 37; educational interpretation 43; re-mediation of 41–47
classrooms 37, 51–66; actors 53; arrangement 55–59, **56, 58, 60**; blackboards 54, 60; Bring Your Own Device (BYOD) model 52, 53, 55–65, **56, 58, 60**; decentralized 64; disappearance 1; materiality 52–53; navigating 65–66; sociomaterial approach 52–54; space 52–54, 63–65; spatial relations 55–59; traditional 56–58, **56**, 63
climate change 161
code 42
cognitive subjectivity, authentic 40
collaborative practices 136–137
collaborative production 72–73
Collective annotation/archival discovery workshop 131–133
collective intelligence 99
communality 74, 148
communal production 74, 74–75
communal space 73–74
communication 176; Fichte's theory of 10–12; networks 174; processes 9, 99–100
community archives 128

computational aesthetics 86–87
computers, operating systems 34n11
connectivity 177; replacement for conversation 174
control: excess of 95, 96; loss of 101; responding to 95–96
convergence culture 47n1
Cramer, F. 70
critical practice 87–88
cultural codes 101
cultural globalization 100
cultural hacking 95–96
culturally emerged nature 101–102
cultural production 68–69, 71–78
culture 93; access to 73; collaborative production 72–73; definition 69
curriculum 37
cyberbullying 175
cyberspace 65, 77, 98–99, 100, 101
Czerki, P. 99

Darstellung 28–30, 30
data 4
datamoshing 88–89
Debray, R. 92, 96
Declaration of the Independence of Cyberspace 98
Decuypere, M. 54
Deleuze, G. 85, 153
Derrida, J. 18, 21n3, 133, 159, 168
deschooling 36–37
desktops 61
detraditionalization 37, 38–41, 41, 42, 46, 47
Dewey, J. 40–41
diaries 134
digital, definition 70
digital devices, diversity 55
digital divide 108
digital gaze 116
digital grammars 133, 134
digital illiteracy 137
digital immigrants 108
digital infrastructures 127, 128
digitalization 70
digital literacy 127–138
digital media 33n4; impact 176–177; networked 177; omnipresence 176–177; ubiquitous 1
digital natives 32, 33n8, 97–98, 98, 101, 107, 108, 114
digital network 4

Index

digital screens 30–32
digital techniques 1
digital technologies: distinguishing 4; distrust 110; rise in 1; ubiquitous 174–176
digital video 88–89
digitization 1, 80, 133, 164–165, 166; archives 127; education impacts 1; literature 2; and social conditions 3
disclosure of the world 23, 29, 32
discourse 15, 18, 21n3
dissimulation 108
Documenta 13 97
do Mar Pereira, M. 129
Drucker, P. F. 92
Dublin Core 134, **135, 136**
Düllo, T. 96
Durham, J. 97–98
dynamic screens 81

education: definition 1, 2; evolutions 2; institutional context 24, 158–160; and post-digital culture 76–78; and screens 76–78; student-centered models 32; teacher-centered models 32; transmission model 32
educational institutions 24, 158–160
educational interpretation 43
educationalists perspective 3; as disclosure of the world 23
educational positioning systems 142
educational settings, sociomaterial approach 54
e-learning platforms 2
Emejulu, A. 127
enclosure 37
environmental agency 75, 84
Eurocentric dominance 96–97
European Commission 140, 142–143
existential perspective 46
expanded cinema 113
experience, authenticity of 37

Facebook 74, 115
Father and Sons (film) 5, 172–174
feedback 144
feminist archival legacies 128, 128–131
Feminist Archive 128, 137–138
feminist information science 129–130
Fenwick, T. 53, 65
Feynman, R. 17
Fichte, J. L. 9, 10–12, 14, 20

fiction theory 163
filmed space 173
films 5
financial support 4
Floridi, L. 123n4
Flusser, V. 27, 28–30, 33n5, 33n7, 41–42, 128, 131, 134, 137, 147–148, 152
Ford Foundation 16
For Now (film) 5
Foucault, M. 13, 14–16, 17, 18, 20, 21n2, 21n3, 33n7, 81, 83, 87, 153
framing 29, 90n1
France 169n2
Frank, J. 175
Freer, J. 129–130
free time 141, 145, 158–60, 166–7, 174
Friedberg, A. 112

gameplay, survival mode 116, 123n14
Gauchet, M 38, 39–41, 43
gaze 59, 63, 111, 133, 173, 174; cinematic 113–114; digital 116; mobile 112–114
Geist 12
generation gap 108
Gibson, W. 98
Giunta, C. 44–46
glitch aesthetics 88–89
Global Contemporary, The 99–100
globalization 164–165; cultural 100
Goffman, E. 4, 18
good life 159–160
Google 89
grammar machines 133
grammatization 144–146, 146, 146–147, 153, 155, 171
Groys, B. 141
Grusin, R. 46
Gumbrecht, H. U. 42–44, 46

hackers 95
handheld devices 30–31
Hansen, M. B. N. 85
Hatsune Miku 68–69, **69**, 71–78; communal production 72–73, 74, 74–75; engagement with 74–75; origins 71–72; songs 72
Havelock, E. 36
Hedinger, J. 97
Heidegger, M. 160–161, 162–163, 163, 168
Herzog, W. 5, 174–176

Hetherington, K. 153
historical being 45
historical consciousness 41
historical thought, crisis of 43
historical tradition 37
historicity 38
history 100; educational interpretation 43; re-mediation of 41–47; and writing 41
homo digitalis 25
homonymy 42
horizontality 55, 61, 62–65, 121
Hörl, E. 87
Human Surge, The (El auge del humano) (film) 5, 176–177
Humboldt, W. von 9, 12–13, 19
hyperconnected life 115–116
hyperconnected reality 123n4
hypermediation 119
Hyper-Reality (film) 5
hypomnemata 46

identification 24–25
identity: building 3; in digital media culture 89; multiple 25
Ihde, D. 33n3
Ilharco, F. 4–5, 19, 27
Illich, I. 25
illiteracy 128, 131
illusion 18
imagination, mobilizations of 137–138
immediacy 32
indeterminate potentiality 141
individualization 65
individualized learning 65, 140
Industrial Revolution 163
information abundance 73
information architectures, social implications embedded in 129–130
Ingold, T. 148
Instagram 74
intelligence 40, 41
intergenerational relations 36
interiorization/exteriorization 133–134
interlacing space 64
International Research Seminars, Making School in the Age of the Screen 4
internet culture 68
Internet of Things 158
Introna, L. 4, 19, 27
inventive intelligence 41
in-visible space 64–65
isolation, space of 64

Kalimtzis, K. 159, 167
Kant, I. 29, 33n8, 102, 159, 169n3
Karlsohn, T. 12–13
kino-eye 33n6
Kittler, F. 9
Knoblauch, H. 19
knots 148–149
knowledge: externalization of. 39; Fichte's theory of 10–12; interiorization/exteriorization 133–134; objectification 39 production 12–13; transfer 80

Lacan, J. 82, 82–83
learning needs, MOOC perspective 142
lecturers, celebrity 17
lectures: 20th century 18–20; academic 9–20; broadcast 13–14; Fichte on 10–12; Goffman on 18; Humboldt on 12–13; as performance 13–17; radio 9; recorded 14–17; rehearsed 19–20; Romantic tradition 10–12, 19; television 16–17; video 17; YouTube 19
Leslie, E. 137
Liebl, F. 96
literacy 133
literature 2
Liverpool Hope University 4
Lo and Behold: Reveries of the Connected World (film) 5, 174–176
looking 107
Lovink, G. 77
LUCA School of Arts Ghent 4
Luhmann, N. 92
Lyotard, J.-F. 169n8

McClintock, R. 37
McLuhan, M. 36, 92, 169n4
maintenant 32, 40–41
Manovich, L. 5, 25, 26, 33n4, 81, 147
Marin, L 145
Masschelein, J. 140–141, 145, 158
Massive Open Online Courses (MOOCs) 1, 17, 140–155; access to 147–148; aims 142; communality 148; computational operations 155; content 148–150; contributions 148–152, **149, 150, 151**; courses 143; design 146–155, **148, 149, 150, 151, 154**; effectiveness 144; feedback 144; grammatization 153, 155; knots 148–149, **149**; learners

142–144; learning in 141–144; learning materials 143; and learning needs 142; media visualizations 153, **154**; monitoring systems 142–143; navigation 149; objective 140; openness 147–148; personalization 142, 144; platforms 142, 144, 147; potential benefits 140, 152–153; practices 144–146; scholastic potential 141; support 143; teachers 143–144; techno-images 147–148, 152
materiality, obliteration of 133–134
materialization 145
Matsuda, K. 5
meanings, negotiations of 73
media culture: identity in 89; media-ecological perspective 80–90; as screen culture 81–82
media-ecological perspective 80–90
media education: case study 107–123; and gaze 112–114; pedagogic strategy 118–119; reversing the perspective 110–111; screen practices 107–110; *Vedozero* (film) 110–123, **115, 117, 120, 122**
media environments 76–78
mediality, changes in 2–3
media of dissemination, dominant 92
mediated behaviour 108–109, **109**
media theory 2–3
media visualizations 152–153, **154**
mediological revolutions 94–95
Melot, M. 32n1
memory practices 3
Mensvoort, K. van 101–102, 102
Merleau-Ponty, M. 30
Meta-Data 128, 131–132, 134–136
Mifsud, L. 66
mirrors 27, 31
mobile gaze 112–114
modernity 23, 38, 95, 100, 164
Modernity; rise of 23
Morin, E. 39
motivation, intrinsic 2
mp3 86–87
multifunctional space 63
museum 31
music videos 88–89

Nancy, J.-L. 160, 161–163, 163, 165
nature 101–102
Negroponte, N. 68

networked individualism 73–74
networked media technologies 177
networked screen culture 68
networked screens 82–86
network structure 77
New Aesthetic 71
new media, pedagogical use of 43–47
New Scientist 16–17
next art and art education: and becoming 94; communication processes 99–100; cultural codes 101; cultural hacking 95–96; digital natives 97–98; dominant culture 98; and Eurocentric dominance 96–97; and the excess of control 96; hero of 95; and the image 101; and nature 101–102; orientation 96; post-art 96–97; postproduction 100–101; time and temporality 99–100; virtual reality 98–99
next art education 92–102; scope 92–94
next nature 101–102
next schools 92–94
next society, the 92, 94–95
Nietzsche, F. 9, 13, 17, 20
nonlinguistic thought 42
Novalis 38
now, the 94; owning 32

off-screen voice 119
onlife 123n4
online access, constant 32
online learning 17 *see also* Massive Open Online Courses (MOOCs)
operating systems 34n11
Ott, M. 84
owning the now 32

paideia 93
paintings 26
Pausch, R. 17
Pazzini, K. J. 82
pedagogy 39–40, 42, 87; hierarchical logic 110; scholastic practices 144–146; use of new media 43–47
peer production 72
perception: modalities of 107; training 108
perception form 28, 29
perceptive experience 107–110
performance 13–17, 19–20
performativity, relation of 75
Perniola, M. 85

personal digital devices 52
personalization 65, 142, 144
personalized education 140–141
perspective, reversing 110–111
Petrarch 44–46
Philosophy of Education Society of Great Britain, Large Grant Scheme 4
photographic images 28, 31
physis 161
place, sense of 112
Plato 159–160
poetization 144–146, 146–147
pointing 19
pop culture 71
post-art 96–97
post-digital aesthetics 177
post-digital culture 69–71; collaborative production 72–73; communal space 73–74; and education 76–78; participation 74–75; screens in 76
post-history 41–47
post-internet art 80
Postman, N. 36
postmodernism 169n8
postproduction 73, 100–101
PowerPoint 18–19
power relations 153
practice, self-definition through 75
presence 29
presence effects 44, 45–46
presentation 28–30
presentification 43, 44–46
Price, S. 73
printing press, invention of 2, 24
private space 64–65
prosumerism 72, 77
psycho-acoustics 86–87

radar 26–27
radical digital citizenship 127
radio 20
radio lectures 9
Rainie, L 73–74
reading 38
reality 27, 29; experience of 27; hyperconnected 123n4; representation of 28; staying in touch with 173–174
reality effect 33n5
realness 31
reflections 31
reflective self, the 9
Reith Lectures 13–14

relevancy 31
representation 28–30; space of 47n5
representativeness 175
Romantic tradition 10–12, 19
Roth, E. 89
Rothe, K. 85–86
Rousseau, J.-J. 23, 102
Russell, B. 13–14, **14**

Saltz, J. 97
scholastic potential 141
scholastic practices 144–146
scholê 145, 158–160, 166–168, 168, 174
school education 1
schooling 36–41; detraditionalization 38–41
schools 4; agency 36; Bring Your Own Device (BYOD) model 52, 53; institutional context 158–160; invention of 145–146; MOOC perspective 142; problem with the new 92–93; reframing 158–168; smart 158; technological transformations 121, 123
screen culture 68; media culture as 81–82; transition to 36
screening technologies 17
screen learning 5
screen practices 107–110, 108–110, **109**
screens 47n5; classic 81; as communal space 73–74; culture of 24; definition 68–69, 76; digital 26, 30, 30–32; dynamic 81; dynamic situation 76; and education 76–78; essence of 19; and experience of reality 27; experiencing 5; as extensions of the body 107–110, **109**; first 27; forms of 4; framing 29, 90n1; function 76; genealogical approach 25–26; handheld devices 30–31; horizontality 55, 61, 62–65; impact 25–32; Lacan's understanding of 82–83; as mirrors 119; networked 82–86; omnipresence 176–177; ontological meaning 31; ontology of 30; perfected 30–32; phenomenological approach 26–27; proliferation of 40; screenness of 25–27; television 26, 28–30; ubiquitous 1, 173; verticality 55, 59–62, 63, 63–65
Second World War 26
seeing 27
seeing-beyond 30

seeing-through 30
Seemann, M. 101
self-creation 10–11, 167
self-definition 75
selfies 108, **109**, 118, 119
self-production 10–11, 167
self-realization 168
self-reflection 10–11
self-regulated learning 144
self, the 10–11, 20
self-understanding 25
self-world-relations 77
Serres, M. 32, 39–40, 41–42
sexting 110
Simons, M. 54, 141, 145, 158
smartphones 30–31, 34n11, 55, 62–63, 165–166
smart schools 158
Smith, T. 164–165
Snibbe, S. 164, 166, 167
social conditions 2–3
social media 173
Social Network Revolution 73–74
social operating systems 73–74
social topology 53–54
social web, the 84
societal change 94–95
sociomaterial approach 52–54
Socrates 42
software 4
Song, Y. 52
Sørensen, E. 54, 61–62
space: boundaries 37; classroom 52–54, 63–65; collapse of 77; interlacing 64; in-visible 64–65; of isolation 64; multifunctional 63; of mutual exclusivity 64; navigating 65–66; private 64–65; relational approach 53; sociomaterial approach 52–54; virtual 113, 147
spatiality 33n8
spectatorship 5
spirit 10
Stalder, F. 69, 70, 74
Sterne, J. 86
Stiegler, B. 24, 36, 84, 128, 131, 133, 134, 145, 146, 163–164, 166, 171
student-centered models 32
subject configurations 3
subjectivation 68, 77
subjectivity 43, 74–75, 77, 80, 85; changes in 2–3

subject matter, involvement 5

tactile vision 31
Taliban, the 97
teacher-centered models 32
teachers: access 59; as monitor of spaces 65–66; MOOCs, 143–144; presence 64; role of 57; space of mobility 59; zone of exclusion 62, 63, 64, 66
teacher training 92, **94**
technê 161
techno-cultural forms 42
techno-images 147–148, 152
technological immediacy 164–166
technology 166; approach to new 164–166; and art 160–163, 168; dark side of 163–164; dominant 24; importance of 23; value-ladenness 162
Technology, Entertainment and Design 166–167
technosphere, the 81–82, 84
TED Talks 19, 166
television 16–17, 26, 28–30, 81, 93
temporal relations 54
Tenen, D. 128, 133–134, 134
textualities 137
theatricality 17
theorizations 4
thinking 24
thinking in unison 13
Thompson, T.L. 62–63
time and temporality 99–100; experience of 173, 174
Tisseron, S. 24–25
topological thinking 53–54
tradition, role of 38
transcendental aesthetics 29
transcendental idealism 169n3
transitory, the 164–165
transmission model, critique of 32
transparency 111, 147
trust 175

UK Women's Liberation Movement 128
universities: disappearance 1; Nietzsche on 13
user-generated content 72

Vedozero (film) 110–123; aims 110–111; cinematic gaze 113–114; diffusion 121; digital gaze 116; editing style 113; as expanded cinema 113; first project

110–114, 116; mobile gaze 112–114; pedagogic strategy 118–119; point of view in motion 112; school environment 114; second realization 114–124, **115, 117, 120, 122**; selfies 119; shooting style 116; vertical format 120–121, 123; voiceover 119; workflow 112, 114–115
veracity 175
Verbeek, P.-P. 160, 161–163, 163, 165, 169n4
verticality 55, 59–62, 63, 63–65, 120–121, 123
Vertov, D. 33n6
video lectures 17
virtual communities 99
virtual encounters 33n8
virtual learning environment 54
virtual reality 98–99
virtual space 113, 147
visualizations 152–153, **154**
Vlieghe, J. 147
vlogs 118, 119

Vorstellung 28–30
Vriend, T. 130

Wallon, H. 31
Web Kids' Manifesto 99
Wellman, B. 73–74
Wellner, G. 34n10
Weyns, W. 164, 165, 166, 169n6
WhatsApp 115
what works approach 2
Williams, E. 5, 176–177
windows 29, 30, 47n5
Windows 34n11
Wissenschaftslehre 11
writing 137; and history 41

YouTube 17, 19, 71, 74, 118, 119

Zahn, M. 75, 76
Zizek, S. 17, 33n9
zone of exclusion 62, 63, 64, 66
zone of glancing 62, 64